Ex Libris

Hywel Gillard.

Rhondda Coal, Cardiff Gold

Rhondda Coal, Cardiff Gold

The Insoles of Llandaff
Coal Owners
and Shippers

Richard Watson

Published with the co-operation and support
of the City and County of Cardiff
Libraries and Information Service

MERTON PRIORY PRESS

First published 1997

Published by Merton Priory Press Ltd
67 Merthyr Road, Whitchurch
Cardiff CF4 1DD

ISBN 1 898937 26 5

Dedication

To Gerry and Rebecca with love

In Memoriam

Brian Jones (1939–96)
who was looking forward to reading this book

Printed by Hillman Printers (Frome) Ltd
Handlemaker Road, Marston Trading Estate
Frome, Somerset BA11 4RW

Contents

List of Illustrations

Figure

Plates

Acknowledgements

Plates 1, 7 and 8 are reproduced by courtesy of the Glamorgan Record Office, which publishes facsimile reproductions of all three items. Plate 6 is reproduced by courtesy of Rhondda Cynon Taff Libraries and is copyright John Cornwell. Plates 10, 14 and 22 are reproduced by courtesy of Cardiff County Council. Plate 12 is reproduced by courtesy of Somerset Record Office. Plate 13 is from the Stephen Rowson Collection. Plate 17 is reproduced by courtesy of the Cardiff & County Club (per Mr Arthur Weston Evans). Plate 19 is reproduced by courtesy of the Living Archive Centre, Barry. Plate 20 is from the Bill Styles Collection.

Descendants of George Insole and Mary Finch

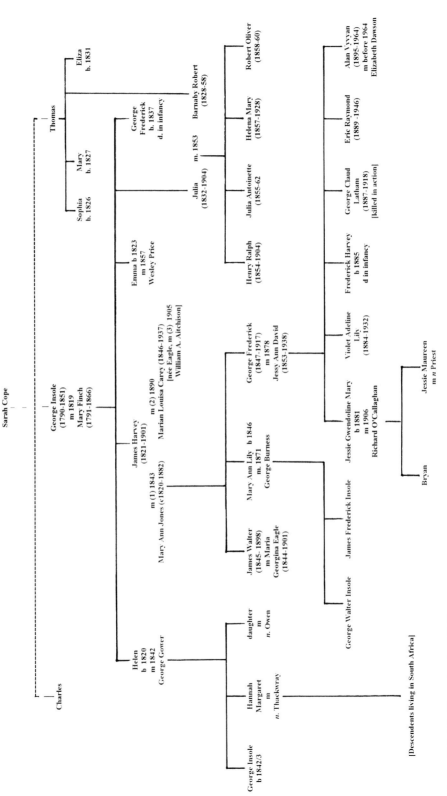

Note: Unverified relationships are shown by a dotted line.

Preface

Although this is primarily a history of the Insoles' businesses, it is also concerned with the life of the family and their connections. The sources, however, are not plentiful and little detailed information concerning their businesses has survived, as their records were destroyed when the firms were wound up. There is even less of their private affairs: they left no letters, diaries or other personal mementoes and, apart from a few important or illustrative incidents, there is little record of their domestic lives. There is no modern holder of any form of family archive.

I have therefore had to rely largely on books and other secondary sources to provide the narrative and, within that, concentrate on those events and topics covered by the primary sources. Among the published material I have been able to use E.D. Lewis's works, in which he cites the firm's letterbooks and accounts, often with quotations, as a quasi-primary source. As the story develops, however, the Insoles' businesses become more and more bound up with the South Wales coalfield as a whole and national issues begin to play a more important part in determining their policies, direction and management. In the twentieth century, in particular, the Insole material consists principally of annual accounts and reports which usually make references to the national situation. I have, therefore, in the later chapters used the secondary sources to describe the broader national background which largely determined the Insoles' fortunes.

The sources have enabled me to compile a narrative of the Insoles' businesses in the South Wales coal industry and to use those episodes and situations which are covered by the primary sources to deal with important topics and developments. The end result is, therefore, not comprehensive but probably sufficiently broad to portray the Insoles' businesses fairly, while describing the salient aspects of the family's private life.

The nature of the sources was one of the reasons why I adopted a narrative rather than a thematic approach. I also felt that the period was long and that both the characteristics of the coal industry and the key issues affecting it would vary considerably over a period of more than a century; those themes, for example, which were important in the 1840s would not always be significant in the 1920s. Chapters 1 and 10, therefore, provide an introduction and conclusion and each intervening chapter covers a defined period; I have dealt with the main themes of the story in those chapters where they seemed to be especially relevant.

I have throughout used the current Ordnance Survey spelling for place-names, except where they formed part of an incorrectly spelt nineteenth-century title. I have used contemporary weights, measures and money values. The Insoles described themselves as colliery proprietors but I have used the more usual term of coal owner to describe them and those like them who both mined and shipped coal. I have described their workers as colliers in the early years and miners later on, following contemporary practice.

This book is based on my M.A. dissertation and I wish therefore to thank Philip Riden, lately of University of Wales, Cardiff, for his assiduous and supportive supervision and for his work in preparing the book for publication. I am also grateful to Ieuan Edwards, the former Cardiff County Librarian, his successor Paul Sawyer, and Richard Phillips for their assistance in publication. My thanks are also due to the staffs of the Cardiff Central Library and of the Glamorgan Record Office for their support and assistance, as well as the staffs of the university libraries in Cardiff and the National Library of Wales, Rhondda Central Library, Merthyr Tydfil Central Library, Birmingham Central Library, Worcester City Library and the county record offices of Worcestershire, Gloucestershire and Somerset. I am indebted also to the staff of the British Red Cross Museum, the Welsh Guards Museum, the library of Trinity College, Cambridge and the Zoological Society of London. I wish to thank Matthew Williams, the Keeper of Collections at Cardiff Castle; William Clarke senior of W. Clarke of Llandaff for access to their records; Nevil James, the Llandaff Cathedral archivist, for advice on monuments and memorials; John Cornwell, for permission to use his photograph of Cymmer Colliery; Ron Clark of Porth and Ewart Richards of Cymmer for their memories of Cymmer Colliery; Arthur Weston Evans for his assistance on the history of the Cardiff & County Club; and Denise Bibby, for assistance with some complex word processing. I am grateful for the encouragement of many friends, particularly Terry Dauncey for reading it, but, above all, I must thank Gerry and Rebecca, my wife and daughter, for their unstinting support and forbearance over the past four years.

Llandaff   *Richard C. Watson*
September 1997

Chapter 1

The Insoles and their World

This is the story of George Insole, an artisan from the English Midlands, who settled in Cardiff and became one of the pioneers of the South Wales steam coal trade, and of his family which built on his foundations and prospered. Insole came to Cardiff in 1827 and, through four generations, the family business expanded from a coal yard beside the Glamorganshire Canal to collieries, docks, railways, farms, country estates and urban building land, which allowed George and his descendants to acquire wealth and social standing and, eventually, to survive the vicissitudes of the coal industry.

The Insole family's fortunes reflect the history of Cardiff and of the Rhondda valleys. In the 1820s Cardiff was the port for the ironworks of the Taff and Cynon valleys but it shipped little coal and handled much less traffic than either Swansea or Newport; it was also a market town for a local area of probably not much more than the traditional six miles radius. By 1880, however, the town had overtaken its rivals and in the following 30 years Cardiff was to develop into the world's largest coal exporting port. By 1913 it had become the centre of the South Wales coal trade and the area's major entrepot, had displaced Bristol from its role as the regional capital of South Wales and was the largest town in the Principality, with the status of a city.

This spectacular progress was partly driven and, to some extent, surpassed by that of the Rhondda valleys. In 1827 there were only two collieries in the Lower Rhondda but, in the second half of the century, the enormous world-wide demand for steam coal and advances in mining technology made it profitable to exploit its deepest seams. In 1913 the collieries of the Rhondda valleys raised 9,000,000 tons of coal for home consumption and export.

The industrialisation of South Wales had been in progress for 150 years when George Insole left Worcester for Cardiff. The origins of this development lay in the area's resources and geography. Its terrain and rainfall allowed water power to be exploited, it had wood for making charcoal, as well as limestone, iron ore and, above all, coal. Furthermore, parts of the coalfield were on the coast, giving easy access to shipping, and it was nowhere more than 25 miles from the sea. Until the early nineteenth century the increasingly rapid industrial development of South Wales had been driven by the metal industries and their use of coke for smelting: first the non-ferrous metals around Swansea and Neath and then the coke ironworks along the heads of the valleys, with the largest concentration of industry and population being around Merthyr Tydfil.

The entrepreneurs who built the metal industries were rich men, often merchants or gentry, who were able to meet the high costs of establishing their works. They regarded coal as a fuel for their furnaces and forges rather than as a profitable commodity in its own right and looked with some disdain on the sale coal trade. The coal owners who followed them came from more modest backgrounds and the cost of entering the coal industry was lower. George Insole was typical of this new class of entrepreneur and the story of his enterprise, difficulties and successes provides an insight into the genesis and early development of the South Wales coal trade. Similarly the way in which his family continued the business illustrates the typical development of successful nineteenth-century British entrepreneurs from industrialists to gentry.

The South Wales coal trade grew from very simple beginnings. In the late nineteenth and early twentieth century triumphalist historians of the industry told stories of the owners of small collieries, or more often their wives, taking coal to the neighbouring town's market or to a regular pitch on the back of a mule or in a hand cart, and selling it to the local people. Where coal was supplied in larger quantities it would be despatched by canal or tramroad and sold to a dealer at the port. Here the coal merchant would stock his wharf and sell cargoes to the captains of itinerant brigs, sloops and other small trading vessels, when they were in harbour. By the beginning of the twentieth century the Cardiff Coal Exchange was the centre of a complex market, involving long-term contracts, spot trading, world-wide chains of coaling stations, overseas agents and specialist dockside tips which screened and loaded coal at Cardiff, Penarth, Barry and the other coal ports on the South Wales coast. The way in which this change occurred provides an understanding of the background to the Insoles' story and includes the development of new marketing and selling techniques and institutions, the effect of competition and co-operation, as well as the identification of the different products of the coalfield.

The Insoles were not just merchants: they were colliery proprietors or coal owners from their earliest days in the trade. The questions that arise from this aspect of their business include the reasons for choosing particular sites for prospecting or colliery purchase, the way in which the collieries were managed and, in the case of new ventures, how a pit was sunk. Working methods and the use of new technology were also important in the development of collieries and in maintaining or enhancing their profitability and competitive position. Safety was a dominant issue, particularly at Cymmer, which experienced one of the worst colliery disasters of the middle years of the nineteenth century.

The coal industry in South Wales was pioneered by freebooting entrepreneurs and their agents who, in many cases, sprung from the new mining communities. They paid sufficient to attract the labour that they needed but paid little regard to the conditions under which their men and boys worked (there were hardly any women or girls employed in the sale coal collieries of South Wales). The colliers were able to obtain some involvement in the selection of officials with responsibility for safety but it was government action that effected and policed the reforms, which were necessary to minimise the risks of a dangerous occupation. A series of Acts of Parliament established HM Inspectors of Mines and gradually strengthened their powers and the rules governing colliery operations. The Insoles' employment practices and their relations with the inspectors illustrate the strength of their commitment, and that of their managers, to the safety of their men and to sound employment policies. The government's involvement in the coal industry eventually, through war and economic depression, led to controls, subsidies and ultimately nationalisation, to all of which the Insole businesses made their response.

The Insoles needed capital for both the coal trade and their colliery operations. George Insole started with very little but the business soon made the family's fortune. Although the role of entrepreneurs in providing capital from their own resources was an important feature of the coal industry in the mid nineteenth century, the coal owners needed other sources. The role of the banks and later the stock market, in financing coal prospecting and colliery development, was important in the growth of the Insoles' businesses, as was the spread of risk arising from joint stock organisation and the security provided by limited liability. The roles of owners, directors, shareholders and banks in bad times as well as in prosperity also need to be established.

The South Wales valleys, outside the iron towns, were sparsely populated before the collieries were opened, and so the new coal owners had to attract a labour force. Unlike many of the new industrial working class, the colliers had a tradition of being consulted by their employers, at least where their safety was concerned. The owners, therefore, required a regular dialogue with their workers and the development of this dialogue and the attitudes of the participants is a recurrent theme in the Insoles' history. It also raises questions about the style of management, the quality of supervision and the training and qualifications of those in charge of colliery operations. The role of the men's representatives and their trade unions is also an important feature of labour relations, as is the way in which the Insoles handled their own workforce.

George Insole had no land when he came to Cardiff but by the end
of the century the family not only had mineral leases for their business
but also extensive holdings of freehold land for living, recreation and
investment. A standard mineral lease had been adopted by most
landowners in South Wales by the time Insole acquired his first colliery
and the identity of the landlords and the terms of each lease can
sometimes be discovered. Of further interest was the practice of sub-
leasing parts of a mineral royalty and the reasons for doing it. Moreover,
in addition to their mineral holdings, the Insoles acquired land, mainly
in Cardiff, for housing development and limited industrial and commercial use. The role of this urban estate is an important element in the
diversification of the family's wealth but their more prominent land
acquisitions were country houses and parkland, farms and sporting
properties, which brought status and a place among the county gentry.

As the valleys were mainly used for pastoral farming before
industrialisation, their transport connections were minimal and primitive
but the movement of coal, in all but the smallest quantities, required
smooth transport at a reasonable cost. When George Insole started his
business the canals and tramroads, which connected the ironworks at the
heads of the valleys to the coastal ports was well established. He and his
family were to see the rise of the railways as successful rivals to the
canals and as replacements for the tramroads, as well as the building of
the docks at Cardiff and other ports. These developments were important
to the Insoles, not only for the services and benefits they provided but
also because of the problems which they brought. In addition the docks
and railway companies were actual or effective monopolies and were
able to dictate to their customers; the extent to which the Insoles were
involved in efforts to break these monopoly powers and to provide
competition is a recurring theme of their story.

George Insole had a reputation for pioneering and his family used his
role in the early steam coal trade as part of their efforts to promote their
products. There were other claimants in the field, however, and in a new
industrial venture, such as the opening up of the South Wales coalfield,
there were many opportunities to be the first to do something. It is
therefore of interest to discover the strength of Insole's claims to be a
pioneer of the steam coal trade. Of further interest is the possible
continuation of this tradition and the question of whether later generations of the family were fired by a similar pioneering spirit.

The success of the Insoles was firmly rooted in the growth of Cardiff
and the Rhondda valleys; Cardiff's growth, particularly in the closing
years of the century, was spectacular. Its success, however, was shared,
as the customs port of Cardiff included Penarth and Barry, which

Cardiff's borough councillors saw as rivals. The role that the Insoles played in the growth of docks and railways indicates their perceived standing in the business community and the influence which they were able to exert in local economic affairs. There was also division among Cardiff's leading citizens between the town, as represented by the borough (later city) council, and the coal and shipping interests of the port, represented by the chamber of commerce. The Insoles' involvement with these bodies demonstrates their commitment, if they had any, to either the townsmen or the docksmen, as the two groups were commonly called. The growth of Cardiff was not just a story of local and international trade; it was also about the spread of urban development, the provision of housing and public services and the growth of fashionable suburbs for the well-to-do. It would be expected that a family with increasing wealth and a desire to make their mark in local society would play a part in such developments.

The growth of the Rhondda valleys was contemporary with that of Cardiff and was, in many ways, the greater change. At the beginning of the nineteenth century Cardiff may have been a small market town but it had the status of a borough; it was the county town of Glamorgan, the seat of a local magnate, the Marquess of Bute, and a port connected with Bristol and the other ports of South Wales, South West England, the western seas of Britain and Ireland. The Rhondda, by contrast, was an area of rural tranquillity and largely remained so for most of the century, although once the coal of the two valleys had been won, industrialisation was rapid. Their development as an urban community, however, was not as richly endowed as Cardiff's, living conditions for the workers were modest, housing was basic and there were fewer public amenities. These tended to be provided not by the leaders of local industry but followed legislation which established local authorities and welfare organisations and by the self-help of the workers themselves. The activities of the Insoles and their local managers in this area sheds light on the roles of the coal owners in the development of mining communities.

George Insole came from the class of independent artisans but, by the end of the century, his family considered themselves to be gentry. They lived in country houses and participated in rural sports and activities, sent their children to public schools and universities and eventually ceded the day-to-day control of their businesses to those who had learnt about collieries and the coal trade as employees and managers rather than owners. This progression was not unusual for British industrialists and the Insoles became very rich. The use which they made of their wealth gives some indication of their status, the influence they could exert and the sort of family they were.

Chapter 2

Beginnings

1827–43

George Insole was born in Worcester in 1790 and his baptism, on 5 December that year, is recorded in the register of St Peter's parish, an artisans' quarter lying to the south of the Cathedral.[1] He was the son of a cabinet maker, William Insole, and his wife Sarah. There is no record of their having married in Worcester but on 20 June 1774 a William Insole was married to Sarah Cope at Pedmore, near Stourbridge on the edge of the Black Country. It is possible, particularly as Insole is an uncommon name, that these were George Insole's parents. Pedmore is about fifteen miles north of Worcester and was, in the late eighteenth century, in the early stages of industrialisation. It may well have had a largely young and shifting population as the number of illegitimate births in the parish register is about one in five of all baptisms. Stourbridge was linked to Worcester both by road and through the canal and river tributaries of the Stour and the Severn.

George Insole probably became his father's apprentice as he is variously described in the parish register as a carpenter and as a cabinet maker. On 11 August 1819 he married Mary Finch at All Saints church in Worcester and they set up home in High Street, close to St Helens parish church, where their eldest daughter, Helen, was baptised on 14 April 1820 and their son, James Harvey, on 2 May 1821. Mary, who could not write, came from Hartpury, a village in north west Gloucestershire, where she was baptised, the youngest of three children of Richard and Ann Finch, on 22 April 1791. Hartpury was a parish of nearly 3,000 acres, containing a manor house, the church and vicarage, a mill, a mason's yard and about eighteen farms. Its nearest towns were the small market town of Newent to the north west and, to the south east, the city of Gloucester which, like Worcester, Stourbridge and Cardiff, was a thriving town and river port on the water highway of the Severn and its tributaries and associated canals. George probably worked with his father, as he is not mentioned separately in trade directories. His father's home was in Foregate Street which extended then outside the northern

---

[1] The area was and still is the site of the Royal Worcester Porcelain Company.

boundary of the city, but was still only a couple of hundred yards from George Insole's home. The city of Worcester was the county town and had, at this time, some 18,000 inhabitants. The cathedral dominated the skyline but there were many other fine buildings, including the Queen Anne guildhall. In addition to being an administrative centre it was an important market town and claimed to have the biggest hop market in the kingdom; the 1820 directory records that 60 per cent of the county's hop harvest was traded in the town. It also had some industry; apart from the usual breweries, warehouses and mills of a country town there were three porcelain works, some forges and, above all, 100 glovers, who were estimated to give employment to 8,000 of the inhabitants. As well as its river and canal transport, it had regular stage-coach and postal connections with London, Bristol, Birmingham, Gloucester and other towns in western England and Wales.

There is little information on George Insole's life and work in Worcester in the following six years, although his second daughter, Emma, was born in the city on 29 August 1823 and was baptised at Angel Street Congregational Church on 25 January of the following year. Before he left Worcester, he had become, according to family tradition, a wood merchant, thus moving back up the supply chain from his trade as a cabinet maker. He would have required some capital for the venture and had, therefore, either been successful in his original trade or had come into money directly or through family connections. He was later to carry out a similar move in the coal business.

In 1827 George Insole moved to Cardiff with his family. They had a choice for the journey, including the river route down the Severn, the road via Gloucester, Monmouth and Newport or the mail coach to Bristol followed by a sea crossing, either directly or on a ferry, either from Aust to Beachley or across the new passage to Portskewett, where there was a turnpike road to Newport. Insole came to Cardiff to set up a partnership with Richard Biddle, who also had a family business in Merthyr Tydfil, as timber, coal and brick merchants. The firm was known as Insole & Biddle and had a yard in St Mary's parish, from which they conducted their business. Its frontage on the canal was 100 ft and its width 400 ft; it contained a dry dock for vessels of up to 80 tons burden, suitable for the repair of canal barges. They also had a brickyard on the moors one mile to the south of the town, containing kilns, sheds and a fireman's cottage in about seven acres and extending from the canal eastwards to what was to be the site of the West Dock. Both properties were leased from the Marquess of Bute, the dockyard on a 61 year lease for ten guineas p.a. and the brickyard for 21 years at £35 8s p.a.[1] Insole eventually settled in the fashionable suburb of Crockherbtown, now Queen Street, at its junction with Park Place, then known as Bradley's Lane. Originally a small community of houses and gardens outside the East Gate of the town, it became a shopping and commercial centre following the opening of the Taff Vale railway station at its eastern end in 1840 and it was renamed Queen Street, at the request of its tradesmen, in the 1880s. Over the years Insole was to extend the gardens of this property, in a thin plot up to the present site of the Reardon Smith Lecture Theatre on the side of the National Museum of Wales. He later gave up or disposed of the land on the corner of Bradley's Lane and Crockherbtown, leaving himself an L-shaped plot, which in recent years was occupied by Seccombe's store. Richard Biddle also had a house in Crockherbtown; although described as a Merthyr Tydfil man, he seems to have had some standing in Cardiff and was a constable in 1829.

Cardiff was not necessarily the obvious centre, at this date, in which to set up a new business in South Wales. Swansea was a larger town, with a growing population of over 13,000, in the western part of the coalfield, an area where both industry and trade were well established and which had gained a reputation for the quality of its steam raising, coking and house coals. Closer still, Newport was of comparable size to Cardiff, with about half the population of Swansea. It was also, with shipments of around 420,000 tons per annum, the leading coal exporting port of the coalfield, ahead of Swansea's 165,000 and Cardiff's 30,400.[2] Newport also had the advantage of being exempt from tariffs in the coal trade to the east of the Holms, an area which included Bristol, Bridgwater and the upstream ports of the River Severn. Cardiff's principal trading role at this period was as the port for the ironworks, from Dowlais to Hirwaun, which used the Glamorganshire Canal and, according to the town's 1829 directory, 60,000 tons had been shipped in the previous year to London, Liverpool, Ireland, Scotland and the Mediterranean. In addition it handled 20,000 boxes of tinplate from Melingriffith and the output of Brown Lenox & Co.'s chain works at Nantgarw. Its coal trade had been around 100,000 tons per annum between 1816 and 1823 but then remained below 30,000 tons until 1828. The town had also an iron foundry, a new dry dock and Guest & Co.'s

---

[1] *Cambrian*, 9 April 1831.

[2] J. Williams, *Digest of Welsh Historical Statistics* (Welsh Office, 1985), I, pp. 318-323: coal shipments in 1828 (tons): Cardiff 30,428, Swansea 165,430, Newport 422,782.

recently erected glass works.[1] Nevertheless, Cardiff's population remained relatively small, although it had grown nearly fourfold since the 1801 census and exceeded 6,000 in 1831. Merthyr Tydfil, however, was by far the largest town in South Wales, with 20,000 inhabitants, and it seems that George Insole's choice of Cardiff was not made on the basis of population, industry or trade. It is probable, therefore, that he or his family already had some well established connections with the town, either directly or, more likely, through his partner, Richard Biddle. Biddle is a name which appears in a number of contemporary parish registers in Worcestershire, so it is possible that, like George Insole, his family was from the county.

The first months of the partnership, from June to December 1827,[2] were successful. Timber sales totalled £1,073 0s 2d but, to modern eyes, they do not seem to have been particularly busy, with only one or two sales recorded each day. The timber was mainly pine or deal and elm, some imported from North America; these were often sold prepared for building which seems to have been their main market. Elm, however, was also used in cabinet making and boat building and pine for cheaper furniture and in cupboards and shelves. It is interesting that building timber, for example boards or laths, was nearly always sold to a householder or a firm, rather than to a contractor, suggesting that the building industry had not yet developed very far in Cardiff.

Among Insole & Biddle's customers were a number of influential people and firms from Cardiff and its hinterland, including the Dowlais Iron Company and William Crawshay & Son, the two largest iron companies of Merthyr Tydfil. Some other customers were Walter Coffin (1785–1867), the Rhondda coal owner, who was to become his rival in the coal trade, as well as a founder of the Taff Vale Railway and MP for Cardiff, E. Priest Richards, a solicitor and member of the gentry family of Plasnewydd, Cardiff, who was the town clerk of Cardiff and, from 1820 to 1867, agent to the second Marquess of Bute (1793–1848), as well as members of the Vachell family, who owned a number of properties in central Cardiff. They also sold timber to the gas company, numerous public houses, tradesmen and shops, as well as cabinet makers and carpenters. Insole & Biddle had an impressive list of customers for a new business, reinforcing the probability that many of connections had been established earlier. In addition to timber, their sales included a canal boat for Walter Coffin, at a price of £100. Canal boats were up to

[1] *Cardiff Guide & Directory* (1829).
[2] Glamorgan Record Office (hereafter GRO), D/D Xcv 1.

60 ft long with a maximum beam of 8 ft 9 in. and carried between 18 and 24 tons, depending on the amount of water in the canal;[1] Insole's boatloads were recorded at between 20 and 24 tons and would have been weighed at the lock and weighing apparatus which was erected on the canal, first beside North Road, Cardiff and then at Crockherbtown in what is now Friary Street.[2] The firm's sales ledger also contains a number of money transactions, involving traders, solicitors, agents and Towgood's the bankers, as well as occasional items for private consumption, such as a flitch of bacon.

In January 1828 the partnership received a setback when a commission in bankruptcy against John and Richard Biddle of Merthyr Tydfil was held in Bristol. The firm of Insole & Biddle, however, survived for a time and from 10 February to 19 May 1829 the day book was recording activities in all parts of the business.[3] The turnover from the sales of timber exceeded that of coal and bricks; the coastal trade in coal was more active in the summer, while at this stage the brick business was busier in the winter. Further activity is recorded for the period from 1 April to 10 September 1830 and they seem to have been busier by this time. Although timber sales had declined to a few orders in the period, the brick trade was brisker, achieving sales of £117 5s 5½d, while the coal trade had grown and Insole spent some time searching out new suppliers and customers, recording travel expenses, of 6d and £25 respectively, for trips to the Rhondda and to Ireland. They also carried out repairs to two boats belonging to the Dowlais Company. The first was a small job for which they charged £1 12s 9d for labour and £2 0s 7d for materials, the second was more substantial and cost £48 2s 1½d. They built a canal boat for Robert Thomas of Abercanaid near Merthyr Tydfil, one of their coal suppliers, for £90 and tendered for a lighter, which would have been used to take coal and iron cargoes out of the canal to larger ships lying in Cardiff Bay. From the entries for wages in their accounts, it seems that the firm did not maintain a staff of its own for this kind of work but hired the necessary labour, including sawyers and shipwrights, when the need arose, paying between 3s 6d and 4s per day to the skilled tradesmen. This is another indication that, among smaller businesses at least, the modern concept of the firm with a full-time, permanent workforce was not yet well established in Cardiff.

Nevertheless Insole and Biddle cannot have enjoyed the happiest of

---

[1] C. Hadfield, *The Canals of South Wales and the Border* (Cardiff, 1967), p. 110.

[2] This weighing machine is now at the Canal Museum, Stoke Bruerne, Northants.

[3] GRO, D/D Xcv 1.

business relationships, for on 1 January 1831 the partnership was dissolved by mutual consent, reputedly on account of the bankruptcy of Richard Biddle, with Insole complaining of Biddle's 'having defrauded me by every means in his power'.[1] This was not, however, the end of George Insole's problems, as a commission in bankruptcy, dated 14 February 1831, was awarded against himself and Richard Biddle.[2] Following the hearing in Bristol, a meeting of creditors was held in Cardiff on 26 March to assent to the sale of the partners' assets; further meetings followed in August 1831 and in January and June 1832 for the payment of dividends from the sale of assets and payments by the firm's creditors and the appropriate certificate was issued in December 1833.[3] George Insole, however, appears to have survived this setback, probably because he had already taken steps to establish his own business outside the partnership. In February 1830 he had acquired a wharf and yard at the southern end of the sea-lock in order to set up in business on his own as a coal shipper.

The presence of coal with iron ore and limestone on the northern outcrop of the coalfield had attracted the eighteenth-century ironmasters to the area. Although they had regarded coal primarily as a fuel for their ironworks, rather than an important commodity in the local economy, by the end of the first quarter of the nineteenth century a large trade in coal from the Monmouthshire valleys had grown up at Newport. In east Glamorgan, however, the iron companies controlled most of the larger collieries and the mining of coal for sale was confined to a small number of pits and levels.

These sale coal collieries served three main markets: the local trade in house coal, known as land sale, the coastal trade in the Severn estuary, around the western seas and to Ireland; and the newer trade in steam raising coal, which extended as far as London. The last was at this time dominated by the semi-anthracite coals of west Glamorgan, shipped mainly from Llanelli and Swansea; Llangennech, Watt's Llanelly, Graigola and Llansamlet, in particular, had well established reputations. The coal trade of Newport and Cardiff was based on its bituminous house coals which were used not only by households for heating and cooking, but also by blacksmiths, commercial undertakings and industry. Newport, with its tariff exemptions and a successful group of coal

---

[1] Insole MSS, Letter Book, cited by E.D. Lewis, 'Pioneers of the Cardiff Coal Trade', *Glamorgan Historian*, 11 (1984), p. 38.

[2] *Cambrian,* 26 Feb. 1831.

[3] *Cambrian*, 12 March, 13 Aug. 1831; 14 Jan., 30 June 1832; 7 Dec. 1833.

shippers and owners, including Thomas Powell (1784–1864), had a commanding position. Thomas Powell was an important figure in the development of the sale coal industry and after his death, in his office at the age of eighty in 1864, his sons formed the Powell Duffryn Company, which was eventually to dominate the South Wales coalfield in the 1920s and 1930s. The trade of Cardiff was in the hands of a number of local merchants, who bought from the small collieries, which were alongside or linked by tramway to the Glamorganshire Canal. Cardiff's leading coal owner at this time was Walter Coffin, who lived in Llandaff and had a well established colliery at Dinas by the lower reaches of the Rhondda Fawr; he had been mining and trading out of Cardiff since 1809. He was joined by Thomas Powell, who in 1828 had sunk a pit at Llancaiach Fawr near Gelligaer, which he had connected by tramroad to the Glamorganshire Canal. In March 1830 Powell leased a 318-ft wharf on the west bank of the sea-lock from the Marquess of Bute, which he linked, by a small tramroad, to a jetty on the Taff, enabling him to load ships either in the sea-lock or on the river.[1]

George Insole set out to sell in four main market sectors: house coal, engine coal for industry, smith's work and the new and growing market for steam coal. In all these he faced widespread competition and his first sales, while still in the partnership, were to local businesses and householders, including many of the firm's brick and timber customers. Soon, however, he was actively seeking both new markets and customers and securing regular supplies of coal. His bituminous coals came from several collieries in the Taff Valley, the most important of which were John Davies's Gelliwion Level near Newbridge (the modern Pontypridd) and David Morley's Craig-yr-Allt Level, on the mountainside opposite Taff's Well, while in 1830 he started to market Waun Wyllt steam coal from Robert Thomas of Abercanaid. His land sale customers were the households, inns, offices, shops and small industrial workshops of Cardiff and the surrounding area. The trade consisted of consignments of one ton or a few hundredweight for individual customers as well as smaller retail sales at the firm's yard. This was a busier trade in 1830 than in the previously recorded years and in April, apart from the retail business, there were over 170 transactions, totalling 154 tons and realising £67 or an average price of 8s 8½d per ton. As the usual retail price in the day book was 9s per ton, Insole seems to have offered bulk discounts.

The coastal trade was not so predictable; the usual method of trading in the early nineteenth century was for the merchants to sell their coal

---

[1] Lewis, 'Pioneers of the Cardiff Coal Trade', p. 31.

on the dock side to the masters of the itinerant sloops, schooners and brigs of the western seas, when they arrived in port. Insole at first followed this practice and his yard was one of a group with an advantageous position at the entrance to the sea-lock. He was not, however, prepared to leave the growth of his business to the vagaries of the ships' voyages and their calls at Cardiff or to the whims of their masters, and so, following the example of his rival, Walter Coffin, he travelled regularly to establish his markets and maintained communication with customers and agents through the post. The high cost of sending letters before the introduction of the penny post in 1840 is well illustrated by a payment of postage for items to Belfast, Dundalk, Enniscorthy and Plymouth, which amounted to 6s 2d. The firm's day book records a number of visits to the ports of the West Country and Ireland, where Cardiff's trade was not affected by the tariff advantages which Newport enjoyed in the Bristol Channel trade. Nevertheless the coastal trade in coal, which included Ireland, was also more seasonal than land sale, with shipping building up in the summer months (Table 2.1).

Table 2.1:
Weekly coastal sales, Insole & Biddle, April–June 1830

Week ending Saturday	Vessels	Volume		Value		
		tons	cwt	£	s	d
1 May	2	28	0	7	17	0
15 May	6	49	12	19	4	3
22 May	7	662	15	183	3	7½
29 May	4	404	0	129	4	0
5 June	2	7	10	3	3	9
12 June	5	386	10	140	12	0
19 June	4	361	0	134	9	6
26 June	4	369	0	134	11	0
3 July	5	389	0	142	3	9
Total for quarter	35	2,657	7	894	8	10½

Source: GRO, Xcv 1, Insole Industrial Records, Insole & Biddle Day Book 1830. There were no coastal sales recorded before 26 April or in the week ending 8 May.

Of these sales, 197 tons 17 cwt were sales to masters which realised £79 3s 10½d, producing an average price of 8s per ton. There were twelve such sales in the quarter, usually for small quantities of a ton or less, although, in the same period, two larger cargoes of up to 108 tons were sold to the 'captain and owners' of the ship rather than to its master alone, possibly indicating the establishment of syndicates of speculative purchasers at the ship's home port. Apart from one cargo sent to Penzance, all the larger cargoes were consigned to customers in Ireland. As well as the main towns of Dublin, Belfast and Limerick, Insole had shipped to customers along the south coast, at Cork, Youghal, Kinsale and Waterford, and at Drogheda, Dundalk and Wexford on the east. In addition he had made sales in the inland river ports of Enniscorthy, New Ross and Clonmel.[1] His customers were mainly local coal merchants but also included a distiller and a brewer. Walter Coffin, however, was already well established in Ireland and Insole's activities presented him with a challenge which marked the start of twenty years of competition between them. The Irish market, however, was buoyant, as the prosperity of the wealthier, and mostly Protestant, classes had been growing since the Act of Union in 1801, which had established free trade between Britain and Ireland. In all, Insole had customers at the Irish ports from Limerick to Belfast and at ports along the English coast as far as Plymouth. The western seas provided the highway for a large trading area which included four of the largest towns in the country, Bristol, Liverpool, Glasgow and Dublin which, with over 200,000 inhabitants recorded in the 1831 census, was then the second largest city in the United Kingdom. Insole's coal was carried on the ships which traded on the western seas, often coming from more distant ports; one of his sales was to a 'Dutchman' and another was carried on the *Hero* of Yarmouth. The majority, however, were from western Britain and Ireland, including in this period the *Amicitia* from Aberystwyth, the *Mariner* from Aberdyfi and the *Thetis*, owned by John Davies of Cardigan, which at that time had the largest registered tonnage of any port in Wales.[2]

Insole was an enthusiastic salesman and a keen writer of advertising notices describing his coals. In 1830 Gelliwion coal, for example, was claimed to be 'excellent for smith's work, gas or coke' and in one of his letters he described Maesmawr as 'a brown ash coal, entirely free from dead slack, superior in quality to any in this neighbourhood'.[3] By the following summer, having weathered the bankruptcy of the partnership, he was once again selling vigorously and wrote: 'The demand for coal from Cardiff I believe was never so great as this summer ... and we

---

[1] GRO, Xcv 1.

[2] *Cambrian Register*, Vol. III, cited by C. Wilkins, *The South Wales Coal Trade* (Cardiff, 1888), p. 318.

[3] Lewis, 'Pioneers of the Cardiff Coal Trade', p. 39.

cannot cope with more than 600 to 800 tons of shipping at a time ... Since I have had anything to do with Gelliwion coal, I have sold more than any other individual that preceded me.'[1]

In 1831 he would have needed all his efforts to recover from the effects of the bankruptcy and to establish himself as an independent coal trader, especially as he no longer had the brick and timber businesses to assist him. The financial results of the firm's coal sales in the second quarter of 1830 were probably of the following order: 2,227 tons of house coal, at a margin of 1s 6d per ton, yielding £167 profit; 430 tons of steam coal at a margin of 4s per ton, yielding £86; and 460 tons of retail sales, at a margin of 2s 6d, yielding £57 10s. the total quarterly profit would thus have been about £310. Given that the winter was a slack time for the coastal trade, they would have been lucky to make £1,000 in 1830, out of which they would have to meet the costs of running the business and have taken their income. As their average weekly sales were less than 240 tons or just over a third of their best week, Insole probably felt that he had the capacity to increase his business and, with more effort and success in his sales campaigns, he would soon be able to prosper.

His optimism was fully justified by his success but is also born out by estimates of his yard's capacity and his probable income. The tonnage of the typical small coal vessel which was used by Insole was between 150 and 200 tons, and so, with a capacity of 600 to 800 tons, he had space at his wharf for four ships at a time. As he was able to load and despatch more than four ships in one week, it is probable that he could accommodate at least two ships in each berth in six days. Any assessment of his wharf's capacity must also take account of the time taken to unload canal boats and to load the ships. In the accounts men are paid for 'wheeling coal on the yard'[2] and it is likely that at this stage of his fortunes he would have used barrows to move his coal. A modern coal merchant would expect to load a 2 cwt barrow in two minutes and Insole's men or the ships' crews would probably have required a similar time, to which should be added about three minutes to push the barrow from the stockpile to the ship, load the coal into the hold and return; a similar time would be needed for unloading the canal boats. A ship's crew of three men in Insole's day should, therefore, have been able to load about 3 tons 12 cwt in an hour, giving them the capacity to load the

[1] Insole MSS, Letter-book, 30 Aug. 1831, cited by Lewis, 'Pioneers of the Cardiff Coal Trade', p. 39.
[2] GRO, Xcv 1.

average 75-ton cargo in just over a day and a half. In addition to loading, the ships' masters would need to take on supplies, carry out repairs and rest or change their crews. Insole would also have needed time to receive new supplies as it would take one man a day and a half to unload a canal boat. It is therefore probable that Insole would have been lucky to get more than four days loading in a week, giving a maximum capacity of 800 tons per week using barrows. If he were working to capacity, and he was given to exaggeration, his weekly gross profit could have been between £85 and £120, depending on the relative quantities of retail sales, house coals, coastal and steam coal. He would have been lucky to achieve this level of coastal sales every week and it is more likely that he would have averaged some lesser figure for the five summer months from mid April to mid September and considerably less in the other seven. Nevertheless, if he achieved 80 per cent success in the summer and only 10 per cent in the other months, he would, with his profits on retail sales, have made a gross surplus of between £2,000 and £2,700 in the year. Out of this he would have to meet the cost of wages, premises, his domestic expenses and such incidentals as the gratuities paid to ships' masters. £2,000 per annum was a good income for a man of business in Cardiff at the time and would have enabled Insole to make the transformation from bankruptcy in January 1831 to colliery owner by January 1833.

Among his early shipments to Ireland, on 26 April 1830, was a cargo of 125 tons for Alexanders of Cork at the price of £40 12s 6d. The word 'Merthyr', which was written in pencil underneath the record of his sale, indicates that the cargo was steam coal and was part of one of George Insole's earliest purchases from the Waun Wyllt colliery at Abercanaid, south of Merthyr Tydfil, in the upper Taff valley. In 1824 Robert Thomas, who came from Llansamlet in west Glamorgan and had worked for a number of years in the colliery of the Cyfarthfa ironworks, had leased the small Waun Wyllt colliery from the Earl of Plymouth. It was a condition of the lease that he was not allowed to build a blast furnace or sell to the ironmasters so that the colliery's output should be confined to the sale coal trade. When he died in 1833, at the age of 58, his widow, Lucy Thomas, continued the business with her son, William. As a widow and a female pioneer she had a unique place in the history of the coalfield, biographers and historians of the South Wales coal industry often calling her the mother of the Welsh steam coal trade. She remained in business with her son for a number of years, moving first to the neighbouring pit at Garth, when the Waun Wyllt lease was not renewed, and then to the Cynon Valley after a leasing dispute with the landowner at Abercanaid, which was not resolved for a number of years. Neither

Robert nor Lucy Thomas could write but they proved to be an enterprising pair. Their first customers were local businesses and householders in Merthyr but they were keen to find a wider market. William Crawshay, Thomas's former employer, was at first opposed to his using the Glamorganshire Canal, in which he was a major shareholder, but eventually relented and on 10 February 1829 the day book of Insole & Biddle recorded the payment of £14 to Robert Thomas for two boat-loads of Waun Wyllt coal. The coal sold readily in Insole's usual markets of South West England and Ireland and Insole, recognising the qualities of the Merthyr Four Foot seam of steam coal and using his increasing knowledge of the national coal trade, probably realised that it would be attractive to the infant steam shipping market, particularly the Thames steam tugs and packet boats. He therefore sought to enter the London market and, on 20 April 1830, took an order from Samuel Welsford of Betts Street, near the London Docks for 120 tons of 'Wain Wilt' coal at 7s 3d per ton, to be delivered within three months. There was, however, some unexplained delay in shipping the coal, although an advance of £3 had been paid to a Captain Thomas, and it was eventually despatched on 12 November on the *Mars* of Shields (master, Captain W. Wright), which was probably larger than Insole's usual freighters as it had to finish loading outside the sea-lock. Insole met all the costs of what was a promotional sale; having paid Robert Thomas 4s per ton and met other expenses, Insole's gross profit was £19 10s, which he complained, 'barely paid the freightage'. The coal, however, was well received and the Thames steam tugs gave publicity to its efficiency and to its smokeless qualities. The following year Insole agreed to supply the London merchants, Edward Wood and Co., of Northumberland Wharf, Strand, with 3,000 tons of Waun Wyllt coal. As a result of the success of the coal 'Merthyr' became the accepted description for Welsh steam coal, giving its name to a number of coals and collieries in the South Wales valleys. George Insole's entry into the trade had been a success and in 1833 he was receiving a boat load a day from Lucy Thomas. He had also entered both the export and Admiralty trades. In 1831 he had sent a cargo of steam coal to Malta and in the same year bunkered HMS *St Pierre*, thus becoming the first South Wales coal owner to supply the Royal Navy. Within a few years Insole was sending cargoes of steam coal to new markets, including Brighton and Ramsgate, as well as further foreign shipments, to Quebec and Alexandria. As Quebec had been the source of some of his timber stocks, he may have had connections there to assist his entry to the coal trade.[1]

It was on these ventures that Insole and his family based his claim to be the pioneer of the steam coal trade to London. This claim was disputed by George Lockett and James Merryweather, two London merchants, who visited Lucy Thomas in 1830 and, reportedly, agreed to take all the coal she could supply. In July 1831, however, Insole wrote to Robert Thomas complaining 'that Mr Noble, Mr Pryde and Mr George Lockett (Junior) are being allowed to ship your coal as well as myself, after you had agreed not to let any other person ship your coal as well as myself'.[2] The argument over who was the pioneer persisted through-out the nineteenth century.[3] Lockett later went into colliery ownership and Merryweather added coal sales to the ironmongery business, which he had opened in Cardiff. Insole's successful entry into the steam coal trade was by no means an easy one and his letters demonstrate the volatile and competitive nature of the business. In July 1832 he told Thomas that he could have sold five times the quantity that he had received but, in the following November, that he must stop sending coal for a little while as it was impossible to sell it in the winter months. In 1833 he complained that Edward Wood was selling steam coal from his rivals, the Llangennech Company,[4] Guest's Dowlais and the Newport coal shippers, at a lower price than Merthyr coal. In 1834 the market was once again buoyant and he was urging Lucy Thomas to send down greater quantities; he had four boat loads (84 tons) in stock and he needed four to five thousand tons; he feared that he might lose the London market to his rivals. These fears, however, were unfounded as the use of steam ships for coastal and river traffic was increasing. By 1836 he was convinced that his Merthyr coal, selling at 8s per ton, had an assured market in London, while in the same year he agreed to supply the Cardiff & Bristol Steam Packet Company with 21½ tons weekly for their channel steamers, the *Lady Charlotte* and *The Prince of Wales*. Nevertheless, in spite of his efforts Insole's sales of South Wales steam coal were still surpassed by those of the Llangennech Co.; even in 1840

[1] Lewis, 'Pioneers of the Cardiff Coal Trade', pp. 43–4.

[2] Insole MSS, Letter-book, 27 Aug. 1831, cited by Lewis, 'Pioneers of the Cardiff Coal Trade', p. 45.

[3] C. Wilkins, *The South Wales Coal Trade* (Cardiff, 1888), pp. 71-6.

[4] J.H. Morris and L.J. Williams, *The South Wales Coal Industry 1844–75* (Cardiff, 1958), p. 22n. The Llangennech Co. was a group of London merchants, shipping from Llanelli, who entered the London steam coal market in 1824 and were the leading shippers of Welsh steam coal to the London market for 20 years.

Insole sold 9,771 tons and Llangennech 17,692.[1]

Meanwhile, Insole was busy in the bituminous house coal trade and was scarcely able to keep up with demand, particularly for coal from the Gelliwion Colliery near Pontypridd, although he had received complaints about breakages in transit. Nevertheless, increased demand and the opportunities offered by the withdrawal of Newport's customs privileges in 1831 prompted him to look for a colliery which he might operate himself and so secure a regular source of supply. On 12 October 1832, following a successful sales trip to Ireland, he made enquiries of Dr John Thomas Casberd of Penmark, who had inherited the property from his mother, Elizabeth, the daughter of Robert Mathew of Maesmawr, about the possibility of leasing the old colliery there, on the west bank of the Taff, opposite Upper Boat. Insole, maintaining an ill-concealed secrecy, purported to write on behalf of 'a relation of mine, a Gentleman of Property, who is inclined to treat for the same'.[2] Coal mining at Maesmawr, in the parish of Llantwit Fardre, is mentioned in Llwyd's *Parochialia,* compiled in 1697, but the colliery in which Insole was interested had fallen on hard times. Output carried on the Glamorganshire Canal had declined from 15,481 tons in 1820, when it was the leading colliery to ship out of Cardiff, to 6,594 in 1830, when its lessee, John Bennet Grover, was in such financial difficulties that he could not pay his workmen. In the same year Grover gave up his lease of his wharf and yard at the sea lock entrance and it was this yard that was then taken over by George Insole. The colliery seems, from the Glamorganshire Canal Co. returns, to have ceased production in 1831,[3] when Grover sought to sub-lease it himself, claiming that between 60 and 100 tons could be raised daily.[4]

Following a survey by the Merthyr mining engineer, William Harrison, George Insole agreed terms with Dr Casberd and in November 1832 reopened the Maesmawr level. He also wanted to open a level from the neighbouring farm of Maesbach, the property of the Marquess of Bute, probably at first to assist in the drainage of the Maesmawr seams. On 26 December 1832 he wrote to E. Priest Richards, the marquess's agent, offering to take at least 30 tons of coal per day[5] 'and as much

[1] Lewis, 'Pioneers of the Cardiff Coal Trade', pp. 45-6.

[2] Ibid., p. 39.

[3] Ibid.

[4] *Cambrian*, 23 March 1831.

[5] Insole MSS, Letter-book, 26 Dec. 1832, cited by Lewis, 'Pioneers of the Cardiff Coal Trade', p. 39.

more as can be disposed of in the Royalty' from Maesbach. He offered
a royalty of 10d per ton for the 4 ft vein and 6d for the 3 ft, with a
wayleave of 1d per ton. Following this offer a survey was carried out by
Robert Beaumont of Llandaff, a mineral surveyor regularly employed by
the marquess. He had carried out a survey in 1830 for a previous offer,
which had come to nothing, although he noted that some of the
Maesbach seams had been worked by Grover. He did not think that the
property was very promising but recommended that a level should be
made, 6 ft 6 in. high by 7 ft wide, in conjunction with Dr Casberd and
that a royalty of 1s per ton for coal drained by the level and 10d for the
rest should be asked. Beaumont believed that Insole's lower offer was
the result of Casberd's charging a wayleave of 2d per ton, which he
thought excessive and advised the marquess, if Casberd would not reduce
it, to build his own tramroad to the canal or to wait for a railroad to be
built. This observation would seem to indicate that a railway in the Taff
valley was being discussed in practical terms, by surveyors and others
concerned with the trade of the valley, at this time.[1] Insole entered into
an agreement with the marquess, although he also spent £3,000 to open
a pit at Maesmawr and does not seem to have worked the Maesbach
seams until the Maesmawr colliery itself was almost exhausted. The plan
of the Taff Vale Railway, deposited with the clerk of the peace in
November 1835, shows no colliery on Maesbach land. On the same plan,
the Maesmawr colliery, on level ground at the southern end of an
eastwards loop in the Taff, appears well-developed with workshops, an
engine house, stores, cottages and a quarry; the colliery was connected
by tramroad to the canal. A surviving account book shows royalties paid
to Dr Casberd until 1840 and thereafter to the Marquess of Bute.[2]
George Insole's Maesmawr colliery provided him with increasing
quantities of coal throughout the 1830s; in 1833 output was 12,943
tons,[3] which by 1839 had nearly doubled to 23,444 tons. He continued
to build up his markets by direct selling to customers both in his
established West Country markets, including Minehead, Bideford, Truro,
Penzance and Plymouth, and in Ireland, which he visited every summer.
He also sought house coal sales with some success in Bristol and
London, building on his established position in the steam coal trade.

Insole's colliery venture proved timely as the 1830s saw a steady
expansion of the iron and coal trades in the Glamorgan valleys. New

---

[1] Cardiff Central Library (hereafter CCL), MS 4.1035, Bute VII.4.

[2] GRO, D/D Xcv 3.

[3] *Cambrian*, 11 Jan. 1834.

ironworks were opened and new coal seams won, in response to the increased demand for iron, particularly for railways, and for coal to provide fuel for new homes, industry and transport. It soon became clear that the Glamorganshire Canal and its sea-lock, with a capacity of 1.5 million tons a year,[1] were becoming inadequate for the growing trade of Cardiff. The two responses to this situation, the Bute Dock and the Taff Vale Railway, were, with the reserves of steam coal in the valleys, to provide the foundation for the success of Cardiff as a port and as the business centre of the South Wales coal trade.

In the 1820s, the Marquess of Bute had been recommended to use his lands to the south of Cardiff to develop a new port for Cardiff. Following a survey by Captain W.H. Smyth to assess the relative merits of the west and east sides of Cardiff Bay, it was decided to build a new ship canal immediately to the south of the town. This scheme, later to become the Bute West Dock, was completed in 1839 and its first ship, the *Lady Charlotte,* the Cardiff & Bristol steam packet, possibly bunkered by George Insole, entered the dock on its formal opening on 6 October 1839. The dock was part of the comprehensive development of a new town on the moors. Houses were built to suit all social classes, although those with the means soon moved away, leaving Butetown to become the town's seamen's quarter. The marquess's housing scheme also put an end to various small scale industries, including ship building, which had formerly occupied the site.

While the Marquess of Bute was building his dock, the ironmasters, whose predecessors had built the canal a generation earlier, were promoting a railway to complement and replace it. The promoters, led by Sir Josiah John Guest of Dowlais (1785–1852), who was the first MP for Merthyr Tydfil, included the colliery proprietors Walter Coffin and Thomas Powell, as well as George Insole, according to nineteenth-century family tradition. The railway's promoters secured Isambard Kingdom Brunel (1806–59) as their consulting engineer and successfully fought off the opposition of the Glamorganshire Canal Company to secure parliamentary approval. On 18 October 1840 the first fifteen miles from Cardiff to Navigation House, Abercynon, were opened and the line to Merthyr was completed in April the following year. The dock and the railway provided Cardiff and its hinterland with the means to begin their spectacular growth in the mining, trading and shipping of coal.

George Insole was in a good position to take advantage of these new developments and by 1841 he was employing 157 men and boys at

---

[1] Morris and Williams, *South Wales Coal Industry,* p. 3.

Maesmawr, putting him among the larger sale coal owners of South Wales. He was also mining on the adjoining Bute land at Maesbach and he owned the neighbouring property of Gedrys Farm, which he probably used for his pit horses and for hay production. The colliery was managed by his agent, Jabez Thomas, who first appears in the firm's records in 1830, receiving a weekly wage of 13s, rising to 15s in a few weeks. Jabez Thomas was born at St Nicholas in the Vale of Glamorgan and was baptised in the parish church on 10 March 1798. While managing the Maesmawr Colliery, he was also a leading member of Carmel, the Methodist meeting house in the parish of Eglwysilan, on the opposite bank of the Taff. He was a trusted servant of the family, putting his management and mining skills at their service until his retirement, as chief agent, in 1877.

During the 1830s coal mining came to be seen as an important contributor to the local economy in its own right, rather than as an adjunct of the iron industry. It was also coming to national prominence and, by 1841, there was sufficient public concern about the employment practices of the ironmasters and colliery owners to warrant the establishment of a Royal Commission to investigate the employment of children in the mines. The commission visited every coalfield and interviewed managers, adult workers and the children themselves. They were more often than not appalled by what they found and their report in 1842, with eloquent comment and vivid illustrations, was followed by the Mines Act of 1842 which prohibited the employment of children under ten underground in collieries and mines. R.H. Franks, the senior commissioner reporting on South Wales, drew attention to the deleterious effect of mine working on the health, vigour and development of the children, their long working hours of up to 14 hours a day, their wages of 2s 6d to 10s per week, which were paid to the father, their meals and holidays and their lack of schooling and religious knowledge, as well as the dangers inherent in the work. He was, however, complimentary about the women's efforts in keeping the children well clothed and regularly fed.

Jabez Thomas was interviewed by the commissioners at Maesmawr, when he commented on the number of public houses in the district, which he believed were better attended than the chapel on Sundays. His statement also included some information about the colliery. The pit was 180 ft deep and the seam 3 ft 8 in. thick. There were two steam engines, one for pumping and one for winding, the cage holding either six men, one man and a horse or a dram of coal weighing 25 cwt. Wages were 18s to 20s per week, before stoppages, which included 3d for a medical fund. These were typical wages in the coalfield. He stated that he would not employ women or children under ten in the pit.

Six boys, among the 27 employed at Maesmawr Colliery, were also interviewed by the commissioners. They were largely uneducated and more ignorant of the letters, numbers and scriptural knowledge about which the commissioners enquired than the children at the nearby Pentyrch Ironworks, where there was a school. The six boys were employed in pumping operations and it would seem that the pit was very wet;[1] the pumping engine was a nine-inch steam forcing pump, which had been bought from the Neath Abbey Ironworks in 1833.[2]

In the early 1840s the production of Maesmawr was beginning to decline and Insole began to look for a new source of bituminous coal. He almost certainly continued to mine Maesbach, at least until 1846, as his books record that he paid royalties to the Marquess of Bute until then. In 1844, however, George Insole moved his mining operations to the Rhondda Valley, where he had been prospecting since 1838.

George Insole's first years in Cardiff had been remarkably successful. He had recovered from a nearly disastrous partnership and built up his coal trading business, while at the same time extending into colliery ownership to give himself, in the bituminous trade, an integrated business from the coal seam to the ship's hold. He did not, however, follow Walter Coffin and acquire his own ships, remaining content to use the vessels which were increasingly attracted to Cardiff for their cargoes. His family surrounded him in his comfortable home with its extended garden, the running of which would have been in the hands of his wife Mary. Their third daughter Julia was born in Cardiff early in 1832 but was not baptised until November, causing the curate who performed the ceremony to note that the child seemed to be ten months old. The baptism was probably delayed while Insole was in Ireland. In 1837 George and Mary's last child, a second son christened George Frederick, was born but did not survive infancy and died on 22 November. Their eldest child, Helen, was seven when they came to Cardiff and so all the family would have been educated in the town; there is certainly no record of their son James being sent away to school. James Insole would probably have joined his father's business on completing his education, although he may have been sent to another coal owner or merchant to learn the trade. During the late 1830s and early 1840s he would have learnt, from training and experience, about the operation and management of the coal trade and a proprietor's supervision of his colliery.

---

[1] *First Report of the Royal Commission on Children's Employment in Mines* (Parl. Papers, 1842), pp. 517–18.

[2] L. Ince, *The Neath Abbey Company* (1984), Appendix 1.

Chapter 3

Into the Rhondda

1843–50

By the end of 1843 George Insole could look back on two eventful years for his family and give thought to his plans for the expansion of his business. His eldest daughter, Helen, had married George Gower, a saddler, in All Saints', Birmingham, on 8 June 1842 and in the following year their first child was born and christened George Insole. When Insole's son, James, had come of age in 1842 he had made him a partner in the business, which was known thereafter as George Insole & Son. Christmas 1843 brought another marriage. Ordinary people had few holidays in the 1840s: Sundays, Christmas Day, Good Friday and Easter Monday were the only ones in the mining districts for owners and employees. On the other hand, the colliers regularly took days off work, particularly Mondays and the day after the fortnightly pay day, and it has been estimated that from the 1840s to the 1860s a typical collier would be absent for between three and six days per month.[1] No doubt the owners also had occasional holidays. Christmas Day 1843 was a Monday, making a two-day break for George Insole, an unwonted period of relaxation.[2] James would not have been at home, however, as on the following Thursday (28 December) he married Mary Ann Jones, the eldest daughter of Thomas Jones of Priory Cottage, Edgbaston, near Birmingham, in her parish church of St Bartholomew. Thomas Jones had been a saddler and ironmonger with premises in Cannon Street, Birmingham, when his daughter had been born on 23 September 1818. There was no railway connection between Birmingham and Cardiff at this date, so it is probable that James had travelled to Birmingham earlier and that his father stayed in Cardiff; George did not sign the marriage register and the witnesses were the bride's father and her younger sister, Sarah Lilly, who was born on 15 May 1824. James and Mary Ann set up home next door to George Insole's house in Crockherbtown. The

---

[1] Morris and Williams, *South Wales Coal Industry*, p. 233.

[2] George and Mary Insole were buried at St Margaret's, Roath, which was traditionally a stronghold of evangelical Anglicanism. It is probable therefore that they worshipped there and that the Insoles' Christmas festivities were muted if not non-existent. After 1872, the parish became a centre of the high Anglican revival.

business, however, was facing fresh challenges and opportunities, which the principals of the new partnership may well have discussed after the honeymoon.

Changes were already occurring in the coal trade and, by the early 1840s, the practice of selling coal to sea captains on the dock side was giving way to direct sales by the coal owners to customers and agents, as Insole had done from his early days in the trade. With the building of the Bute Dock, he acquired a wharf alongside his rivals, Thomas Powell and Walter Coffin, which would eventually replace his yard on the canal. He also moved into new offices in Bute Crescent, a row of large terraced houses built close to the pier head as part of the development of Butetown. In the early 1840s Cardiff's coal trade was dominated by Thomas Powell and Walter Coffin (Table 3.1).

Table 3.1: *Cardiff's major coal shippers, 1839*

Shipper	*Tons of coal shipped from Cardiff*
Thomas Powell	61,917
Walter Coffin	51,100
George Insole	23,444
Morgan Thomas	14,924
Lucy Thomas	17,097
John Edmonds	14,073
Duncan & Co.	13,386

Source: W.H. Smyth, *Nautical Observations on the Port and Maritime Vicinity of Cardiff* (Cardiff, 1840), p. 11.

Insole's canal shipments were less than half those of his two main competitors, although he may have handled much of Lucy Thomas's 17,000 tons, bringing him into contention with Coffin, who was his strongest rival in the Irish market. He was still operating Maesmawr Colliery and, from 1840, Maesbach, as well as selling steam coal from Lucy Thomas's Graig pit. In addition to the output of his own pits, he sold bituminous coals from a number of other collieries in the valleys of the Taff and its tributaries, including small quantities of No 2 Rhondda from Richard Lewis, who operated a small level at Cymmer, for which the following prices were recorded in the firm's day book:

19 July 1843	£26 7s
27 August 1843	£25 0s
3 September 1843	£30 0s[1]

By the end of 1843 it was becoming clear to the Insoles that they needed a more plentiful supply of Rhondda coal if they were to compete successfully against Walter Coffin. Throughout his operation of the Maesmawr colliery, George Insole had found Coffin a vigorous competitor. The Irish, in particular, although one of Insole's most successful markets, were buying 'Coffin's Coal', the No 3 Rhondda seam, although it was 1s per ton more expensive than Maesmawr. Insole had been visiting the Rhondda since at least 1830 and he seems to have been seriously prospecting there from about 1838. In the summer of 1844 George and James Insole made an extensive visit to Ireland, during which they met customers in many parts of the country, who again confirmed the high reputation of Coffin's coal.

Once they had returned they took immediate steps to acquire a source of Rhondda coal. On 25 September they leased for seventy years the mineral rights beneath 375 acres of land at Cymmer, including Richard Lewis's level, from Evan Morgan of Tyn-y-cymmer Farm. The annual sleeping or dead rent, i.e. the minimum rent payable regardless of production, was £126 and the royalty was 6d per 2,520 lb of large coal; this was probably the local colliers' ton, which varied from district to district, but it was also the weight of the Welsh ton, the measure used in the steam coal collieries until the Mines Regulation Act of 1872 required all returns to use the imperial ton of 2,240 lb.[2] Insole was now able to reassure his customers that he would soon be selling Rhondda coal from his own colliery. On 19 October 1844 he wrote to T.C. Armitage, a Dublin merchant and distributor of Welsh coal on the Irish market, letting him know that he would have the same coal as Coffin, which he claimed was known as the best in the kingdom for coking or smith's work and was, as he put it, 'suitable for Ireland'. He had previously made similar claims for his Maesmawr coal but the trade was highly competitive. On 24 December George Insole wrote again to Armitage, telling him that he was about to start working Cymmer coal and in the same month the Insoles opened the South Cymmer Level to the No 2 Rhondda seam, near Richard Lewis's level, which then ceased produc-

---

[1] Insole MSS, Day Book 1843, cited by E.D. Lewis, *The Rhondda Valleys* (1959), p. 46.
[2] R.H. Walters, *The Economic and Business History of the South Wales Steam Coal Industry,1840–1914* (New York, 1977), p. xv.

tion.[1] On 29 October 1844 the Insoles had appointed Armitage as their agent in Ireland for three years from 1 January 1845, 'to carry out their instructions, promote their interest and extend their connexion to the utmost of his ability throughout Ireland' for an annual salary of £120 and 20 tons of coal a year, 'to be put free on board ship at Cardiff ... in lieu of all charges for stationery and so forth'. The agreement, however, did not prove a happy one and they were soon engaged in an acrimonious dispute which ended in court in the summer of 1850. The Insoles had employed Armitage and paid his salary for one year but had then ceased to use his services and had forbidden him to act on their behalf. They also withheld his 20 tons of coal. Armitage sued for the coal, affirming also that, although he had always been ready to fulfil the agreement, he had not been paid for the second and third years. His action failed; the Insoles' argument that he should have sent a ship or named one at Cardiff to receive the coal being upheld by the three judges.[2]

Although the Insoles continued to work Maesmawr it was reaching exhaustion, with output for the year ending 30 June 1844 being only 1,449 tons.[3] It seems that George Insole's offer to the Marquess of Bute had born fruit, as they also operated the Rhyd-yr-helig Colliery at Maesbach. On 15 May 1846 the Taff Vale Railway Company agreed to build a siding to 'Messers Insoles' colliery at Maesfach' and on 14 July the same year the company served a notice on the Insoles with regard to the effect of their workings on the railway at Willowford, or Rhyd-yr-helig in Welsh, an old crossing point on the River Taff, where the railway runs close to the Maesbach colliery.[4]

During 1845 and 1846 the Insoles worked the South Cymmer Level but with less success than they had hoped. Their difficulties increased when, in December 1845, they met the Dinas Fault, which dropped the coal measures ten yards.[5] Faulting was a frequent problem in the South Wales coalfield, creating uncertainty for owner and collier alike. Although they drove through the fault and continued to work the seam on the other side, the Cymmer enterprise was not fulfilling the Insoles' earlier expectations.

Nevertheless, the demand for coal was growing rapidly, not only in

[1] Insole MSS, Letter Book, 24 Dec. 1844, cited by Lewis, *Rhondda Valleys*, p. 46n.

[2] *The Law Journal Reports*, XXVIII, 1850, pp. 202-4; *Cardiff & Merthyr Guardian*, 27 July 1850.

[3] Lewis, 'Pioneers of the Cardiff Coal Trade', p. 41.

[4] Public Record Office (hereafter PRO), RAIL 684/2, 31 May 1844 – 5 July 1849.

[5] Insole MSS, Letter Book, 18 Nov. 1845, cited by Lewis, *Rhondda Valleys*, p. 48.

established domestic and industrial markets but also in the new industries of gas production and railways. Gas companies had been formed in the towns of South Wales since 1821, when the Swansea and Cardiff companies were established.[1] They were promoted to provide street lighting but they connected private houses, business premises and public buildings on the line of the gas main. Gas and coke making required bituminous coal and, in the early years, railway locomotives were fuelled with coke rather than the steam coal which they were to use later in the century. In order to satisfy all their customers, the Insoles needed a more productive source of bituminous coal than the South Cymmer Level; they also needed to win the No 3 Rhondda seams. In 1847, therefore, they sank their first shaft, the No 1 Pit, to the No 3 Rhondda, which they found 80 yards below the No 2 Rhondda. This came to be known as the Cymmer Old Pit and within a year was in full production, 4,575 tons of coal being sent to Cardiff during the months of July to September 1848.[2] Demand still seems to have outrun supply, for in December 1848 George Insole wrote to one of his long-standing customers, Henry Morgan, regretting that he was unable to send him a cargo of Cymmer coal since he did not have enough. He also explained that the great demand and the slow turn-around of ships at the docks made it 'a task to please everyone'.[3] This letter not only demonstrates the strength of demand at the time but also shows that the Bute Dock was already having difficulty in dealing with the volume of traffic.

A further demand on the Insoles' resources came from their decision to begin coke production on their own account, a process for which No 3 Rhondda was very suitable. In July 1848 they built 36 coke ovens at Cymmer for £1,440[4] and in January 1849 they hired sixteen ovens at 5s per week each from the Taff Vale Railway Company, although these were given up the following May.[5] In 1850 they submitted a tender to the railway company for the supply of coke for three years. The prices in their tender were 9s per ton using their own ovens or 10s 6d if using the railway company's. On 5 February 1850 their 9s tender was accepted by the Taff Vale board and on 20 March it was reported to the directors that the Insoles had signed a three-year contract. Other coke customers

---

[1] R. Jones and C. G. Reeve, *A History of Gas Production in Wales* (Cardiff 1978), p. 22.

[2] Insole MSS, Account Book, 1848, cited by Lewis, *Rhondda Valleys*, p. 48.

[3] Insole MSS, Letter Book, 4 Dec. 1848, cited by Lewis, 'Pioneers of the Cardiff Coal Trade', p. 42.

[4] Insole MSS, Letter Book, 1 Aug. 1848, cited by Lewis, *Rhondda Valleys*, p. 48.

[5] PRO, RAIL 684/2.

included the ironworks at Aberaman owned by the ironmaster and coal owner, Crawshay Bailey (1789–1872), the Aberdare and Gadlys brick companies and the Woolwich Arsenal, as well as the Royal Dockyards and a number of railway companies.

Two years later, in November 1852, James Insole contracted to make a weekly delivery of coke for seven years to the Bristol & Exeter Railway Company at the Great Western Dock in Bristol. The contract provides some insights into both the operation of a new market, employing the latest technology, and the vendor's careful scrutiny of the supplier's methods. The coke was to be made with No 3 Rhondda coal, to be burnt at the rate of 15 hours per ton and to be cooled with salt-free water. Insole's coke making was to be inspected and regularly supervised by the railway's locomotive engineer, who also decided the exact weekly quantity between the agreed limits of 190 and 230 tons. Insole also had to deposit a stock of 2,000 tons at the railway's Bristol wharf. The coke was to be screened on board at Bristol by Insole, using his own two inch and seven eighths inch screens, into coke boxes provided by the railway. Prices were 16s 3d per ton for large coke, 10s for small and 1s for dust (less than seven eighths of an inch) but any coke which had had contact with salt water was to be rejected. There were also break clauses and penalties, in case of default by Insole, as well as actions to be taken in the event of a strike. The railway could terminate the contract after three, four or five years by giving six months notice and paying £3,000, £2,500 or £2,000 respectively. These amounts were much less than the income which Insole received from the contract: depending on the proportion of large coal, an average quantity of 210 tons per week should have be realised between £7,500 and £8,500 per annum.[1]

The Insoles' coke sales added a third market to those for bituminous and steam coal, in which they were already established. The 1840s saw a rush to win the steam coal seams in the Cynon Valley, where Lucy and William Thomas had opened Lletty Shenkin Colliery in 1843, although it is not clear whether the Insoles sold much of this coal. They did, however, become agents for the Aberaman Merthyr Steam Coal of David Williams.[2] This pit, at Treaman in the Cynon Valley, was sunk in 1847 and its opening coincided with the first Admiralty trials of steam coals, carried out by Sir Henry de la Beche and Dr Lyon Playfair.[3] The trials

[1]   National Library of Wales (hereafter NLW), E.D. Lewis Collection, Agreement between J.H. Insole and the Bristol & Exeter Railway.

[2]   Lewis, 'Pioneers of the Cardiff Coal Trade', p. 47; David Williams was also known by his bardic title Alaw Goch and was to be associated with the Insoles for a number of years.

[3]   *First Report on Coals suited to the Steam Navy* (Parl. Papers, 1847–8), p. xxviii.

proved not only the advantages of Welsh steam coal, in almost every respect, over its rivals, from Scotland, Lancashire, Derbyshire and above all Newcastle, but also the pre-eminence of Aberaman Merthyr among the Welsh coals. In March 1848 George Insole was told that 'Aberaman Merthyr Steam Coal' had been added to the list of coals specified in the Naval Command and in April to that of the Controller of Victualling of Her Majesty's Navy. George Insole used these endorsements to publish a pamphlet, advertising Aberaman coal which included tables of the results taken from the trial report.[1] The naval trials provided a fresh stimulus for the growth of George Insole & Son in the rapidly develop-ing market for steam coal. To the new Admiralty orders were added sales to the merchant marine, including the Royal Mail Steam Packet Company and the Peninsular & Oriental Steam Navigation Company. A further change for the business was the impetus given to its export trade. By the end of 1848, with their pamphlet translated into French, they were shipping Aberaman coal to Nantes, Brest, Calais, Marseilles and Corsica. In the next year, in addition to their established home, Irish and French markets, they sent cargoes of both steam and house coals to the Mediterranean (including four cargoes a week to Malta), to South America and to Singapore. Exports were further assisted by the repeal in 1845 of the export duty of 2s a ton on coal carried in British ships and in 1850 of the 4s a ton paid on coal carried in ships of countries without a reciprocal treaty with the United Kingdom. In 1850 the Insoles' sources of supply were further increased by the sinking of the Deep Duffryn Colliery at Mountain Ash by David Williams. It is possible that he received some assistance from George Insole and in 1852 James Insole bought shares worth £6,000 in the venture.[2]

The Insoles' bituminous coals from their Rhondda colliery were in great demand and between 1845 and 1850 they extended their mineral holdings at Cymmer. They leased the mineral rights of Bedw Farm, covering the valley to the south of their Tyn-y-cymmer holding, from the Phillips estate. Then, in August 1850, they signed a lease of the mineral rights of Glynfach, on the mountainside to the south of Bedw, for 40 years from 1 May 1850, from Sir Thomas Digby Aubrey of Aylesbury, the descendant of a Glamorgan gentry family. This lease appears to have been for an annual rent only, an older style of agreement, which by this time had been largely superseded by the mineral lease for royalties, which had become a standard for the coalfield. George Insole's earlier

---

[1] See Appendix D.

[2] Insole MSS, Day Ledger, June 1852, cited by Lewis, *Rhondda Valleys*, p. 48n.

leases were of this type. It is probable, however, that the annual rent only applied while Insole was winning the coal, for by the 1860s he was paying royalties on all coal raised.

By 1850, the Insoles' mineral property covered 1,300 acres of what is now the village of Cymmer. Expansion on this scale called for large sums of money, not only to finance the investment itself but also for working capital. Morris and Williams estimate that the cost of sinking a 90 fathom shaft, about twice the depth of the Old Pit, was £1,500 and that pumps and engines could cost a further £2,500.[1] By 1848 the Insoles' inventory of fixed plant at the Old Pit exceeded £5,000[2] and included a 17 in. pumping engine, built by J. T. Price's Neath Abbey Ironworks.[3] Their payments for capital items had increased fivefold in two years, from £133 in July 1846 to £660 in July 1848.[4] At the pioneering stage of the development of the coalfield, from which it was starting to emerge in the 1840s, capital investment largely depended on what was called the abstinence of the entrepreneur, that is the ploughing back of profits into the growth of the business. These profits were large for the successful and returns of 20 per cent were expected in what was a risky business. Nevertheless the proprietor's profits were not always sufficient and speculators like the Insoles relied upon their banks for long term credit and for the discounting of bills to reduce their need for working capital. The Insoles' bank was the West of England & South Wales District Bank, which had opened a Cardiff office in 1834. George Insole was a well established and trusted customer by the time that he moved to the Rhondda and the bank 'gave him every assistance', the contemporary euphemism for overdrafts and loans.[5]

Although the Insoles' acquisition of a mineral lease at Cymmer in 1844 gave them access to the coal seams which they needed to increase their sales, it brought them serious transport problems. Richard Lewis had brought his coal to the canal in carts along the parish road, in effect a narrow track along the valley floor, but this method would have been inadequate for the quantities which the Insoles planned. At that time, according to most authorities, the only serviceable road route from Cardiff into the Rhondda Valleys was through the town of Llantrisant, over Llantrisant Common and to the west of Mynydd-y-glyn, although

[1] Morris and Williams, *South Wales Coal Industry*, p. 138.

[2] Lewis, 'Pioneers of the Cardiff Coal Trade', p. 47.

[3] Ince, *Neath Abbey Company*, Appendix 1.

[4] Lewis, *Rhondda Valleys*, p. 47.

[5] Ibid.

George Yates's map of 1799 does show two roads from Newbridge up the lower Rhondda Valley, one on either side of the river. One of these was probably the 'narrow delightful sylvan path' referred to by a earlier traveller.[1] Coffin's tramroad carried passengers to Newbridge on market days from Cymmer and Dinas, providing a less arduous journey than the road to Llantrisant. Both he and Insole had their own personal trams.

Walter Coffin was at this time both the deputy chairman of the Taff Vale Railway Company and Insole's chief rival in the Rhondda. In October 1840 the railway began work on the one-mile Rhondda branch, to link up with Walter Coffin's tramroad, which was opened as far as Eirw in June 1841, at a cost of £7,417.[2] It did not carry passengers in its early years, although after Coffin's tramroad ceased to run beyond the railway terminus at Eirw, a horse-drawn omnibus service was provided from Dinas via Cymmer to Newbridge on market days.

The value of a rail link to the colliery proprietors was increased by the installation of coal handling equipment by the Taff Vale at the dockside in Cardiff, which was in operation in 1842.[3] Nevertheless, at this time the coal trade of Cardiff was still lagging behind that of both Newport and Swansea, even after the opening of the Bute Dock. In 1842 Cardiff exported 245,800 tons of coal, compared with Swansea's 511,300 tons and Newport's 555,800 tons,[4] and it was not until 1844 that the dock trade overtook that of the canal. It was, therefore, in the interests of both the coal owners and the Marquess of Bute that more coal should be brought down to Cardiff. In 1846 the Taff Vale leased the Aberdare Railway and started bringing the steam coals of the Cynon Valley to Cardiff, while in the same year the two companies made a compact to protect their interests. In 1849 the Taff Vale Railway leased the Bute Dock, further cementing the interdependence of the two undertakings and giving them control of the transport and shipment of the larger part of Cardiff's coal trade.

These developments, however, did not give George Insole the direct connection from Cymmer to Cardiff which he needed. When he acquired the lease of the Cymmer property, he was already a customer of the Taff Vale, presumably from his Maesmawr and Rhyd-yr-helig collieries. Both were close to the railway line which, unlike the Glamorganshire Canal, was on the same side of the River Taff as the collieries. The Insoles first

[1] J.T. Barber, *A Tour through South Wales and Monmouthshire* (1803), p. 70.

[2] Lewis, *Rhondda Valleys*, p. 116.

[3] Morris and Williams, *South Wales Coal Industry*, p. 102.

[4] Williams, *Digest of Welsh Historical Statistics*, I, pp. 318-320.

appear in the railway's advertised accounts in the *Cardiff & Merthyr Guardian* on 13 January 1844, when they were charged £9 2s out of the railway company's revenue for the week of £553 11s 1d. By the end of the year they were sending more than £25 worth of coal per week on the railway, out of its total weekly business of over £800.

In December 1844 the Insoles and other colliery owners in the Lower Rhondda wrote to the directors of the Taff Vale Railway, asking them to extend the Rhondda branch in order that they might be able to bring their coal down the railway. The letter was probably drafted by Insole, as it appears in the firm's letter book and its promises seem to reflect his confidence and optimism. The writers promised:

> If you will so far accommodate us as to extend the line now asked for, we will *guarantee* to bring down 100 tons of coal a day as the minimum quantity, but we do not hesitate to say that quantity shall be increased three times in twelve months after the line is made, independent of the traffic made by other parties.[1]

The matter was referred to the railway's superintendent, George Fisher, to report back but no immediate report seems to have been forthcoming.[2] At least two of the Taff Vale directors, Walter Coffin and Thomas Powell, were competitors of the writers and may have been keen to keep them waiting; on the other hand, they both had long experience in the coal trade and may have been sceptical about these optimistic forecasts.

Over a year later, in its edition of 23 January 1846, the *Cambrian* reported that a special general meeting of the Taff Vale Railway Company had been held in Bristol to approve a proposal to prepare a parliamentary bill for an extension to the Rhondda branch.[3] The directors were anxious to prevent the rival Rhondda & Ely Valley Junction Railway, a broad gauge line to be linked to the South Wales Railway, 'going over the mountain and robbing them of mineral ground' which they 'looked on as their own'.[4] The new rival railway was at this stage only a proposal, one of many in the growing rail mania of the time.

[1] Insole MSS, Letter Book, 12 Dec. 1844, cited by Lewis, 'Pioneers of the Cardiff Coal Trade', p. 41.

[2] PRO, RAIL 684/2.

[3] The Taff Vale at this time held its shareholders' meetings in Bristol, no doubt an indication of where most of its stockholders came from as well as a recognition of the city's old role as a regional capital. By contrast the Penarth Dock & Railway Company, formed some twenty years later, held its meetings in Cardiff.

[4] *Cambrian*, 23 Jan. 1846.

The Taff Vale's survey had estimated costs of £86,900 for the Rhondda
Fawr branch of nine and a half miles and £41,600 for the Rhondda Fach
branch of five miles. In addition they were seeking approval for a branch
line of nearly two miles, costing £2,600, along the south bank of the
river to Cymmer and thence to Dinas. The low price may have assumed
the use of the bed of Coffin's tramroad. It was proposed to finance the
bill with a one-for-five rights issue. The proposal was supported by the
meeting and subsequent technical amendments were approved by a
further Special General Meeting in the following June.

In February 1846, less than a month after the approval of the board's
plans, David James, who had a colliery at Porth, on the opposite side of
the river to Cymmer, objected to the railway making the Cymmer branch
a 'public road', on account of his agreement, probably for a wayleave,
with the Insoles. James Insole, who was attending the meeting on behalf
of the firm, said that he had no objection to striking the clause for
making the Cymmer branch from the bill. At the next board meeting on
17 March 1846, however, George Insole attended, said that his son 'did
not understand the question to be as read' and affirmed that he wanted
the Cymmer branch 'to be made as in the bill'. No resolution is recorded
in the minutes.[1]

On 15 May 1846 George Insole again attended a meeting of the board
to discuss a letter which he had written asking for a loan of £500 to
build a branch railway to Cymmer. This would probably have been a
private line from the colliery to the Taff Vale's Rhondda branch,
crossing the river at Porth and passing over David James's mineral land.
Local tradition had it that Insole was reluctant to have this line on
account of the obligation to pay a wayleave to James.[2] It was common
practice, as the Rhondda was opened up, for the colliery proprietors to
build private lines to the Taff Vale railway, which the company then
bought or leased. The loan was agreed, with the condition that the
Insoles bought the sleepers, chairs and rails from the railway company.
The loan was to be at 5 per cent on unspecified security and the
necessary arrangements were to be made by the Parliamentary Committee and the parties' solicitors. On 14 July the Insoles wrote to the railway
to say that they were ready for the sleepers but the company asked them
to provide their security. A fortnight later the Insoles asked for the loan
of the sleepers but the company was only prepared to sell them, albeit

[1] PRO, RAIL 684/2.

[2] NLW, MS 437E, M.O. Jones ('Nil Desperandum'), 'Coal Industry in the Rhondda'
(Treorchy Eisteddfod, 1895).

at cost price and subject to security. Nothing seems to have come of these proposals for, at the Taff Vale board meeting on 11 November 1846, the Insoles sent a further letter asking for a branch to Cymmer. The minutes note that the company was proceeding with the parliamentary bill for the Rhondda branch, the plans of which included both the line to Cymmer along the south bank of the river and the line across Porth land.[1] In the meantime the Insoles had to make their own arrangements to get their coal from the colliery, partly by tramroad and then by hand cart over a wooden bridge, where it was loaded into carts and taken along the parish road to Eirw.[2] The parish road was still a narrow track and was not widened until the 1860s. This method put the Insoles at a disadvantage as it involved small loads and excessive handling with the risk of breakage. The use of Coffin's tramroad, which was refused, would have been helped, since each tram held 50 cwt and a team of four horses could draw between twelve and fifteen trams.

Another special general meeting of the shareholders of the Aberdare and Taff Vale railway companies, which approved the leasing of the former, was held in December 1846. The terms of the lease were that the Taff Vale Company would pay an annual dividend of 5 per cent of the Aberdare Company's capital in 1847, rising by 1 per cent per annum to 10 per cent from 1 January 1852. At this meeting a Mr Hamlen, a Taff Vale shareholder, criticised Walter Coffin for not allowing the Insoles to use his tramway, on the grounds that it would interfere with his traffic. Hamlen further criticised Coffin and the 'freighting directors', such as Thomas Powell, for not building a Rhondda branch in the first place. He considered that 'all men were too selfish to be judges in their own cases' and accused Coffin of behaviour which was 'not fair or tradesmanlike'. Walter Coffin defended himself by saying that George Insole was 'a strange man'.[3]

The Rhondda branch was eventually built over the next ten years. It was a highly speculative move by the Taff Vale, as there were no collieries or prospectors in the upper Rhondda in the 1840s and in the 1850s the company offered a reward of £500 for the first steam coal to be won in the Rhondda valleys. The Rhondda Fawr branch on the north bank of the river was completed as far as Dinas in May 1849 but a year later there was no progress on the Cymmer branch on the south bank and George Insole wrote to the railway company, asking for this branch to

[1] GRO, Q/DP/61, 97A.

[2] 'Excursion to Cymmer Colliery', *Trans. Cardiff Naturalists' Society*, XV, 1883, p. 42.

[3] *Cambrian*, 18 Dec. 1846.

be built immediately. The directors called for plans, which they received on 6 June 1850. They then asked for further information on the cheapest way to get coal from the collieries on the south bank of the Rhondda Fawr to their railway and decided to seek counsel's opinion as to whether they could be compelled to build the branch. At last on 9 July 1850 they decided to approach the landowners to discuss routes and wayleaves.

The delays in getting adequate transport for their Cymmer coal were not the Insoles' only problem with the Taff Vale Railway Company. In June 1844 the directors instructed their secretary to write to the Insoles explaining the steps which they were taking to ensure that delays in returning their wagons would not be repeated. A year later, however, the Insoles again complained about delays, which they blamed on a dispute over the terms under which they had leased sixteen trucks in the previous October at 7s per week each. They asked for new terms and a dispute ensued over payments for the wagons. At the August board meeting an agreement for the Insoles to hire 29 wagons at £12 per annum was confirmed, so there had been some improvement in the terms of hire. At the end of November 1846, however, the Insoles returned their wagons to the company. In April 1847 the Insoles sent a list of demands to the railway. They wanted a siding for Cymmer coal, revision of charges, wagons for Aberdare coal and room at the dock. They also specified where in a train they wanted their trucks marshalling. The directors passed these matters to George Fisher, adding that the Insoles must pay the usual rate for wagons. By December the Insoles were being told not to use their trucks for third parties but who the third parties were was not revealed.[1] In November 1849 the Insoles complained about breakages at the dockside and asked for the exclusive use of two staithes, which the company refused, suggesting that they use a moveable shoot to reduce breakages. A month later they asked the company to sell them 200 wagons, presumably to cope with the rapid expansion of their business, which followed the naval trials. They offered to pay in quarterly instalments and to pay interest at 7 per cent but the company refused, on the ground that they did not have enough wagons themselves. In September the following year the Insoles wrote that they had agreed to hire 200 wagons from 'parties in Newcastle' for five or ten years at £8 per annum each.[2]

When the Insoles moved to the Rhondda, Cymmer was a small hamlet

[1] PRO, RAIL 684/2.
[2] PRO, RAIL 684/3, 19 July 1849 - 29 May 1856.

in a rural setting with only a few houses and farms and an Independent chapel, which had been opened in 1743. Although they had come to an established community and a number of their Maesmawr workers came with them, they still needed more men to work the colliery. In addition there was insufficient housing for a mining village, even at this early stage. It was therefore necessary for the Insoles to try to recruit workers from neighbouring valleys, who could walk over the mountain or up the valley to work and, for those who came to settle, they had to build houses. After the sinking of the Cymmer Old Pit, 50 miners' cottages were built at Cymmer and others at Bedw and Glynfach, when the land became available. Another group of cottages, known as America Fach, was built on the north side of the river at Porth.[1] The houses were small terraces of two-storey houses of traditional design but, rather than the traditional stone shingles, the Insoles used Bangor slate for the roofs.

Colliers' wages fluctuated considerably in the 1840s; having been between 18s and 20s per week in 1841, they were between 10s and 12s in 1843. By 1846, however, they had recovered to between 21s and 23s and by 1850 had reached 30s per week in Aberdare.[2] The 1840s were not a period of peaceful industrial relations. The experience of low wages in the earlier part of the decade would not have been quickly forgotten and by 1847 all the Rhondda colliers were reported to be in a trade union, except those at Dinas where Coffin would not employ union members.[3] There had been Chartist activity in the Lower Rhondda in 1839 and the owners often considered any unrest among the colliers to be a Chartist plot. The newspapers also carried news of the Rebecca Riots in West Wales, which must have added to a feeling among the ruling classes that there was widespread and possibly revolutionary unrest among the people. A number of strikes occurred in the Lower Rhondda including one at the Insoles' colliery at Cymmer in 1849. In February that year the Insoles drew up and agreed with their colliers rules and regulations for the Cymmer Colliery.[4] In July the same year the colliers came out on strike and a small group, selected by the owners and their manager, Jabez Thomas, were charged with breaching their contracts. The case was heard before the Llantrisant magistrates and, although the accused colliers did not attend, they were sentenced to a month's imprisonment, as an example to the others. The exemplary

---

[1] Lewis, *Rhondda Valleys*, p. 49.

[2] Morris and Williams, *South Wales Coal Industry*, p. 218.

[3] *Cardiff & Merthyr Guardian*, 18 Sept. 1847.

[4] See Appendix C.

nature of this 'lenient' punishment was, however, ineffective and the men stayed out. A further group were charged but they attended the court and were defended by John Owen, a solicitor from Pontypool, who was well known for his success in representing the miners of South Wales, before Henry Austin Bruce and two clergymen. Jabez Thomas was cross-examined by Owen, who accused Thomas of having deceived him and of being untrustworthy. James Insole was in court to hear not only this robust questioning of his colliery manager but also Bruce's criticism of clause eight in the rules which allowed appeals by the men only to the proprietors, whose decision was to be final. The dispute concerned the cutting of underground roadways, which did not appear in the rules. After some argument and negotiation in the court, James Insole agreed to pay his men the same rate as the Dinas colliers and the men decided to return, although not until their fellow workers had finished their sentences.[1]

The 1840s were a time for family life as well as work for the Insoles. George and Mary's eldest daughter Helen, following her marriage to George Gower and the birth of her eldest son at their home in Canton, had two daughters. She does not appear, however, to have settled in Cardiff and she and her husband played little part in the family's coal owning affairs. James and Mary Ann Insole had three children, all born at Crockherbtown: James Walter, usually known by his second name, in 1845, Mary Ann Lilly, known as Mary Ann, in 1846 and George Frederick, who was called Fred, in 1847. George Insole himself was elected to the borough council, as one of the six members for the South Ward, on 1 November 1845 and ten days later he was elected to the Navigation and Harbour Committee. As well as being a knowledgeable member, this position may have helped him in his business. Membership of the council, however, does not appear to have been an arduous responsibility; Insole attended about half its meetings and of these a number had no business to discuss.[2] He was, however, a member of a local delegation which met Thomas Webster Rammell, the superintending inspector of the General Board of Health, when he carried out a far-reaching enquiry into the sewerage, drainage, water supply and sanitary condition of the town, an enquiry that was strongly but ineffectually opposed by Priest Richards, who was still town clerk.[3]

---

[1] *Cardiff & Merthyr Guardian*, 11 Sept. 1849.

[2] GRO, B/C 4, Cardiff Borough Council Minutes.

[3] D.C. James, 'The Genesis of Sanitary Reform in Cardiff, 1774–1850', *Welsh History Review*, 11 (1982–3), 61–3.

George Insole had been suffering from heart disease for many years according to his death certificate. His condition cannot have been alleviated by his apparently stressful life and on Christmas Day 1850 he suffered what was probably a stroke which left him paralysed. He did not recover and one week later he died. The following announcement was made in the *Cardiff & Merthyr Guardian* in its next issue:

> January 1st at his residence, Crockherbtown, Cardiff, George Insole Esq. aged 60. Mr. Insole was an enterprising and extensive coal proprietor and was mainly instrumental in developing the resources of one of the most important mineral districts in this county. By his death a vacancy is occasioned in the representation of South Ward, Cardiff.[1]

The newspaper did not publish an obituary and the notice in the *Cambrian* was even shorter, describing him as 'an enterprising and extensive coal proprietor'.[2] The funeral took place three days later at St Margaret's Roath, where a memorial was later erected. He had had an eventful and successful life, becoming a coal owner when past forty years of age. In spite of his heart problems he was a vigorous entrepreneur, who died a wealthy man. In his will his share of the colliery was to be offered to his son at valuation and the rest of his property was left to his wife for her lifetime and then, in equal shares, to his four surviving children. James Harvey accepted the offer and thus became the sole proprietor of George Insole & Son.

[1] *Cardiff and Merthyr Guardian*, 4 Jan. 1851.

[2] *Cambrian*, 10 Jan. 1851.

Chapter 4

Success and Disaster

1851–62

George Insole's will left his widow and daughters well provided for and presented his son James with a big opportunity. Although the will was not proved until 12 December 1855, he was the sole surviving partner and quickly took charge of the business. The demand for coal was increasing at home and abroad, with the growth of towns, the expansion of industry, the spread of railways and the development of steam ships. All tariffs on foreign trade had been removed and Britain's rulers saw her leading the world into a new age. 1851 was the year of the Great Exhibition, a time of optimism and self-confidence for the British, particularly the innovators and entrepreneurs of the Industrial Revolution. Energy was one of the most important elements of industrial success and in the second half of the nineteenth century energy meant coal.

By the time of his father's death access to the Taff Vale Railway from the Cymmer colliery had been achieved and James Insole set out to increase the output of his mineral holdings at Cymmer. In 1851 he sunk a new pit about a mile upstream from the Old Pit, on a narrow piece of land between the foot of the mountain and the Rhondda Fawr River. This was known as the Upper Cymmer Colliery and was quickly brought into operation. In 1860 Insole leased it to T.C. Hinde, a coal owner in the Neath Valley, who continued to operate it for a number of years.[1] He had already, on 30 May 1854, secured permission to sub-lease part of the Glynfach minerals, which he held on a 40-year lease from Sir Thomas Aubrey.[2] He then sub-leased this part of the mineral property for a dead rent of £200 p.a. to Richard Ellis, a Cardiff merchant, who opened a level to No 2 Rhondda. Sub-leasing was useful both for Sir Thomas Aubrey and for Insole since more capital was brought in to exploit the minerals but, as landowner and chief lessee, they were still left with a regular income. It is also probable that part of the agreement with Ellis would have nominated or at least given preference to the firm of George Insole & Son as the shipper of the coal.

---

[1] D.R. Phillips, *History of the Vale of Neath* (Swansea, 1925), p. 247.

[2] GRO, D/D Au 182.

Insole continued to develop the Cymmer colliery as fast as he was able and in 1853 he started to sink a second pit, the New Cymmer, 100 yards from the Old Pit.[1] The sinking was completed in 1855, making more of the No 3 Rhondda seam available. The Crimean War had broken out in 1854, increasing the demand for coal and raising its price. In 1850 the Old Pit had employed 80 men and boys, mining 23,656 tons in the year.[2] In 1855, however, Insole doubled the workforce to 160 and increased the working area by a third, having pushed through a fault, which dropped the seam by sixteen feet, some 1,000 yards from the pit bottom. The length of the underground airways was now 10,325 yards or nearly six miles but no steps were taken to increase the ventilation of the pit. It still had a single shaft, which was divided by a brick and timber brattice into a downcast and upcast. The shaft was oval in section, 16 ft x 9 ft 6 in. with the brattice 2 ft from one end, reducing the downcast to 11 ft 10½ in.[3] The usual method of ventilating pits at this time was still the 'North of England' technique, imported from Belgium in the eighteenth century, in which a furnace at the base of the upcast was used to draw air through the pit. As the length of the airways increased, through roads, headings and stalls, a complex system of doors was required to maintain adequate ventilation. Even so accumulations of gases could occur and sometimes ignite as they passed over the furnace in the return air current. The Cymmer Old Pit was equipped with a furnace and had 72 doors. The downcast was also used to lower and raise men, horses and trams of coal. Some collieries in South Wales, including Thomas Powell's Gelligaer Colliery in 1849 and John Calvert's Gyfeillion Colliery in 1851, had already replaced their furnaces with fan systems and the Old Pit's ventilation attracted criticism. Insole's sole priority, however, seems to have been to get the coal out as fast as possible, in order to take advantage of higher prices. By 1854 No 3 Rhondda was selling at Cardiff for 10s 6d per ton, an increase of 1s 6d per ton or 17 per cent, while maximum wages had increased by 10 per cent from 20s to 22s per week.[4]

Not only did wages lag behind prices but employment was irregular and on annual contracts at the discretion of the employer. In addition

[1] *Cardiff & Merthyr Guardian*, 2 Aug. 1856.

[2] Insole MSS, Account Book for the Cymmer Collieries, March 1851, and Royalty Account for year ending 31 Dec. 1850, cited by E.D. Lewis, 'The Cymer (Rhondda) Explosion 1856', *Trans. Hon. Society of Cymmrodorion*, 1976, pp. 128–9.

[3] *Cardiff & Merthyr Guardian*, 16 Aug. 1856.

[4] Insole MSS, Cymmer Colliery pay sheets, 1848–55, cited by Lewis, 'Cymer (Rhondda) Explosion', p. 128.

working hours were six twelve-hour shifts per week, the underground distances which had to be walked before a collier could start working and earning were greater, living conditions were poor and the work itself was dangerous. There was moreover no compensation for injuries and a life of poverty on parish relief was often the result of disabling accidents. Combining these conditions with the autocratic behaviour of James Insole and his manager, Jabez Thomas, it is not surprising that disputes occurred. Insole, however, was making large enough profits at Cymmer to enable him to invest in David Williams's Deep Duffryn Colliery and to build himself a house in the newly fashionable suburb of Llandaff. Jabez Thomas was left in control at Cymmer, as the manager of the colliery with wide powers of discretion and as a leader in the local community. Neither Insole nor Thomas appears to have been in the least unsure, let alone embarrassed, by their patent priorities, their approach to business and their attitudes to their employees; in this they were probably typical of the owners and managers of the new industries who were to enrich themselves in the years of Victorian prosperity and largely determine attitudes in society towards industry and commerce, the privileges of capital and the obligations of labour.

The rapid development of the Cymmer Colliery, as indeed of many other South Wales collieries at that time, was causing concern also to HM Inspector of Mines, newly appointed under the Coal Mines Act of 1850. This Act was the first serious attempt to legislate for greater safety in collieries. It was the result of pressure from the press and the public, which followed reports of accidents in the 1840s and the failure of the measures introduced in the 1842 Act to make much headway in improving safety. The 1850 Act instituted a government inspectorate and, with further Acts in 1855 and 1860, introduced safety procedures and gave approved colliery rules the force of law.[1] The first government inspector for South Wales and the West of England, appointed on 12 November 1851, was Herbert Mackworth (1823–58), a descendant of the Neath industrialists, the Mackworths of the Gnoll, but more importantly a graduate of King's College, London and a trained engineer with experience of colliery management. Mackworth was well aware of the dangers and the risks which both management and colliers ran in

---

[1] Morris and Williams, *South Wales Coal Industry*, p. 184: 'This Act [Mines Act, 1850], tentative at first and limited to five years, was epoch making. Not only did it involve government control of underground mining, a wholly male and preponderently adult occupation, but it also both laid the foundation for the development of a safety code and, as accidents could not be wholly prevented, ultimately led logically to the introduction of workmen's compensation.'

winning coal in the pits of South Wales. Explosions in the Cynon Valley, at Lletty Shenkin in 1849 and at Middle Duffryn in 1850, had claimed 52 and 13 lives respectively, while soon after his appointment he gave evidence at the inquest on 65 men and boys killed in another explosion at Middle Duffryn in May 1852. At this time there was less experience of deep mining in South Wales than in other coalfields, owing to the popularity of levels; furthermore, the sandstone roof of the No 3 Rhondda gave a false sense of security and shortcuts were taken, which sometimes led to roof falls. Although the dangers of firedamp or methane gas were recognised in the steam coal collieries, the No 3 Rhondda was not considered a dangerous or 'hot' seam. The inspectors were an innovation in 1850 and were not welcomed by all the colliery owners and managers many of whom, including Insole and Thomas, appear to have tried to ignore their new obligations. Nevertheless, as the inspectors visited more collieries and, in particular, investigated disasters and attended coroners' hearings, they learnt more about the management and practice of coal mining and the need for better safety procedures. Their annual reports during the 1850s drew attention to poor management in the South Wales collieries, especially underground.

Herbert Mackworth complained in his reports that he had been set a very difficult task; it would take, in his estimation, four years to visit each pit in his district. He seems, however, to have had concerns about the Cymmer Colliery from an early date. On 8 July 1852, after his appearance at the inquest which followed the second explosion at Middle Duffryn, he sent James Insole a copy of his report on the disaster with a letter drawing attention to the need for adequate ventilation and for effective safety rules.[1] Nothing came of these proposals and Insole was later to say that he could not remember receiving the letter.

Eighteen months after, on New Year's Day 1854, having just secured a return to work after a strike, Jabez Thomas decided to make a complete change in the underground management, following the emigration to Australia of William Mills, the colliery's experienced underground agent and overman. He discharged two firemen, with four to five years' experience, in whom the men had confidence, on the grounds that 'they were not proper men' and that he needed 'to secure his authority'. He did, however, give the men excellent 'characters'. He then appointed as firemen two inexperienced men of his own choosing from Dinas, a non-union colliery. It was at the time normal practice, when selecting firemen, for the men to nominate a short list of possible candidates, from

---

[1] *Reports of Inspectors of Mines* (Parl. Papers, 1856), pp. 118–19.

whom the manager made his selection. Having been deprived of their usual participation in a matter affecting their safety and having no confidence in the new men, the colliers went on strike and stayed out for 22 weeks. It seems likely that Insole, or probably Jabez Thomas, either recruited new workers or was able to persuade some of the colliers to work, as a detachment of police was sent from Neath to Cymmer on 31 March in expectation of a riot by the striking colliers, who were protesting at the colliery gates against those who were working. The men eventually returned to work only under legal coercion from Insole.[1]

On 28 March 1854 Herbert Mackworth had called at Cymmer. As Jabez Thomas was away ill he inspected the pit with David Thomas, the acting manager and the overman, Rowland Thomas Rowland. He was obviously not happy with the pit and, although he was not empowered to issue a caution about a pit which was not working, he left some recommendations with the two men. These contained instructions on dividing the airways in the pit and reducing the number of doors, the use of safety lamps rather than naked lights and the need to connect the old workings to the New Pit shaft when it was completed.[2]

In May 1854 a new underground agent, Edward Hay, was appointed following an advertisement placed by James Insole. The agent was not, in modern parlance, a line manager but gave instructions and advice on the working of the seams and handled the administration, pay and accounts of the colliery. He also was reported to have recommended linking the two pits but Jabez Thomas seems to have resented what he considered Hay's interference.

On 20 October following Mackworth again visited Cymmer and found that no action had been taken on his recommendations. He decided that a clear set of rules was needed and, taking advantage of a resolution of a national meeting of coal owners earlier that month supporting the adoption of colliery rules, he sent a copy of model rules for the Cymmer colliery to Insole.[3] Mackworth's hand was strengthened by the 1855 Coal Mines Act, which gave government approved rules the force of law. These were not a set of nationally enforceable rules but a procedure by which the owner, with or without the advice of the local inspectors, drafted a list of rules for his colliery and sent them to the Home Secretary for approval. They had to be printed in Welsh and English, distributed to the men and read to them sufficiently regularly to ensure

---

[1] *Cardiff & Merthyr Guardian,* 2 Aug. 1856.

[2] *Reports of Inspectors of Mines* (Parl. Papers, 1856), p. 119.

[3] Ibid.

that the workers, many of whom were illiterate, understood them.

Mackworth's efforts still seemed in vain. In June 1855 Morgan Richards, one of the new firemen, came to the office and reported having seen 60 yards of 'fire' in the main headings, which were part of Morgan Rowlands's district. Rowlands, a 25 year-old fireman, who felt that this was a slur on his competence, contradicted Richards's report and a fight took place. Jabez Thomas intervened and grappling with Richards threw him out of the office. Although Edward Hay confirmed the presence of firedamp, both Richards and Rowland Thomas Rowland were dismissed. Jabez Thomas now appointed Rowland Rowlands as the new overman; he was Morgan's brother, a man with five years' experience as a collier but none as a fireman. Morgan Rowlands kept his position as fireman and was joined by his brother-in-law, William Thomas, and David Jones.

Two months later, on 20 August, an explosion of firedamp occurred at Cymmer New, when one man was killed. As a result Mackworth visited the colliery, to find that his recommendations had been only 'very partially carried into effect'. He referred Hay to the rules, which he had sent the previous year and left him another copy. On the following day he gave evidence at the inquest on the dead collier to the effect that the accident could have been avoided if his proposed rules had been followed.[1] On 25 November he received an assurance from Hay that Insole had sent rules to Cymmer.

On 1 January 1856 Mackworth's district was split; he retained Monmouthshire, Somerset and Gloucestershire, while Thomas Evans, a 28 year-old engineer from Dowlais, took over responsibility for the rest of South Wales. Mackworth wrote a special report on the Cymmer Colliery for Evans. In the following month Edward Hay resigned to take up a new post, probably to the relief of Jabez Thomas, who appointed David Grey as underground agent. It was normal practice at this time for the owner to appoint underground agents, as had happened when Hay was appointed, but on this occasion the task was left to Jabez Thomas.

In April the rules for Cymmer Colliery were approved by the Home Secretary but were not issued to the men until June. There were still shortcomings: although they were printed in Welsh and English, they were not read to the men and they excluded rules on gas, firedamp and lights, which Thomas had had removed for the original on the ground, it appears, that the No 3 Rhondda was not a fiery seam. The failure to have the rules read regularly to the men was a serious breach of the law as many of them were illiterate or incapable of understanding a complex

---

[1] Ibid., p. 121.

document. On 11 July David Grey, who did not enjoy the best of health, left Cymmer for a more congenial post, leaving the colliery without an underground agent.

This was the latest in a series of events which put Cymmer Old Pit at risk. Insole's drive for production and profit, his habit of ignoring warnings and advice, Jabez Thomas's insensitive attitudes in disputes and in the management of the colliery, the appointment of inexperienced officials, a cavalier attitude to the men's safety and the almost universal belief that No 3 Rhondda was a safe seam, all conspired to make Cymmer Old a disaster waiting to happen.

On Tuesday 15 July 1856 at 3.30 a.m., about first light at that time of year, the firemen went down the pit to check that it was safe for working. William Jones noticed firedamp in one of the stalls in the new workings and he placed some crossed timbers at the entrance, as a warning to the colliers not to enter. He returned to the surface after some two hours inspection, told the other fireman, Morgan Rowlands, what he had seen and went home to breakfast. Morgan Rowlands, however, did not report the presence of firedamp to his brother Rowland, the overman, since David Morgan, who normally worked the stall, was away at the seaside. Rowland Rowlands accordingly allowed work to start and at 6.30 a.m. about 130 men and boys went down the pit. Among them were two boys who were sent to work in David Morgan's stall.

An hour later there was an explosion in the Old Pit. Jabez Thomas, who was at the New Pit, came to the pit head but did not descend; he was said to have asked first about the fate of the horses. Rowland Rowlands left the office and went down the pit. He found some survivors near the bottom of the shaft and then started to discover the dead; he had to return to the surface twice because of the poor air in the pit.

On the surface a large crowd quickly assembled and rescuers went down into what was still a foul and dangerous atmosphere. During the day men came to help from the Cynon Valley and by 9 o'clock that night 112 bodies had been recovered. Only twelve survivors were brought up, one of whom died later. A further body was found on the Wednesday. All through the day coffins were made in the colliery yard and the dead were taken to their homes, some as far as Pontypridd and Aberdare.[1] Among the early arrivals on the scene were the reporters from the *Cardiff & Merthyr Guardian*, the *Cambrian* and the *Monmouthshire Merlin*, who wrote graphic descriptions of the scene at the surface

---

[1] The distance to the town of Aberdare was a long walk and the use of the name by the coroner and the newspapers possibly referred to all the communities in the Cynon Valley.

and the situation underground, where the dead were often found huddled together. They also noted that eight of the pit's twelve horses, valued at £30 or £40 each, were killed. Thomas Evans, the local inspector of mines, went down in the afternoon but he was overcome by the bad air and had to go home to recover. Henry Naunton Davies (1828–99), the surgeon at Cymmer who attended the colliers, also came to help.[1] He noticed that 36 of the dead showed signs of burning, five had been injured but the rest had died of suffocation from the after damp, a poisonous mixture of gases including carbon monoxide, which was left after the explosion.

With 114 dead, the disaster was the first in Wales with more than 100 fatalities and the worst that had been known in Britain. Many of the dead were boys or young single men: 34 were under the age of sixteen, including fifteen door boys who had not reached their twelfth birthday. Others had dependent families: the explosion left 32 widows, of whom five were pregnant, and 92 orphaned children, including seven in one family. There were a further thirteen adults and eleven children who had been dependent on a collier's earnings. The effect on the village was devastating and the sense of shock spread quickly through the coalfield. The news travelled further and the next day the question of the causes and consequences of the disaster was raised in the House of Commons.

On Wednesday 16 July the inquest was opened at the Tynewydd Inn at Porth by the North Glamorgan coroner, George Overton, a local landowner with interests in ironworks.[2] A jury of eighteen was sworn and they went to view the bodies. Newspaper reporters accompanied them and described the scenes of mourning in harrowing detail; they also commented upon the cleanliness and tidiness of the miners' houses. Having viewed the bodies the inquest was adjourned to Monday 29 July.

As well as shock there was anger: Daniel Maxey, one of the jury, made an impassioned plea for an immediate and independent examination of the pit as soon as he was sworn. There was considerable unrest among the colliers and others at the pit head, who blamed the management of the colliery for the disaster. In consequence, a large contingent of the county police was sent to the village early on the Thursday morning, in case there was more unrest. On Thursday, however, all was quiet; it was the first day of the victims' funerals which were reported to

---

[1] H.N. Davies was the son of Dr Evan Naunton Davies (1801–50), who was the surgeon at Dinas and, like Walter Coffin, a prominent Unitarian.

[2] The account of the inquest is based on reports in the *Cardiff & Merthyr Guardian* and the *Cambrian*, 19 July–29 Aug. 1856.

have had a pacifying effect on the community. James Insole paid all the funeral costs.

The public response to the disaster was immediate. Meetings were held at Pontypridd, Cardiff, Newport, Merthyr and Bristol, where subscription lists were opened. The meeting at Pontypridd raised £1,200 including £500 from James Insole. There were, however, successful objections to the nomination of Insole to the committee. A suggestion at the meeting that any payments should be in addition to parish relief, at that time 10s per week for a widow and three children,[1] was strongly opposed by Walter Coffin and defeated. As it turned out, the trustees of the relief fund proved themselves every bit as parsimonious as the poor law guardians. The most spontaneous response was from the Society of Locomotive Engine Drivers and Firemen on the Taff Vale Railway, who asked the superintendent, George Fisher to deduct a day's pay from each man for the fund, since they also worked in a dangerous occupation. The directors of the railway agreed to donate £200 at their September meeting.

On Monday 28 July the inquest reopened at the Butchers Arms in the centre of Pontypridd. A tent with room, it was said, for several hundred had been erected but there was still not enough room for everybody. The coroner was to be assisted by a government assessor, a barrister called Poulden; Mr Huddlestone appeared as counsel for James Insole and the managers, John Owen for the bereaved families, while Thomas Evans, the inspector, was joined, on the instructions of the Home Secretary, by Herbert Mackworth and Joseph Dickenson from Manchester. Also present were the colliery proprietors, David W. James and David Williams, the Bute Trustees' agent, W.S. Clark, and a number of mining engineers. The jury of eighteen included one gentleman, two drapers, an ironmonger, a tailor, a maltster, two publicans, including the landlord of the Butchers Arms, a contractor, an overlooker, a foreman, a fireman, a carpenter and five colliers. The inquest was to take thirteen days, lasting until 22 August.

Opening the inquest, the coroner recalled previous explosions at Lletty Shenkin and Middle Duffryn, and was reminded by Joseph Dickenson of recent disasters at Haswell (93 dead) and Wallsend (103). Overton had presided at the Middle Duffryn inquest in 1852 and was not sympathetic to careless and cavalier behaviour by owners or managers. He was also aware of the widespread belief among the colliers, firemen and overmen

---

[1] Llantrisant Vestry Book, Aug. 1856, cited by Lewis, 'Cymer (Rhondda) Explosion', p. 126.

in the valley that the No 3 Rhondda seam was safe from firedamp. He also reminded the jury that the Coal Mines Inspection Act gave properly approved colliery rules the force of law, although he thought that the Cymmer rules were lenient. As well as the legal representatives, he allowed the government assessor, the inspectors and the jury to question witnesses, some of whom were called a number of times.

The first witness was James Insole, who gave information about the colliery and its managers. He then disclaimed all responsibility for the management of the colliery, which he said he left to Jabez Thomas, whom he considered a fully competent colliery manager. He added that he would never refuse money for safety. John Owen raised the issue of the 1854 strike, when he had represented the men, which had been a consequence of Jabez Thomas's management appointments; Insole, however, claimed that it was not relevant to the inquest and did not respond. In answer to Mackworth's questions he said that he could not recall having received his letters. He had left the letter from the Home Secretary approving his rules at home and had to return at lunch-time to collect it. After his appearance he took no further part in the inquest.

In the afternoon Dr Henry Naunton Davies, the surgeon, described the effects of the explosion on the victims and gave his opinion that most had suffocated. John Williams, a mining engineer who had carried out an examination of the colliery, then described the pit and its method of working. On the next morning, Rowland Rowlands gave his account of the explosion and of his search for survivors, after which the inquest was again adjourned to Monday 11th August in order to allow the injured, who would provide first-hand evidence, to get better.[1] When the inquest reconvened John Owen complained that a man, who had leave to inspect the pit from the coroner, had been prevented from doing so by James Insole. The coroner upheld the complaint. The inquest then heard from the colliers who were underground when the explosion occurred, including two boys of about thirteen and two adults, one of whom was badly injured. A third boy was still not sufficiently recovered to be able to speak. The adults confirmed that their candles had had caps on their flames, a recognised sign of gas, on a number of occasions but they had not reported the incidents as they felt that nothing would be done.

Jabez Thomas was questioned a number of times. At first he claimed to be responsible only for surface activities and said that Rowland Rowlands was in charge of all underground working. At a later appearance, however, he changed his mind and said that he was in

---

[1] *Cardiff & Merthyr Guardian*, 2 Aug. 1856.

charge of all departments. He confirmed that the workings of the New
Pit and Old Pit were only about 20 or 30 yards apart but that nothing
had been done to connect the two airways. He was evasive in giving
evidence both about his relations with Hay and Grey and about his
distribution of the rules, although under further questioning he admitted
that he had not had the rules read to the men as the law required. He
must, however, have been aware of the lack of opportunities for
elementary education and the consequent illiteracy among the workforce
at Cymmer. He was a leading member of Bethlehem, the Calvinistic
Methodist Chapel, which had started a small day school in 1852,
financed by a stoppage of 1½d in the pound per week from the Cymmer
workmen.[1] David Grey and Edward Hay were restrained in their
evidence and neither thought that Cymmer was a 'fiery' pit. Two
independent witnesses were called. David Lloyd, a colliery manager, said
that in his opinion Cymmer was better than some pits he knew but he
thought that a six-mile air flow without a division was too long. William
Bedlington, a mineral surveyor at Abersychan Ironworks with 30 years
experience, was near Cymmer on the day and had offered to help. He
said that the airways were insufficient and that the explosion could have
been avoided with better ventilation but he also thought that David
James's pit at Porth was just as bad; he would not have worked David
Morgan's stall except with safety lamps and he blamed the overman for
sending the boys there.[2]

The last week of the inquest included the testimony of the firemen
and of the inspectors of mines. The firemen gave their accounts of the
events of the morning of the disaster, including David Jones's report to
Morgan Rowlands and Morgan's to his brother the overman. The
inspectors were very critical of the ventilation of the pit, the use of
naked lights and the generally lax attitude of the managers and workmen
to safety. In the opinion of Thomas Evans the Cymmer Old Pit required
35,000 cubic feet of fresh air per minute but the actual quantity was
7,648 cu. ft, of which only 1,011 cu. ft reached the southern workings
where the explosion took place. The coroner in his summing up was
equally trenchant in his guidance to the jury. He reminded them that the
cause of death by suffocation was not in question and that they only had
to decide if any were responsible. He dealt with recent cases and
summarised his view of the law as follows: 'If a man takes upon himself

---

[1] W.J. Rees, 'Cynnyrch yr Anghydffurfwyr yng Nghymoedd y Rhondda', *Trafodion Cym-
deithas Hanes Bedyddwyr Cymru*, 1961, cited by Lewis, 'Cymer (Rhondda) Explosion', p. 140.
[2] *Cardiff & Merthyr Guardian*, 9 Aug. 1856.

an office requiring skill or care, and if by his ignorance, carelessness or negligence, he cause the death of another, he will be guilty of manslaughter.' After half an hour's retirement the jury returned verdicts of manslaughter, on the grounds of negligence, against Jabez Thomas, Rowland Rowlands, Morgan Rowlands, William Thomas and David Jones. The verdicts were supported by seventeen of the eighteen jurors, the dissenter being William Rosser, a fireman from Gyfeillion. At this time it was not common for coroners' juries to bring in verdicts of manslaughter in colliery accidents and this decision was widely applauded. The coroner himself commended the jury and the verdict was welcomed by the local community, the public and the press, including, on 30 August, *The Times*.

The trial, however, did not take place until the following year, at the Glamorgan Spring Assizes on 7 March before Sir William Watson.[1] At first the indictment was considered by a grand jury, whom the judge advised to dismiss the case, as Jabez Thomas could not be considered responsible for underground activities and no direct case of omission had been brought against the other men. Except in the cases of William Thomas and David Jones, the jury ignored the judge and returned a true bill of indictment against Jabez Thomas and the two Rowlands brothers on a charge of manslaughter. The trial then followed and the judge continued to appear to act in the interest of the defendants by insisting that they would have to be shown to be directly responsible for the charge to be proved. He also attacked the inspectors who were giving evidence, ridiculed their opinions and questioned the need for their jobs. He directed the jury to discharge Thomas and advised them to acquit the other two, which they did.[2]

The people of the community and especially the families of the dead felt angry, frustrated and bitter at the verdicts. These feelings, added to the horrifying nature of the explosion itself, perpetuated the memory of the disaster. E.D. Lewis, writing of the days immediately preceding the First World War, recalled how old miners, including his great-grandfather, John Price, Trebanog, 'still remembered with awe and bitterness the great Cymer explosion of 15 July 1856'.[3] Herbert Mackworth felt that

---

[1] Sir W.H. Watson (1796–1860) had served as an officer of foot and dragoons in the Napoleonic Wars, after which he entered Lincoln's Inn and was called to the bar in 1832. His first wife was the sister of William (later Lord) Armstrong, the Northumberland industrialist. He was Liberal MP for Hull 1854–6. He died at Welshpool in March 1860, after suffering an apoplectic fit at the end of his charge to the grand jury *(DNB)*.

[2] *Cambrian*, 6 March 1857.

[3] Lewis, 'Cymer (Rhondda) Explosion', p. 161.

little benefit had accrued to the district from the verdicts and he noted in his report that those colliers who had spoken up at the inquest had found it difficult to find work afterwards and one had applied to him for assistance.[1] On the other hand some good did eventually follow the Cymmer Colliery disaster. The use of naked lights was reduced, although the colliers' habit of buying cheap safety lamps and opening them to provide more light still persisted. Eventually in the 1870s the Insoles equipped each collier with a secure safety lamp and prosecuted anyone tampering with them. The New Cymmer pit was connected to the Old Pit workings early in 1857, its shaft becoming the downcast, and in the mid-1870s a Waddle fan, 45 ft in diameter with a capacity of 250,000 cu. ft per minute, was installed to replace the furnace system of ventilation.

The disaster's legacy of mistrust and betrayal probably added to the bitterness of the Rhondda miners' strike of 1857–8 and helped to give the Cymmer colliers a leading role in it.[2] The dispute began with the reduction in coal prices caused by the fall in demand which followed the end of the Crimean War in 1856. On 26 November 1857 the steam coal colliery owners decided to reduce wages by 15 per cent. The men resolved to resist, first in the Cynon Valley and then in the Rhondda, and were soon joined by the workers in the bituminous collieries, so that by the end of the year between 6,000 and 8,000 men were out on strike. The dispute lasted until after Christmas, in spite of the owners' threat to add a further 5 per cent to the reduction. At last troops were called in to enforce a return to work and at a mass meeting at Cymmer the strikers decided to resume work with a 20 per cent reduction in wages.

Parliament, meanwhile, continued to legislate for greater safety. The Mines Regulation Act, 1860 increased the scope of colliery rules and the penalties for infringement, gave greater protection to workers and effectively excluded boys under twelve from working underground. Its provisions were reinforced by a further Act in 1862 and ten years later the Coal Mines Regulation Act of 1872 extended the scope of rules, gave more protection to boys and required managers to be certificated. Existing managers, including Jabez Thomas, were given certificates without test or examination. It was not until 1877 that a qualified mining engineer was appointed to manage the Cymmer undertaking, which had been one of Herbert Mackworth's original recommendations over twenty years before.

Those who had lost their bread-winner in the disaster became

---

[1] *Reports of Inspectors of Mines* (Parl. Papers, 1856), p. 124.

[2] Lewis, 'Cymer (Rhondda) Explosion', p. 156.

dependent on parish relief and small grants from 'The Cymmer Widows' and Orphans' Fund'. Neither the insurance companies and provident associations nor voluntary organisations for mutual assistance like the Oddfellows had made much progress in the Rhondda Valleys at this time. Nevertheless both were to become more active following the disaster and the Merthyr Tydfil branch of the Oddfellows organised a summer fete to raise money for the widows and orphans.

The Cymmer explosion took its place in the history of the South Wales coalfield, not only as the first disaster with more than 100 killed but also as an example of the single-minded greed of the owner, the incompetence of the management and the failure of the legal system to provide effective control over those who would exploit their employees so blatantly for their own ends. Furthermore, the fact that the first language of most of the colliers was Welsh and the coroner's and the court's proceedings were in English could only have increased their alienation from the system. In retrospect the stubborn ignorance of the colliers concerning the safety of the No 3 Rhondda seam also seems incomprehensible to modern ears. It is a story which highlights the competitive and demanding nature of the coal industry in what was a relatively recently worked section of the coalfield in the booming but ruthless early years of the sale coal trade. Nevertheless, some of those involved, George Overton, the coroner, Herbert Mackworth and the other inspectors, John Owen, the bereaved families' solicitor, and William Bedlington, the veteran mining engineer, showed that there were those in positions of power and influence, who opposed the outlook and practice of the industrialists of the day. The Cymmer disaster had also, if only briefly, alerted people outside the coal industry to conditions within it.

While these events were taking place in the Rhondda, James Insole's domestic life was undergoing some changes. At the time of the 1851 Census he was living in Crockherbtown with his wife and three children, now aged six, four and three, with a cook, housemaid and nurse. He also had a visitor, Thomas Webb Jones, probably his wife's brother, a saddler and ironmonger from Birmingham. His mother was living next door at George Insole's old house with her two unmarried daughters, Emma and Julia and her 22-year old nephew, Robert Barnaby Insole. He was the son of George Insole's brother Thomas, who was a Worcestershire farmer. Robert worked with his cousin James in the family firm of George Insole & Son at their office, 17 Bute Crescent, and was described in the census return as a coal merchant.[1]

In 1852 James Insole moved to Old Penhill House, Llandaff, where he was looking for a site for a new home. Llandaff had been described as very much impoverished in 1829[2] but by 1850 its lack of a passenger railway made it attractive to the carriage class. On 13 October 1853 Robert Insole married his cousin Julia at Llandaff Cathedral. At the time the only part of the cathedral that was available for services was the Lady Chapel, the rest of the building being in the process of restoration by John Prichard (1817–86), the diocesan architect. As Julia's parish church was St John's Cardiff, the reasons for the marriage taking place at the partly reconstructed cathedral, in the middle of building operations, are not known; it may, however, have been the choice of her brother, who would have given her away and who now lived in the cathedral parish. Robert and Julia set up home in Hastings Villa, Crockherbtown close to Windsor Place. In the following summer their eldest son, Henry, was born, followed in 1855 and 1857 by their daughters, Julia Antoinette and Helena. By 1858, they had moved and their son Oliver was born that year at 50 Windsor Road, Penarth. Their married life, however, was to be short; in the same year Robert contracted an intestinal disease, made his will on 13 October and died, two weeks later, on 28 October 1858. His death was followed by those of two of his children, Oliver on 5 February 1860 and Julia Antoinette in early December 1862. They were all buried at St Augustine's, Penarth as were Julia and their surviving children, Robert and Lena, neither of whom married. Throughout the 46 years of her widowhood, Julia remained in Cardiff, first in Crockherbtown and later at 38, The Parade in Tredegarville, but had no interest in the family business. She did, however, own property in the town and she had some dealings with her brother in the course of managing her affairs. On 30 October 1857 her elder sister, Emma, who was by this time 33 years old, had married Wesley Price of Cardiff House at the Wesley Chapel off Charles Street in Cardiff. Emma appears to have had no business arrangements with the family and eventually moved to Torquay.

In 1855 James Insole bought some land from Revd C.W. Evans on the southern slope below Fairwater Road in Llandaff and instructed the London architect, William Gilbee Habershon, who had then recently opened an office in Newport, to build a house for him.[3] Habershon drew up his plans and invited tenders which were reported in the trade press

---

[1] *Ewan's Cardiff Almanack & Guide* (1855).

[2] W. Bird, *Cardiff Guide & Directory*, 1829.

[3] Lewis, 'Cymer (Rhondda) Explosion', p. 133n.

to range from £1,950 to £2,972.[1] The building, known as Ely Court, a typical double gabled mid-Victorian house, was completed in 1856 or 1857 and by 1858 the family had moved in. It was to be considerably extended over the next sixty years to become the building now known as Insole Court. In 1857 James Insole became a borough magistrate, a reflection of his standing in the town. He undoubtedly had aspirations to join the gentry but, although he now had a gentleman's residence in the county, he did not become a county magistrate for another ten years.

Although his colliery and house building must have preoccupied him, James Insole would have spent most of his time in Cardiff, mainly at his office or in meetings connected with the coal trade. He normally visited his colliery one day a week and the business of making contracts and trading in coal, which occupied the other five days, was probably more congenial to an aspiring gentleman. He was shipping also out of Newport and Swansea, where he had an agent and in 1858 he was chairman of a meeting of shippers of Merthyr and Aberdare steam coal at the port of Swansea, which called on the South Wales and the Vale of Neath railway companies to reduce their freight charges and agreed other moves to bring coal shipping at Swansea more in to line with Cardiff.[2]

Next to coal, his most important business concern was transport, specifically railways and docks. Although he now had a rail link from Cymmer to the sea, the minute books and correspondence of the Taff Vale Railway in this period still contain records of minor disagreements and quarrels with Insole. Like many coal owners he was frustrated by the inflexibility of the railway company and by congestion at the docks. The Bute Trustees did take steps to increase capacity but the coal owners considered them tardy and insufficient. In 1852 work started on the Bute East Dock and in 1856 the Bute Tidal Harbour, later incorporated into the Roath Basin, was opened. The East Dock was completed in 1858 but by then a group of coal owners had taken matters into their own hands.

On 10 October 1855 a meeting, attended by Crawshay Bailey, Thomas Powell, his son Thomas Powell junior, and Samuel Dobson, a Cardiff consulting engineer, was held at Bailey's house in London.[3] This was the first meeting of what became the Ely Tidal Harbour & Railway Company, which planned to build a wharf on the eastern bank of the river Ely, with connections to the Taff Vale Railway and possibly to both the South Wales Railway and the Glamorganshire Canal. It was the

---

[1] *The Builder*, 28 July 1855.

[2] *Cambrian*, 3 Sept. 1858.

[3] PRO, RAIL 561/1.

first attempt by the coal owners to break the monopoly of the Taff Vale
Railway and the Bute Dock. Crawshay Bailey and the others all
subscribed and agreed to approach other prominent figures in the coal
trade, including James Insole. Dobson was to prepare plans, maps,
commercial assessments and other statistics. A circular letter was sent to
potential investors, calling a meeting at the Cardiff Arms Hotel on 23
August 1855. James Insole was at the meeting and was elected a director
of the company. The company's share capital was to be £100,000 in
£100 shares, of which Insole had 50. The railway line was to run from
the Taff Vale at 'Mr Booker's weir' to the east bank of the Ely estuary.
The weir is near what is now Radyr station, then known as Penarth
Junction, and was the off-take for the feeder for Melingriffith tinplate
works, of which Thomas William Booker was the managing director.

Meetings were held throughout the winter of 1855–6 and much time
was spent in negotiation with the trustees of Lady Harriet Windsor
(1797–1869), on whose land the proposed tidal harbour would be built.
The directors had decided not to proceed with either a canal branch or
a junction with the South Wales Railway, which was still broad gauge.
They also increased the share capital to £130,000 and started work on
the preparation of a parliamentary bill. James Insole and Benjamin
Matthews, the Insole family's solicitor, were sent to open discussions
with the Taff Vale Railway. Further meetings were held in London in
April 1856 with Lady Bute and with officials of the Board of Trade
before the bill completed its passage. During the summer, in spite of
opposition from Lady Bute, the Ely Tidal Harbour & Railway Act
became law and work could now begin in earnest. In September a more
formal organisation was adopted. The Hon. Robert Windsor-Clive MP
(1824–59), who was Lady Harriet Windsor's eldest son, was elected
chairman, and Crawshay Bailey, who was now an MP, deputy chairman.
James Insole was a member of the Finance Committee. On 24 October
1856 tenders were invited for building the railway and harbour on the
east bank of the Ely, while on 3 November Samuel Dobson was told to
carry out a survey for a branch line crossing to the western side of the
river and leading to a dock under the lee of Penarth Head. By 1
December eight tenders had been received and James Rennie's was
accepted for £91,000. In what would today be a highly irregular
proceeding he made a new offer below his tender when he met the
directors. On 10 December an extraordinary general meeting agreed to
prepare a parliamentary bill for a line on the west bank of the Ely and
a dock at Penarth. The capital for the new undertaking would be
£175,000, with shares being offered first to existing shareholders. On 6
January the share capital was raised to £185,000.

On 27 February 1857 at the second ordinary meeting at the Cardiff Arms Hotel the directors reported that the current works were supported by the Admiralty and should be completed by 30 June 1858. Furthermore, the Penarth Harbour Dock & Railway Bill had been read twice and had also been approved by the Admiralty. James Insole was a member of the company's parliamentary committee for the Penarth Dock Bill.

Early in 1858 the Taff Vale Railway made its first approaches to the new railway with a view to making an operating agreement, by which the Taff Vale would have worked the railway. This could have been beneficial to the Penarth Railway as the Taff Vale had experience and expertise in what was still a new industry for which good staff were not easy to find. In May, for example, the directors were looking for a resident engineer as they did not have confidence in the contractors' site managers. Discussions continued with the Taff Vale throughout the spring and summer but without agreement. On 14 September the directors resolved to work the line themselves. It seems that the Taff Vale was only prepared to offer a short term agreement, while the Penarth directors wanted a more permanent arrangement. By this time James Insole's attendance at board meetings had become less regular and he had two differences with his fellow directors. One concerned a demand that the railway acquire some land to give him access to the line and the other his lateness in paying for shares. They do not seem to have been resolved until well into 1860. In spite of these differences Insole was re-elected to the board at the end of his initial term.

On 13 March 1859 the directors decided to open for traffic on the following 1 June but it was not until September that the line was ready and the Ely Tidal Harbour was opened. The water area of the harbour was 26 acres and it had ten coal staithes, each capable of shipping 140 tons per hour, with space for 30 or 40 more on a waterfront of 12,000 feet. It was also equipped with three steam cranes, each capable of moving 50 tons of ballast per hour.[1]

During the next five years the company concentrated on establishing their trade and building Penarth Dock. On 2 January 1860 the directors strengthened their commercial position at the mouth of the Ely, when they subscribed £15,000 to the Ely Valley Railway.[2] In 1862 they eventually reached an agreement with the Taff Vale to lease the

---

[1] A. Bassett, 'The Port of Cardiff and the Aberdare Steam Coal Field', *Trans. S. Wales Inst. Engineers*, IV, 1864–5, p. 104; E.L. Chappell, *History of the Port of Cardiff* (Cardiff, 1939), p. 87.

[2] PRO, RAIL 561/1.

undertaking for 999 years for a perpetual dividend of 5¼ per cent. They also had a dispute with their contractor which ended in the Court of Chancery, which authorised the board to complete the work themselves.[1] Eventually, by the summer of 1865, the western branch railway and the dock were completed, bringing the total cost of the two ventures to £775,000. The new dock was 2,100 ft long and 370 ft wide and was entered through wrought iron lock gates 60 ft wide, a lock 270 ft long and a basin of 400 ft by 330 ft. The south side of the dock was equipped with twelve hydraulic coal drops or tips, with space for six more.[2]

The formal opening of the Penarth Dock took place at high water, about 7.30 a.m., on Saturday 10 June 1865. Extensive preparations were ordered by the board. Samuel Dobson was to test the machinery and the dockmaster was to have all the gatemen and other workmen well drilled in their duties. All directors were to be at Penarth by 7 a.m. and they were each allotted two spare tickets for a formal breakfast, which was provided for 350 people, including two representatives of the Taff Vale who had six tickets each. Refreshments were also provided for gunners and bandsmen, about 50 in all, and every man in the company's employ received a shilling to mark the occasion.[3] The dock was more favourably sited than the Bute Dock in relation to the steep tides of the Severn Estuary and 275,333 tons of coal were shipped in the remaining six months of the first year. Five years later their annual export coal trade was 1,230,404 tons, which by 1881 had risen to 1,880,482 tons. In 1880 the Penarth Dock was extended from 21 to 26½ acres at a cost of £250,000 and coal exports reached a peak of 4,525,910 tons in 1913.[4]

The Penarth Dock and Ely Tidal Harbour provided much-needed outlets for the coalfield, although they were at first seen as rivals by the Bute Trustees and the Taff Vale Railway. Following the agreement with the Taff Vale, however, the new scheme was integrated within the overall management of Cardiff's docks. If the purpose of the railway's coal owner founders was to provide a counterbalance to the monopoly powers of the Bute Trustees and the Taff Vale they were unsuccessful, but if they were merely seeking to increase the capacity of the port of Cardiff they achieved their objective, at least in the short term.

---

[1] Chappell, *Port of Cardiff*, pp. 87–8.

[2] Bassett, 'The Port of Cardiff', p. 103.

[3] PRO, RAIL 561/3.

[4] Chappell, *Port of Cardiff*, p. 89.

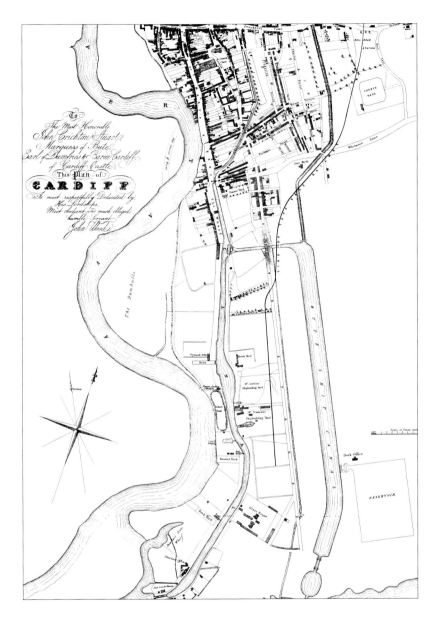

1. Detail from John Wood's plan of Cardiff of *c.* 1840, showing 'Crockherb Town' (the modern Queen Street) at the top (where George Insole had his house) and the sea-lock at the southern end of the Glamorganshire Canal at the foot. Insole's coal yard lay alongside the canal near the sea-lock, opposite the Dowlais Iron Co.'s offices. *(Courtesy Glamorgan Record Office)*

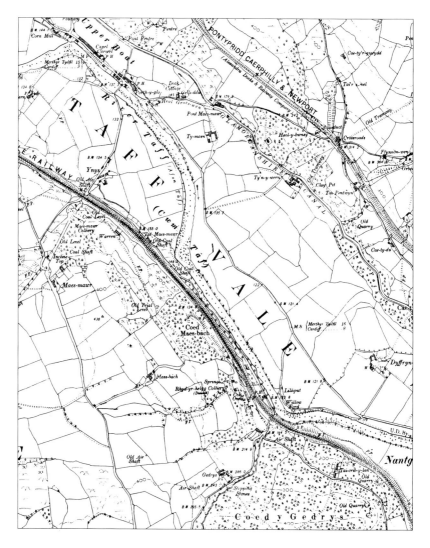

2. Detail from Ordnance Survey 1:10,560 map of 1901, showing Maesmawr in the Taff valley north of Cardiff.

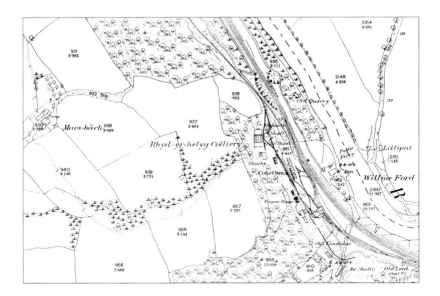

3. *Above:* Detail from Ordnance Survey 1:2500 map (1874), showing Rhyd-yr-helyg Colliery, Maesbach. *Below:* Copy of a map prepared for George Insole of Cymmer Levels, 1843 *(From E.D. Lewis,* The Rhondda Valleys)

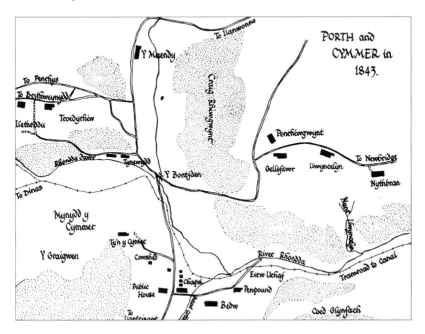

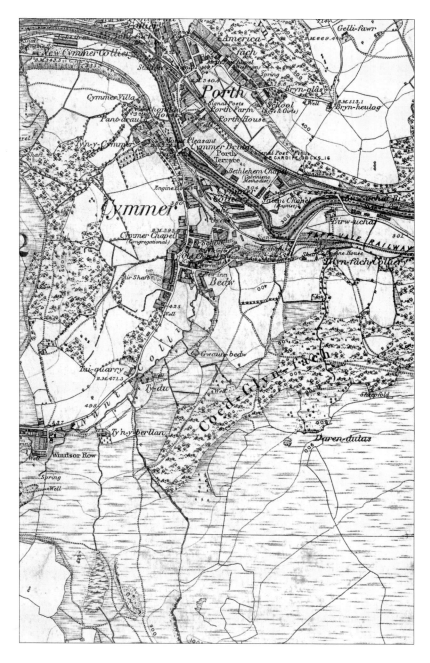

4. Detail from Ordnance Survey 1:10,560 map of 1885, showing Cymmer and Porth in the lower Rhondda valley.

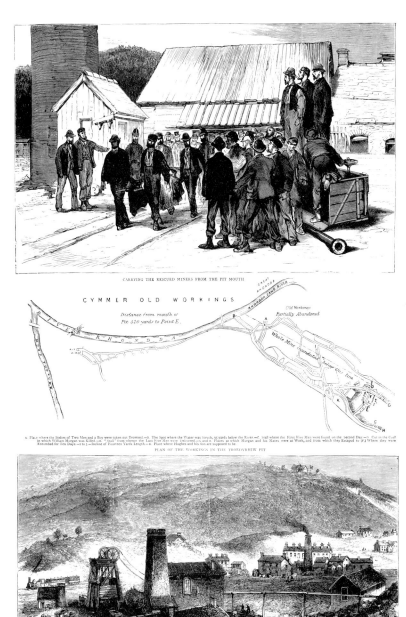

CARRYING THE RESCUED MINERS FROM THE PIT MOUTH

CYMMER OLD WORKINGS

Distance from mouth of
Pit 520 yards to Point E.

Old Workings
Partially Abandoned

A. Place where the Bodies of Two Men and a Boy were taken out Drowned.—B. The Spot where the Water was Struck, 95 yards below the River.—C. Stall where the First Five Men were found on the second Day.—D. Cut in the Coal in which William Morgan was Killed.—E. "Stall" from whence the Last Five Men were Delivered.—G and H. Places at which Morgan and his Mates were at Work, and from which they Escaped to (F.) Where they were Entombed for Ten Days.—I to J.—Incline of Fourteen Yards Length.—K. Place where Hughes and his Son are supposed to be.

PLAN OF THE WORKINGS IN THE TROEDYRHIW PIT

5. Illustrations accompanying a report on the Tynewydd Colliery disaster, from *The Graphic*, 28 April 1877.

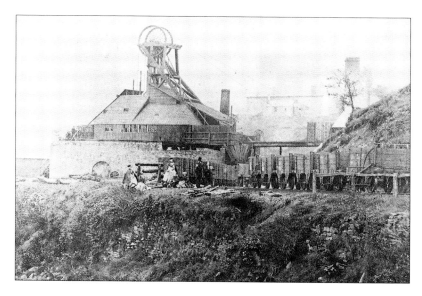

6. Photograph of Cymmer Colliery, *c.* 1860. The family group, shown in the enlargement below, has not been identified. They appear well-to-do and therefore their inclusion seems odd, unless they had some connection with the colliery. It may be Jabez Thomas and his family but he was probably over 60 at the time. James Insole, however, was nearly 40 and it is possible that the picture shows him and his family. *(Courtesy Rhondda Cynon Taff Libraries, copyright John Cornwell)*

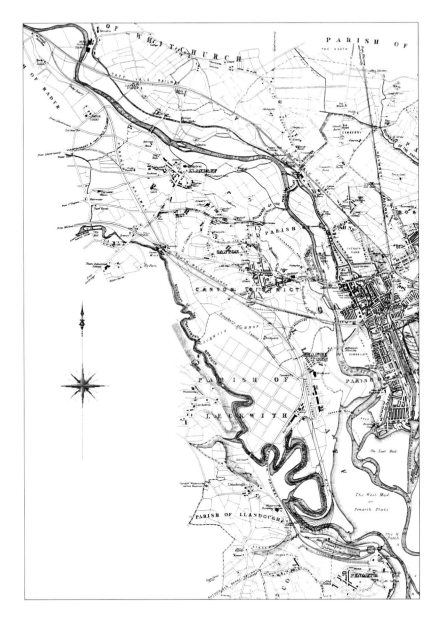

7. Detail from Thomas Waring's map of Cardiff and district (1869), showing the Penarth Railway, Ely Tidal Harbour and Penarth Dock. *(Courtesy Glamorgan Record Office)*

8. Detail from 'An Impression of Penarth Dock, 1865', a watercolour by G.H. Andrews, showing the dock on the left and Ely Tidal Harbour in the centre. *(Courtesy Glamorgan Record Office)*

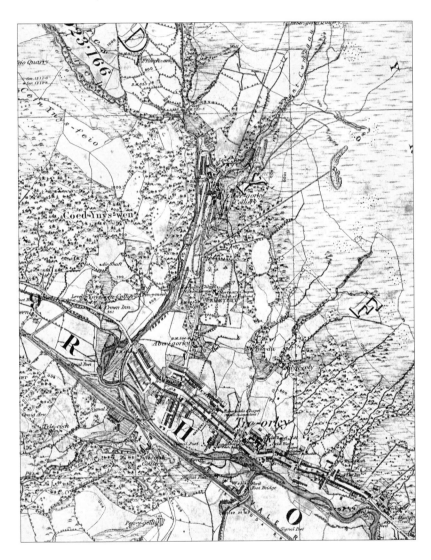

9. Detail from Ordnance Survey 1:10,560 map of 1884, showing Abergorci and Treorci in the Rhondda Valley.

10. Photographs of Cymmer Colliery, from George Insole & Son's booklet, *Cymmer Steam Coal* (1880). *(Courtesy Cardiff County Library)*

Chapter 5

The Search for Steam Coal

1862–74

In the early development of the South Wales coalfield, coal was won in those areas where the seams outcropped or were close to the surface, that is in the western part of the coalfield and on its northern and southern rims in Glamorgan and Monmouthshire. Throughout the coalfield the coal seams change from being bituminous and friable in the south and east to anthracitic and hard in the north and west, these changes often occurring within the same seam. The bituminous coals contain between 84 and 91 per cent carbon and anthracite over 93 per cent. Between these two and generally at a lower depth the seams become what came to be known as steam coal, combining a carbon content of between 91 and 93 per cent and the smokeless qualities of anthracite with some of the friability of the bituminous coals. In practice the coal's carbon content produced intense heat, which its relative softness allowed it to release quickly as it expanded and 'cauliflowered'.[1] Furthermore the coal produced little smoke and when large coal was used no clinker and very little ash.

This coal, with its combination of high calorific value and relatively clean operation, was an ideal fuel for steam engines, which were the main source of power in industry and transport in the second half of the nineteenth century, and an enormous demand was created which increased, seemingly inexorably, until the First World War. Steam coal from South Wales, shipped mainly through Cardiff, was the leader in the market and the growth of the trade, from its beginnings in the 1830s to its peak in 1913, was the basis of Cardiff's own economic growth, prosperity and regional pre-eminence. Ultimately, however, this dependence on a single product made the mining valleys, the docks and railways and the city itself vulnerable to changes in fuel technology and markets.

By the 1850s the markets for steam coal were well established. Twenty years earlier marine steam engines were considered more suitable

---

[1] R.H. Walters, *The Economic and Business History of the South Wales Steam Coal Industry, 1840–1914* (New York, 1977), p. xv.

for inshore vessels and coasters than for ocean-going ships. The steam boats on the Thames had been the target of George Insole's early ventures with Lucy Thomas's steam coal and by 1842 it was estimated that some 5,000 steam ships were afloat on the river on any summer day. They included government packets, coastal traders, passenger ferries, tugs and pleasure steamers.[1] By 1850 Admiralty trials to find the best fuel for the Royal Navy, and the improving reliability and performance of steam powered vessels established the future of the steamship in sea transport. By the 1880s steamers had overtaken sailing ships as carriers in the Cardiff coal trade (Table 5.1).

Table 5.1: *Coal shipments from Bute Docks, Cardiff, 1865–82*

Year	By steamer (tons)	By sailing ship (tons)
1865	275,000	1,942,063
1873	1,186,175	1,322,545
1882	3,959,121	1,621,397

Source: E.D. Lewis, *The Rhondda Valleys*, p. 135.

The demand for steam coal was further increased by the establishment of a world-wide chain of bunkering stations or depots, as steamship lines vied for supremacy in carrying passengers and cargoes around the world. Steam coal also supplanted coke as the preferred fuel for railway locomotives. By 1850 Britain had a national railway network and the period 1850–70 saw the spread of industrialisation in Europe and the construction of European railway systems. Overseas the countries of South America, the Mediterranean and Asia were trading with Britain, overwhelmingly sending their goods in British ships and, with the spread of industry and railways, increasing the market for South Wales coal. Throughout the expansion of the steam coal trade France remained the largest overseas market for the South Wales coalfield, followed by other Mediterranean countries and South America.[2]

Steam coal prices also played a part in encouraging investment in collieries and in stimulating coal production. Between 1840 and the end of the century there were a number of periods when steam coal prices rose above the range of 7s to 8s per ton.[3] These were in the early 1840s, 1852–6, short periods between 1863 and 1865, 1870–5 (including an average price for 1873 of 23s 3d per ton, which was not surpassed until

---

[1] *Cambrian*, 28 May 1842.

[2] Walters, *South Wales Steam Coal Industry*, App. 11.

[3] See Appendix B.

1916) and 1889–94. These price rises were caused by an imbalance of supply and demand, to which the coal industry was particularly sensitive. The coal owners and shippers did not maintain large stocks of coal, as it was liable to deteriorate and sudden or rapid increases in demand could often not be met by an equivalent increase in production. Variations in demand were usually a product of the business cycle, sometimes aggravated by external events. The Crimean War (1854–6) caused an increase in demand and the Franco-Prussian War (1870–1) a dislocation of the French market. From the late 1890s prices increased steadily in most years until the First World War, reaching 17s 6d per ton in 1914.

In 1864 further trials of steam coals were conducted, partly in response to the influence of MPs from north east England seeking the reinstatement of Newcastle coals in the Royal Navy's steam fleet. As a result the Admiralty issued new rules for the supply of coal to the ships of the Royal Navy, which stipulated that all steam coal contracts were to be two-thirds Welsh and one-third Newcastle.[1] This proved impractical and in 1872, following many complaints, the Admiralty reverted to all Welsh for its steam coal contracts.[2] A number of further Admiralty tests of South Wales steam coals followed throughout the 1870s, enhancing their reputation. Following Britain, which was the world's leading maritime power, the governments of other countries also specified South Wales steam coal, including France, Italy and the Netherlands, as did many steamship lines. In forty years Welsh steam coal had established a world-wide reputation as the leading fuel for steam raising, making fortunes for some and providing dangerous, unhealthy and hard work for many.

George Insole's role in the steam coal market had always been as a shipper rather than a colliery proprietor. He appears to have had adequate and reliable sources of supply, including the Thomas family, David Williams and the Plymouth Ironworks. James Insole, on the other hand, seems to have decided to take a more direct approach. His first venture, with David Williams in the Deep Duffryn colliery at Mountain Ash, did not last long. His £6,000 investment in 1852 had been made during the sinking of the pit, which lasted from February 1850 to January 1855.[3] Output reached 150 tons per day by 1857 but the pit had problems with ventilation and Williams had been served with a notice from the Home

---

[1] *Cambrian*, 3 June 1864.

[2] Lewis, *Rhondda Valleys*, p. 136.

[3] Walters, *South Wales Steam Coal Industry*, p. 22.

Secretary that the colliery was unsafe. As the warning was issued on the advice of Herbert Mackworth it must have originated in 1855, the last year for which Mackworth was the inspector for Glamorgan. Nothing, however, was done for well over a year. It may be that the Cymmer disaster had persuaded David Williams, possibly after discussion with James Insole, to sell the colliery or he may not have had the capital to effect improvements. Whatever the reason he put the colliery on the market and in August 1857 Deep Duffryn was sold to John Nixon (1815–99) and his partner, William Cory, a London coal merchant, for £42,000. Nixon was a mining engineer from County Durham, an innovator who pioneered the sale of South Wales steam coal in France and introduced new working methods and machinery in his collieries. He installed ventilation fans and winding engines at Deep Duffryn and within two years raised its output from the 150 tons per day, which David Williams had achieved, to 1,000 tons.[1]

For the next five years James Insole continued to sell steam coal from other coal owners' collieries, confining his own mining operations to the bituminous seams at Cymmer. At this time the mining of steam coal in the Rhondda, as opposed to the Cynon Valley, was seen as a risky venture, because of the depth of the seams and the capital required to win the coal. The Rhondda coal owners preferred to continue to mine the bituminous seams of the upper coal levels, which were proven and profitable. Nevertheless the exploitation of the steam coal measures of the Rhondda had already begun, although for the first ten years of their development, from 1854 to 1864, progress was slow with few of the colliery proprietors taking part. The 1857-8 coal strike, which began in the steam collieries of the Cynon Valley and then spread to all the pits in the Rhondda, did nothing to encourage them to speculate further. The lack of commercial success at the only steam coal pit in the Rhondda valleys, the Bute Merthyr at Treherbert, was another warning of the difficulties and uncertainties which faced the prospector for steam coal in the Rhondda of the 1850s.

Ironically the opening of the Bute Merthyr Colliery was the result of pressure from outside the coal trade to prove steam coal in the Rhondda and to encourage its exploitation. In 1850 the Taff Vale Railway offered £500 to the first person to sink a pit 120 yards below the river level in the upper reaches of the Rhondda Fawr. The Taff Vale, whose line reached only as far as Dinas in the lower Rhondda, were concerned

---

[1] J.E. Vincent, *John Nixon. Pioneer of the Steam Coal Trade in South Wales* (1900), pp. 168–9.

about potential competitors at the upper end of the valley, with rival plans for railways both over the mountain to the Vale of Neath and from Tonypandy to the Ely Valley and the South Wales Railway.

In 1845 the Marquess of Bute had acquired Cwm Saerbren farm and its mineral rights from William Davies for £11,000, on the advice of William Southern Clark (1817–64), the chief agent of the Bute mineral estate. The Bute Trustees decided to take up the Taff Vale Railway's challenge and on 16 October 1851 began sinking a pit at Cwm Saerbren. This was an unusual course of action for a landowner in South Wales where, in contrast to the practice in some other coalfields, landowners had for many years normally leased rather than worked their mineral holdings. At first the Bute venture was a success and on 7 April 1853 the Upper Four Feet seam was proved at a depth of 125 yards. An upcast shaft was sunk and on 21 December 1855 the first steam coal raised in the Rhondda valley was sent from Cwm Saerbren to Cardiff. At the time the railway ended at Gellideg and so the first part of the journey was made in carts. The Bute estate had won the Taff Vale's £500 and the railway was completed to Cwm Saerbren (the modern Treherbert) in August 1856,[1] although the pit, known as the Bute Merthyr Associated Colliery, was not commercially successful until the mid-1860s.

By 1860 only two other steam coal collieries had opened in the Rhondda, at Tylacoch (1855) and Ynysfeio (1859).[2] At the same time James Insole's sources of steam coal were becoming less secure, Deep Duffryn had been sold and the Aberaman seams were becoming less productive. In 1862, therefore, he tried to prove steam coal at Cymmer, spending over £500 between November 1862 and June 1863. The seams, however, were thin and unworkable; they were probably those lying between 50 and 100 yards below the No 3 Rhondda: the Hafod, Abergorci, Pentre and Gorllwyn.[3] In 1863 Insole started to prospect for steam coal at Abergorci in the upper Rhondda Fawr, not far from the Bute Merthyr Colliery at Cwm Saerbren, and he reached the steam coal measures in 1865. On 2 June 1862, before beginning his search at Cymmer, he had acquired the Abergorci level from Houghty Huxham for £7,000.[4] Huxham, who had been the first manager of the Bute Merthyr Colliery, Thomas Hopkin and William Morgan of Aberdare had opened the level on an old colliery site in September 1859. They had been

---

[1] D.S.M. Barrie, *The Taff Vale Railway* (Oakwood Press, 1982), p. 16.

[2] Lewis, *Rhondda Valleys*, p. 92.

[3] Insole MSS, Ledger, Nov. 1862–July 1863, cited by Lewis, *Rhondda Valleys*, p. 71.

[4] Ibid., Cymmer Ledger, 2 Jun. 1862, cited by Lewis *Rhondda Valleys*, p. 75.

working the No 3 Rhondda and this may have been an indication to
Insole that the steam coal seams at Abergorci would be at similar depths
to those at Bute Merthyr, rather than the depths of around 200 yards,
where he had been prospecting in the lower Rhondda. The purchase of
Abergorci may have been something of an opportunist venture as James
Insole was Huxham's mortgagor and he may have acquired the colliery
partly by repossession. Probably by November 1862 Insole had
abandoned his prospecting at Cymmer and concentrated his search for
steam coal on Abergorci, where he sunk a pit.[1] After two years his
efforts were rewarded and the steam coal seams were won. Output at the
colliery increased rapidly (Table 5.2).

Abergorci colliery was situated about 100 feet above Treorci in the
narrow Nant Orci valley. It had no branch railway or siding in Insole's
time but it did have a lengthy tramroad: this ran from the Abergorci
quarry high on the mountain, down to the colliery, where there was a
small network of track and sidings, and thence down the valley to join
the Taff Vale Railway. Once the steam coal seams had been reached the
colliery provided Insole with a valuable and plentiful source of supply,
under his direct control, for the best part of ten years.

Table 5.2: *Coal Output at Abergorci Colliery, 1864–72*

Year	Tons
1864	18,827
1865	30,874
1866	95,946
1867	84,598
1868	117,154
1869	132,343
1871	95,162
1872	142,055
1873	134,408

Source: NLW, XAC 259 R47 L67, E.D. Lewis Collection,
Return of coal raised in Ystradyfodwg parish.

The years from 1864 until 1914 were a period of spectacular growth
in the Rhondda coal industry, for the first twenty years through new
leases and sinkings and for the remaining thirty largely through the
expansion and exploitation of existing mineral holdings. By the end of
the 1870s the two valleys had been transformed, as speculators and
prospectors realised their potential. In 1874 Idris Williams, the assistant

---

[1] Ibid., Cymmer Ledger, 14 Nov. 1862, cited by Lewis *Rhondda Valleys,* p. 75.

overseer of the poor in the parish of Ystradyfodwg, noted that the coal raised in the collieries of the parish had increased, from 404,448 tons to 1,850,022 tons, in the previous ten years as a result of increased output and new pits.[1] By 1875 the output of coal in the Rhondda valleys had outstripped output in the Cynon Valley: by 1884 the Rhondda's 5,600,000 tons was double the Cynon Valley's 2,300,000 and one-fifth of the output of the entire South Wales coalfield.

The attractions of the Rhondda for prospectors were its newly proven and probable coal reserves, the strong and growing demand for steam coal and the promise of firm and often increasing prices which it could command. Moreover, improved working methods and the widespread use of mechanical power for ventilation, winding and underground transport were enabling productivity to increase. The railway network was also improving, giving access eventually to all the main South Wales ports. Many of the new collieries were owned by large companies, including substantial figures such as David Davies of Llandinam (1818–90), a railway contractor, who was attracted to the coal trade by prospects in the American market, and the Cory brothers who, like the Insoles, had started in the coal trade as shippers. The Rhondda steam coal industry was strong enough to withstand not only the vagaries of the business cycle but also general depressions in trade, such as followed the failure of the discount house of Overend, Gurney & Co. in 1866 and the collapse of the South Wales iron trade in the 1870s.

In the early 1870s James Insole decided to dispose of the colliery at Abergorci, possibly in order to finance further prospecting for steam coal at Cymmer and thus to concentrate all his mining activities on one site. In 1873 the colliery was sold to Burnyeat, Brown & Co., a firm of merchants and industrialists from Whitehaven and Liverpool, through their Cardiff shipping agent J.B. Ferrier jun. The firm had been formed in January of the same year to acquire the Lletty Shenkin colliery for £200,000, which had a claimed output of over 240,000 tons per annum.[2] The steam coal from Abergorci continued to be referred to as Insole's Merthyr and the new owners had offices next door to George Insole & Son, at 5 Bute Crescent, for which they paid James Insole rent.

On 6 December 1875 the search for steam coal at Cymmer began again and in eighteen months brought great success. In the spring of 1877 the Two-Foot-Nine seam of steam coal was won, at a depth of 299

[1] NLW, XAC 259 R47 L67, E.D. Lewis Collection, Return of coal raised in Ystradyfodwg parish.

[2] *Colliery Guardian*, 12 Dec. 1873.

yards. Sinking continued throughout the summer and three further seams
were won: in June the Four-Feet at 321 yards, in July the Six-Feet at 340
yards and in August the Nine-Feet at 370 yards. Having sunk 1,000 feet
below their current working of the No 3 Rhondda, they had now four
excellent seams within some 200 feet. The firm produced a promotional
booklet advertising their steam coal with a history of the firm and an
account of the search for steam coal at Cymmer, which was in a second
edition by 1880.[1] The Insoles now had an assured source of supply for
both house and steam coals, which was to last until 1939. During that
time they continued to extend their operations and to take on new leases.

James Insole's search for steam coal was not a period of harmonious
industrial relations. Although the early 1860s were comparatively free
from strikes,[2] considerable distrust must have persisted between the
colliers and their employers, not least at Cymmer where memories of the
1856 disaster and the colliers' defeat in the 1857–8 strike would still
have been fresh. As a result, when the owners increased wages by 5 per
cent in November 1863 and by 10 per cent in March 1864, it only served
to convince the men that the owners could afford to pay more and
agitation started. The National Miners' Union had been established in the
north of England and its meeting at Leeds in the same month was
attended by John Griffiths, a delegate from the Rhondda. The owners
also used this period of strong trade to combine and on 14 March 1864
the Aberdare Steam Collieries Association was formed. In 1870 it was
extended to the Rhondda owners and renamed the South Wales Steam
Collieries Association. In June 1866, facing a demand for an increase in
wages and concerned about the effects of the failure of Overend, Gurney
& Co., the house-coal owners set up the South Wales Bituminous
Collieries Association.[3] James Insole did not join either of these
associations or their successors and the Insole businesses remained
outside any combination of owners for many years.

As the pits became deeper in order to reach the steam coal seams,
working conditions became more dangerous and between 1867 and 1871
there were four explosions in the Rhondda valleys, killing 270 men in
all. In the face of increasing dangers underground, the strength of the
owners and their reluctance to grant increases in wages, particularly from
1870 when coal prices were rising, the colliers' sense of grievance
mounted. The National Miners' Union could not deal with wages and

[1] George Insole & Son, *Cymmer Steam Coal* (Cardiff, 1880) (copy in CCL).

[2] Lewis, *Rhondda Valleys*, p. 161.

[3] Morris and Williams, *South Wales Coal Industry*, pp. 267-8.

made little headway in the Rhondda but in 1869 a new union, the Amalgamated Association of Miners, was formed in Lancashire and quickly spread to other coalfields. By 1871 there were about 12,000 miners from the Cynon and Rhondda valleys in the union.

On 27 February 1871 the coal owners gave notice of a reduction of wages by 10 per cent, although the price of coal was rising sharply. The Amalgamated Association of Miners replied with a demand for a 10 per cent increase, which the Steam Collieries Association rejected on 20 May. On 26 May 11,000 men in all 26 collieries in the Cynon and Rhondda valleys belonging to members of the association stopped work. James Insole, not being a member of the association, was at first unaffected by the strike but almost immediately declared a lock-out in sympathy with the owners' association at Abergorci. The owners resorted to importing blackleg labour using well-known strike breakers to hire men, women and boys from England to work in the mines. In order to accommodate them striking miners were evicted from their homes, behaviour described by E.D. Lewis as 'industrial bourbonism', which turned public opinion against the owners. The strike lasted three months until in August the owners conceded the men's demand for arbitration and work was resumed. On 1 February 1872 the arbitrators announced their decision, awarding a 2½ per cent increase to the men. One of the union leaders and a miners' delegate on the arbitration committee was Lewis Morgan from Abergorci. In 1873 a strike in the ironworks' pits went to arbitration, which again found in favour of the men. Although defeated, the owners were able to take advantage of an extraordinary boom in coal prices, which reached 23s 3d per ton in 1873. In March 1874 the owners' association was reconstituted as the South Wales Coal Owners' Association, its enlarged membership representing 70 per cent of the output of the coalfield, but the firm of George Insole & Son was not a member. In 1874 the coal boom came to an end and prices fell by nearly half to 12s 6d per ton. On 1 December 1874 the owners announced a 10 per cent reduction and the men resisted. After a five-month strike the owners increased the reduction to 15 per cent and the men were defeated, returning to work on 29 May with a 12½ per cent reduction. Agreement was reached, however, on the introduction of the Sliding Scale of Wages, which linked the workers' pay to the price of coal and regulated colliery wages for 27 years. Three months later the Amalgamated Association of Miners became insolvent and was dissolved. The Rhondda miners, however, formed their own union, Undeb Glowyr Dyffryn Rhondda, and in February 1877 they invited William Abraham, known as Mabon, (1842–1922) to be their full-time paid agent. This small beginning in the Rhondda led to the formation of

Cambrian Miners' Association and ultimately to the South Wales Miners' Federation, which represented the men in the years leading up to the First World War.[1] James Insole stayed outside the owners' associations but, at least at this time, he does not seem to have taken advantage of his independence to strike a bargain with his workers, as some other Rhondda coal owners did. On the contrary, he supported the owners' association without having the benefits of membership, including indemnity in the event of strikes. A possible reason for what seems an illogical position may have been that he saw himself primarily as a shipper, using his own coal where possible but having other sources of supply, for example the Plymouth Ironworks, to see him through lean periods; he would not have wanted to undermine the position of those who would be potential suppliers when he was in greatest need. He may, however, have been an independent man who did not like to lose his freedom of action, particularly if he felt that the other owners might try to fix prices and control output. Jabez Thomas's attitude may have been important, as he was still responsible for Insole's colliery operations, and he appears to have been a taciturn and rather surly man, who would prefer to act alone, although E.D. Lewis describes him as 'somewhat chastened' following the Cymmer disaster and his subsequent trial.[2] Whatever the reasons, James Insole kept out of any association of owners, although in later years his successors at the collieries and the docks did join.

His other business interests also provided distractions from the coal trade. George Insole & Sons were described as ship owners in Wakeford's *Cardiff Directory* of 1863 but not in that of 1874. James Insole owned 30 £5 shares in the Cardiff Steam Navigation Co. and it may have been this modest investment which occasioned the entry, as the Insoles are not recorded as owning ships at any other time. The Insoles seem normally to have chartered ships or sold directly to shipping lines. By the early 1860s James Insole seems to have had a less active role in the Penarth Dock & Railway Company than in its early days. Also, after the agreement with the Taff Vale in 1862 and the opening of the Penarth Dock in 1865, the board had no involvement in the running of the railway, harbour or docks and indeed had very little to do at all. Another venture in which he took part was the Cardiff Baths Co., of which he was chairman, holding an investment of £100 in £10 shares out of its total capital of £2,500. The company built and ran the Guildford Street

[1] Lewis, *Rhondda Valleys*, pp. 164–5.
[2] Lewis, 'Cymer (Rhondda) Explosion', p. 161.

baths, which opened on 1 May 1862. Its advertisements offered turkish baths, hot water baths, first and second class swimming baths and a tepid plunge. They also announced that 'reduced second class tickets are issued by the Ladies Sanitary Association in charitable cases'.[1] This was not, however, a successful venture and the baths closed after less than ten years, eventually being taken over and run as a public amenity by the Cardiff Borough Council. James Insole's standing among the Cardiff docksmen was recognised by his election as the first president of the Cardiff Chamber of Commerce, which was founded in 1866 and incorporated in 1880. He remained a director of the Chamber until 1887 and a member until his death. His sons joined in 1870 and Henry Lewis in 1872, when Walter Insole was a vice president. The brothers' membership ceased in 1878 but Fred rejoined in 1887. James Insole does not appear to have been very assiduous in his attendance, going to one or two meetings out the usual dozen or so held every year. It may well have been that the topics discussed were rather mundane and, in his view, more appropriate to his managers than to a coal owner and aspiring country gentleman.

By this time, in addition to his activities in the coal industry, Insole had made considerable acquisitions of land and properties in Cardiff and the surrounding district as well as in the valleys.[2] In 1864 his holdings included houses, farms and industrial properties. His home, Ely Court in Llandaff, was valued at £7,337 and Pencisely Farm, another house in the parish of Llandaff with land to the south of Ely Court, was worth £8,171. Both these houses were for his or the family's own use but he also had investments in houses and land, which provided him with an income. Of these his properties in Canton, Ely and Llandaff had a value of £5,532 and those in Bute Street and Bute Crescent by the docks of £3,662. The Canton property included Harvey Street, named after himself, which is now a car park, but the Insole Arms, a public house rebuilt early in the twentieth century, still stands. Harvey Street consisted of small terraced houses, which helped to provide homes for many of the Irish community in Canton. He was later to own terraced houses in Grangetown and these developments would be much needed at a time when there was, in Cardiff, a shortage of soundly built working class housing.[3] His property outside Cardiff and its immediate environs included Llantrisant House with 62 acres and houses and cottages with

[1] *Cardiff & County Calendar* (1868).

[2] CCL, Insole MS 4.734.

[3] M.J. Daunton, *Coal Metropolis. Cardiff 1870–1914* (Leicester 1977), pp. 97–105.

a value of £6,306 and a moiety of the Caergwaner estate at Llantrisant. He held Bedw Farm at Cymmer and Abergorci Farm, the land on which his colliery buildings and workers' houses were built. His land holdings in June 1864 were valued in total at £32,000.

In the same year his company shareholdings were worth £15,000. More than half this amount was accounted for by his investment of 86 shares of £100 each in the Penarth Harbour, Dock & Railway Company, then valued at £8,880. These were showing a small premium on their purchase price, possibly reflecting the initial success of the Ely Tidal Harbour and the forthcoming opening of the Penarth Dock, which had an advantage over the Bute Docks as, being closer to the mouth of Cardiff Bay, ships were able to leave and enter for a longer period at each high tide. He also held railway shares worth a total of £5,460 in the Taff Vale Railway (£3000), the Monmouthshire Railway & Canal Co. (£1,000), the Bristol & Exeter Railway Co. (£960) and the Ely Valley Railway Co. (£500). Other companies in which he held shares were the Cardiff Steam Towing Co. (£100) and the Rhymney Iron Co. This last shareholding and that in the Monmouthshire Railway may indicate that he handled the iron company's sale coal; the value of his 30 shares of £50 each was only £776 or just over half their book value. All his shareholdings appear to have been in firms of which he was a director or with which he had commercial dealings.

Table 5.3:
Capital not employed in the coal business, 1860–64

Date	Capital
June 1860	£41,000
June 1861	£53,000
June 1862	£60,000
June 1863	£66,000
June 1864	£72,000

Source: CCL, Insole MSS, J.H. Insole's Private Ledger.

His land and shareholdings grew throughout the early 1860s as he took his profits from his collieries and coal trading. Between June 1860 and June 1864 he increased his 'capital not employed in the coal business', as he described it, by some 75 per cent (Table 5.3).

While searching for steam coal and increasing his income as a rentier rather than an entrepreneur, James Insole was, in the typical British fashion, also adding to his status as one of the district's emerging gentry. At the time of the 1861 Census he was in residence at Ely Court with his wife, Mary Ann, and her sister, Sarah Lilly Jones. Sally Jones, as she was known, was to stay at the house for the rest of her life, no doubt acting as housekeeper to her sister and brother-in-law. Also at the Court was Insole's nephew, George Insole Gower, who was eighteen years old and described as a 'scholar'; he was the son of James's elder sister Helen. The household had three living-in servants and the coachman's family of nine occupied the small lodge on Fairwater Road. None of the Insole children was at home for the Census. In January 1861 the boys had both been sent to the recently founded Cheltenham College, a popular school with the rising middle class of Cardiff. Walter, who was sixteen, stayed until June 1863 and Fred until June 1865, when he was approaching eighteen. Neither went on to university but appear to have been sent to other firms in the coal trade, sometimes well away from Cardiff, before being taken into the family business.

In the ensuing ten years a number of changes took place in the family. On 17 August 1866 James Insole's mother Mary, died at the age of 74 and was buried with her husband at St Margaret's, Roath. In 1869 his elder son Walter married Maria Georgina Eagle from Dublin. They set up home in Pencisely House where they were living at the time of the 1871 Census but Insole's other two children Mary Ann, now aged 24, and Fred, 23, who were not yet married, were living at Ely Court with their parents and aunt. A new coachman with a family of five was living in the lodge. As on other occasions none of the Insole's domestic servants at the previous census were still in their employ and they do not appear to have had any long-serving domestic staff until the end of the century. Soon after the census, on 19 April 1871, Mary Ann married George Burness of Leytonstone, some ten years her senior, at Llandaff Cathedral. He was a London coal shipper in the family firm of James Burness & Sons, who had offices in Leadenhall Street and in Insole's property at 5 Bute Crescent, Cardiff.

In 1869 James Insole had formed a family owned company to run the Cymmer Colliery and had taken Fred into the ownership of this enterprise. Walter was also given a share but in the 1871 Census, whereas Fred was described as a colliery owner, Walter called himself an annuitant, presumably denoting that he preferred to see himself as a gentleman of independent means rather than as a colliery owner or coal shipper. By 1874 the Insoles' business was profitable and still forward looking; it was also able to support a standard of living far beyond the world into which James Insole had been born in Worcester fifty years before. They were, however, only on the threshold of developments in the business and in their private lives, which would bring even greater wealth and enhanced social standing.

Chapter 6

A New Generation

1874–83

By 1875 a number of changes had been made in the organisation of the Insole businesses. Until 1874 Hunt's *Mineral Statistics* show that the Cymmer and Abergorci collieries were owned by Geo. Insole & Son, often listed as Insole & Son, the partnership established by George Insole in 1843, when he brought his son James into the business. In the 1874 return the Abergorci colliery was owned by Burnyeat, Brown & Co. and the Cymmer colliery by Insole & Son. From 1875 until 1881 *Mineral Statistics* record George Insole & Co. as the owners of the Cymmer Colliery, which by now included the Upper Cymmer and Glynfach pits. According to E.D. Lewis, Insole & Son was a company incorporated in 1869 under the Joint Stock Companies Act of 1856, although there is some doubt on this point.[1] By 1880 James Insole's accounting journal referred to the Cymmer Colliery Co. as the operating company at Cymmer and in 1883 he recorded the receipt of bills of exchange in payment for his sons' and their partner's shares in the company. Whatever its legal status, it seems certain that a separate business was set up to run the collieries, either as an unregistered joint stock company or a partnership, while coal trading at Cardiff Docks remained the responsibility of the firm of George Insole & Son, which was a partnership throughout its existence.

A number of events probably gave rise to the reorganisation of the businesses. James Insole's sons Walter and Fred had joined the firm; William Henry Lewis, an employee of George Insole & Son, had made his mark in the coal trading business; and James Insole himself retired from the management of both undertakings. After leaving Cheltenham College both Walter and Fred Insole had been trained in the coal trade through an informal apprenticeship, Fred with Galbraith, Pembroke & Co., shipowners of London.[2] This was probably considered sufficiently thorough for the direction of the businesses to be left to them, although

---

[1] Lewis, *Rhondda Valleys*, p. 86. No company of this or a similar name can be found in the printed index to companies registered between 1856 and 1920 at the PRO.

[2] *Western Mail*, 12 Feb. 1917.

they were joined by W. H. Lewis as managing partner at the docks and as a director of the Cymmer colliery company.[1] Lewis was born on 8 March 1840 in Cardiff, the son of Rees Lewis, a prominent Nonconformist, and had been educated at Montague House, at that time a well regarded school in Cardiff. He then went to France for two years, where he learnt French and Italian. He was an accomplished harpist who won prizes at eisteddfodau and, like James Insole, he surrounded his home with a beautiful garden. It had been suggested in his youth that he might make a living as a professional musician but he decided to pursue a career in commerce and he joined George Insole & Son in 1864.[2] In ten years he had become an experienced coal trader and had risen to be a partner in the firm. From the start, both George and James Insole had themselves run the shipping office, one of the oldest in Cardiff, but now, in the third generation, control passed to a professional manager who had worked his way up through the business. This was not an uncommon development in the coal trade.

In the Insoles' shipping office at 3 Bute Crescent, a three-storey building close to the headquarters of the Bute Docks, Henry Lewis and the Insole brothers would have had control of the enterprise. The area between the Glamorganshire Canal and the Docks, which was Cardiff's principal business district, was small enough for all things necessary for the day's work to be readily at hand. They would decide upon sales policy and maintain contact with their suppliers, customers, business associates and agents. They would enter into long-term contracts with shipping lines and railways and make spot sales and purchases, as well as sending cargoes to replenish their bunkering stations. During a working day they would supervise the movement of their coal from railway wagons to ships' holds and negotiate with ships' captains, railway officials, coal trimmers and dock staff.

Coal sales were negotiated at one of two prices, either free on board (f.o.b.) or cost, insurance, freight (c.i.f.). F.o.b. sales did not involve any further responsibility for the colliery company or the shipper once the coal had been loaded into the ship's hold. It was the method used in early coal sales when the traders would sell cargoes of coal to ships' captains on the dockside. It was still common among traders in the 1850s when they walked up and down outside their offices in Bute Crescent looking for business, a procedure described by Matthew Cope, a Cardiff coal owner whose father lived at 12 Bute Crescent, when writing after

[1] Walters, *South Wales Steam Coal Industry*, p. 170.
[2] *Western Mail*, 25 Oct. 1905.

the First World War.[1] Used by a number of colliery companies which did not have their own agents at the docks, this price was used for spot trading and was the usual quoted price for coals. A variation of f.o.b. was f.o.t. (free on truck), which was often used in sales to railways or when a coal consignment was transported entirely by rail to the customer. C.i.f. sales, on the other hand required the shipper to arrange the entire cost of acquiring the coal from the colliery and delivering it to its destination. It was used by the larger shipping firms and colliery companies, giving them both control of the operation and more opportunities for profit.

Although, by the 1880s, the coal shippers and traders had well established offices around the docks, much business was still conducted in the open air, often in the park in the centre of Mountstuart Square. An enterprising Cardiff businessman, Frederick de Courcy Hamilton, having frequently seen coal shippers making deals under umbrellas in the square, decided 'to give the docksmen shelter'.[2] He acquired the open land in the middle of the square and in 1883, much to the annoyance of some of the residents, commissioned Edwin Seward to design a coal exchange. The building was completed in less than three years and the Exchange opened for business on 1 February 1886. It was run as a private venture by de Courcy Hamilton, who invited the coal traders to join the Exchange Club, which gave them admittance to the floor. This was a central hall, with a high ceiling and two galleries, containing offices and rooms for letting; the trading floor itself was to open from 12 noon to 1 p.m. daily. The venture proved to be a success and the Exchange became the centre of the South Wales coal trade.[3]

Colliery companies that had been started by firms of shippers and merchants usually sold their coal through the trading arm of their business at the docks, and the Insoles were among the longest standing in this group at Cardiff. Coal sales were normally made by annual contract and, by end of the century, these accounted for 75 to 80 per cent of Cardiff's coal trade. Tenders were invited for contracts and were advertised at the Coal Exchange and in the press, most commonly in the autumn. A well established firm with its own source of supply, such as George Insole & Son, would have secured nearly all its business through contracts, many regularly renewed. They would only have used spot

[1] M. Cope, '85 Years in Newport and Cardiff', a series of articles in the *Western Mail*, 21 March–5 May 1928 (bound set in CCL).

[2] D.G. Moore, 'Cardiff Docks' (bound series of articles from *Cardiff Business* in CCL).

[3] C. Evans, S. Dodsworth and J. Barnett, *Below the Bridge* (Cardiff, 1984), pp. 26–7.

transactions at the Coal Exchange in emergencies or to gain a short-term advantage. The spot market was the field of the middlemen, who made a living at the edges of the market and were regarded with some disdain by the more substantial firms.

As managing partner and thus the firm's agent at the port of shipment, Henry Lewis would have been responsible for ensuring that the coal was of proper quality and that its loading was fast, careful and efficient. It was also important that the turn-round of consignments was as quick as possible in order to minimise the delay to the colliery's wagons. The coal was screened first at the colliery to eliminate small coal and had to be clear of shale and clod, and then at the dockside in the mechanical coal tips which were used to transfer coal and coke from the railway wagons to the ships. Once in the hold it was spread evenly to trim the ship by the coal trimmers, an independent-minded group of workmen, who negotiated their rates directly with the coal owners and shippers and did not readily join forces with the organisations of other dock workers or seamen.

Lewis's skills were probably not only those of the trader but also of the administrator, as the growing complexity of the coal trade required good office procedures to handle orders, tenders, contracts and invoicing. George Insole & Son maintained a relatively small staff at their offices in Bute Crescent but some other firms, particularly those which diversified into shipping like Powell Duffryn and Cory Bros, built up very large administrative and clerical staffs.

By the 1870s the Insole business was situated at the heart of the South Wales coal trade, since steam coal, from the Taff, Cynon and Rhondda valleys, had put Cardiff ahead of Newport as the leading coal exporting port of the region. There had been five colliery sales agencies in each port in 1844 but by 1913 Cardiff had 74 and Newport 32. In total Cardiff had 113 coal exporting firms in 1913.[1] It was, in part, Cardiff's position at the centre of steam coal movements that enabled the port to dominate the trade and its Coal Exchange to become the market-place for the South Wales coalfield.

Cymmer Steam Coal, their promotional book published in 1880, was George Insole & Son's advertisement for their product and was illustrated with photographs of various parts of the colliery and of its plant and heavy equipment. It related the history of the Insole business and the growth of the steam coal trade, described the colliery and the coal seams and extolled the qualities of its steam coal. According to the

[1] Walters, *South Wales Steam Coal Industry*, p. 306.

book even the dust of Rhondda steam coal would burn, giving it an
advantage over Aberdare steam coal, in value for money, of some 10 per
cent. In their example 4s per ton could be saved on a consignment of
1,000 tons of steam coal sent to a remote depot at a price of £2 per ton.
They also included testimonials from shipowners at Liverpool and
Palermo, a list of their agents and bunkering stations, as well as the
names of some of their principal customers. They had agents at Rouen,
Le Havre, Paris, Milan and Messina and their customers included the
following shipping lines:

> Allan Brothers & Co., Liverpool
> British India Steam Navigation Co.
> British Ship Owners Co., Liverpool
> Ducal Line of Steamers, London
> Ismay, Imrie & Co., White Star Line, Liverpool
> J. & V. Florio, Palermo
> Mississippi & Dominion Co., Liverpool
> Orient Company, London
> Peninsular and Oriental Steam Navigation Co.

The firm was also included in the lists of suppliers to the navies of Italy
and Spain as well as the Royal Navy. Their bunkering stations were at
Gibraltar, Malta and Aden, to supply the shipping lines to the Mediterranean, the South Atlantic and the Far East.[1]

By this time James Insole had retired from the mining and shipping
firms, probably in 1874 or 1875, but had not left the coal business
altogether. He still retained the mineral leases at Cymmer and Glynfach
and sub-let the coal measures to the Cymmer Colliery Company and
others. He usually charged a royalty of twice that which he paid to the
landowner. He hired mineral surveyors to prospect for coal, entered into
new mineral leases himself and then offered the opportunity of new
winnings to his lessees. In effect he had abandoned the role of industrialist for that of surrogate landowner.

James Insole had been encouraged in his aspirations to join the gentry
when he was made a county magistrate in 1867. His rising status was
further acknowledged in 1872 when he received a grant of arms.[2] His

---

[1] George Insole & Son, *Cymmer Steam Coal* (Cardiff, 1880) (Copy in CCL).

[2] Grant of arms, 15 April 1872: INSOLE. Azure, a griffin passant, in chief three leopards'
faces jessant-de-lys or. Mantling: azure and or. Crest: upon a wreath of colours, a griffin passant
or, charged on the body with two pheons and resting the dexter claw on the leopard's face.
Jessant-de-lys azure. Motto: Soyez Ferme.

livery was blue with gold facings, reflecting the blue and gold in his achievement. Its principal feature was the griffin, which he used in decorating the extensions and embellishments which he was soon to make to his property in Llandaff.

In 1873 James Insole started rebuilding Ely Court in the style of the Gothic Revival, which had been favoured by the architect William Burges (1827–81) in the rebuilding of Cardiff Castle for the third Marquess of Bute (1847–1900). Insole employed the architect, George Robinson and his 22-year-old assistant Edwin Seward, to extend the south-facing garden front of the house and to erect a 70 ft tower with a slate roof and an oriel window. This tower possibly contained a summer smoking room as in the tower at Cardiff Castle and, as it was built on rising ground, it would have provided fine views for Insole's guests as they smoked their cigars. He obtained these from George Insole & Son and they were probably a small by-product of the shipping business. The gardens were laid out and stocked by the Cardiff firm of Treseder and contained wooded shrubberies, an orchard, a formal garden with a fountain, walks and terraces, greenhouses and what may have been a tennis court or croquet lawn.

In 1875 he further enhanced his gentry status by acquiring a sporting property in the Brendon Hills of west Somerset. On 25 November at an auction in London he bought the Luxborough Estate, including Chargot House, described as 'a picturesque and commodious shooting box' by the selling agents. The house had a drawing room, a dining room with vaulted ceiling, a morning room, and sleeping accommodation for fifteen, with bedrooms, dressing rooms and running water on two floors. The estate extended through a number of small parishes in the Brendon Hills and included the lordships of the manors of Luxborough and Withiel Florey and the advowson of Withiel Florey, including the great tithes which were commuted to £155 per annum.[1]

The estate as advertised was over 7,000 acres[2] and had been owned by Sir Thomas Buckler Lethbridge, a member of a local gentry family which had a baronetcy but probably not much money. The estate villages had little good agricultural land and were surrounded by wooded hills and moorland. It was, however, for its game rather than its rents, that it was valued and it is still, by local repute, one of the foremost shooting

---

[1] Somerset Record Office, DD/DP 14/3.

[2] Cf. J. Bateman, *The Great Landowners of Great Britain and Ireland* (1883), p. 237, where J.H. Insole is credited with 7,201 acres in Somerset (gross annual value £5,077), and 1,107 acres in Glamorgan worth £4,100 p.a.

estates in the country. The estate, at the time of the sale, also had iron ore beds leased to the Ebbw Vale Iron Co., with a claimed yield of about £500 per annum. The original agreement with the company had been made on 24 June 1853, for a royalty 1s per ton (of 2,520 lb) or 8d per ton for white iron or carbonate, with a dead rent of £50 per annum.[1]

When James Insole bought the estate from Sir Thomas's trustees, it was in the occupation of Charles Lethbridge, then in his late thirties, who had recently come into the estate following the death of his uncle Ambrose Lethbridge in 1875. Ambrose and Charles Lethbridge were both lineal descendants of Sir Thomas and had been made tenants for life under the terms of his will. Ambrose appears to have had some ailment, as his nephew Charles was granted power of attorney for his uncle in 1872.[2] Following the sale of the estate to Insole, Charles moved away and was living in Dorset in 1877.

There is no surviving record of the price which James Insole paid for the estate but its value on the death of Ambrose Lethbridge was £66,796, incurring £8,350 duty on Charles's succession. The rental value of the estate was assessed at £5,497 gross, £4,177 net. If the former was the sum paid for the estate, Insole's net income from rents and royalties would have been 7 per cent.[3] He was, however, to find that he was faced with considerable expenses in the first years of his ownership. Ambrose Lethbridge had only had the estate since 1871; he had found it in a dilapidated condition and had spent £6,520 on repairs in 1871–5. Insole's solicitor, Benjamin Matthews, had agreed with the vendors' solicitors, J. & C. Longbourne of Lincoln's Inn Fields, to leave repairs out of the contract in December 1875, as there had been an agreement with the tenants that repairs would be made over a period of years. It does not seem to have been easy for Insole to get the work completed satisfactorily, if at all, and by 1878 he was in dispute with some local firms, having paid for repairs which he claimed had not been done.[4]

Nevertheless, James Insole was now a landowner in Somerset as well as Glamorgan. He was lord of the manor, patron of an advowson and owner of land and minerals. He seems to have been interested in the possibilities of developing the mineral estate, as he had a survey carried out in the early 1880s.[5] Insole's elder son, Walter, had a taste for the

[1] Somerset RO, DD/DP 15/10.

[2] Somerset RO, DD/DP 14/13.

[3] Somerset RO, DD/DP 14/12.

[4] Somerset RO, DD/DP 14/13.

[5] CCL, Insole MSS, 4.734.

life of a country gentleman[1] and he lived, for part of the year, at Chargot in the early 1880s, although by the end of the decade the local directories show that James Insole was in occupation.[2]

In 1877 James Insole ordered further additions to Ely Court from Edwin Seward; he was now a partner in James, Seward & Thomas, one of Cardiff's foremost firms of architects. He added a north wing in what was considered the Swiss style, with half-timbered cladding on the upper floor intersected by tall gabled windows, which rested on stone corbels and had elaborately decorated bargeboards. This wing contained some domestic quarters on the ground floor but the upper floor seems to have been a billiard room, at that time a common and even essential feature of the house of an industrialist with pretensions to join the gentry. The wing created an open courtyard with a central circular flower bed outside the main entrance to the house, creating a similar effect to the entrance to St Fagans castle. As well as the two griffins by the drive, Insole embellished the outside of the house with decorative stonework, which was carried out by W. Clarke of Llandaff, a firm still in business today. Extensive alterations were made to the interior of the house to continue the gothic theme, including ornately carved doors with worked brass fittings, a large stone fireplace in the entrance hall, walls painted with medieval designs and an alabaster balustrade on the staircase. On the newel post at the foot of the staircase was a magnificent gasolier, a griffin holding a pole or simple flambeau which provided a flaming light. This and most of the decoration has disappeared but in two rooms some survives: the library or study on the first floor has a vaulted ceiling with painted borders, scrolls and mottoes. On the ground floor the old dining room (or winter smoking room) has panelled walls and a carved wooden ceiling with an elaborate buffet in an alcove on the end wall. The walls are surmounted by a frieze depicting the four seasons, painted by Fred Weekes, who had painted the same subject, but with less vitality, in the smoking room at Cardiff Castle. By now James Insole could afford to employ some of the foremost artists and craftsmen in South Wales.[3] Seward wrote that the total cost of his work for James Insole at Ely Court was £10,000 and he also did work on Pencisely House. As well as the work on the house Insole made improvements to the grounds and in 1879 he acquired some land to the south of the property facing Ely

---

[1] *Western Mail*, 5 May 1898.

[2] *Kelly's Directory of Somerset* (1875, 1883, 1889 and 1897 eds.).

[3] Information on the architectural history of Ely Court has been kindly supplied by Matthew Williams, Keeper of Collections at Cardiff Castle.

Road. Here he built a new lodge house and entrance with a second sweeping carriage drive which passed over a mock bridge, with griffins on the pillars at one end, close to the house.

James Insole's income had grown to meet these commitments. Table 6.1 shows his income and expenditure for the year 1 July 1880 to 30 June 1881.

Table 6.1: *J.H. Insole's income and expenditure 1880–1*

Income	£	Expenditure	£
Colliery royalties	8,398	Colliery royalties	3,550
Sale of cottage	20	Colliery expenses	27
Dividends	1,099	Salaries & pensions	1,566
Interest received	6,101	Interest paid	2,043
Luxborough Estate	5,727	Luxborough Estate	3,378
Rents (net of tax)	2,111	Legal fees & costs	844
Ty Fry Farm & Wood	712	Ty Fry Farm & Wood	1,698
Pencisely Farm	752	Pencisely Farm	463
Sundry debtors	60	Ely Court	897
		Sundry expenses	540
Gross income	24,980	Total expenditure	15,006
Less expenditure	15,006		
Net income	9,974		

Source: CCL, Insole MSS, J.H. Insole's Journal (1880–92).

James Insole received colliery royalties mainly from the Cymmer Colliery Co., whose payments of £7,097 14s 2d made up 86 per cent of the total. Other lessees were Morris Brothers and Down & Co., who successively worked the Glynfach colliery and David Joseph who worked the Upper Cymmer level. Insole normally received double the royalty which he paid, typically 1s per ton for large coal and 6d per ton for small, as against 6d and 3d paid to the principal lessors. The two landowners who received his royalties were Josiah Lewis for Tyn-y-cymmer and Charles Aubrey Aubrey (formerly Ricketts) for Glynfach; this implies either that the Bedw minerals had been worked out or that the land had been acquired by Lewis or Aubrey.

His dividend income came from a number of companies, mostly railways and utilities. The railways were the Taff Vale, Penarth, Ely Valley, Rhondda Vale & Hirwaun Junction and the Somerset & Dorset. He had shares in the Ystrad [Rhondda] Gas & Water Co., the Chepstow Water Co. and the Cardiff Hotel and held Rhymney Iron Co. debentures and Spanish Government bonds. His shareholdings were no longer confined to his suppliers, customers and business associates, as had been the case in the 1860s, but being largely in utilities and government bonds show that his diversification was concentrated in relatively secure investments.

He paid a salary of £250 per annum to Henry Lewis, possibly for acting as his agent and supervising the keeping of his books, and a pension of £100 per annum to Jabez Thomas who had retired in 1877. He paid fees to the firm of Brown & Adams, mineral agents, and to W. Peile, a mineral surveyor, for work at Luxborough and Glynfach. His largest payment to an individual person was an allowance of £1,000 per annum paid to his daughter, Mary Ann Burness, who was living near London with her husband and their children.

He seems from his interest accounts to have been a borrower and lender on a considerable scale. Apart from regular payments to his two widowed sisters, Emma and Julia, to his son-in-law, George Burness, and to his bank, 75 per cent of his interest payments were on two loans of £20,000 each due to Elder & Maitland at 3¾ per cent and 4 per cent. His own lending was in the main connected either with the coal trade or with family affairs. The largest loan was about £50,000, assuming an annual interest rate of 5 per cent, to Burnyeat, Brown & Co. Ltd, who acquired the Abergorci colliery from Insole in 1873. He also lent £20,000 to the Cymmer Colliery Co. and £10,000, increased in 1881 to £21,500, to George Insole & Son. Among his smaller loans were £8,300 to T.E. Heath & Co., the patent fuel manufacturers and predecessor of the Star Patent Fuel Co. Ltd, of which Insole became a director, buying fifteen £100 shares, some 10 per cent of the capital, when the company was set up in 1887.[1] He also made loans to Peile, his mineral surveyor, and to Henry Lewis. It seems probable that Lewis was James Insole's protégé and that the loan may have been made to enable him to buy his share of the businesses; in reorganising the business, Insole had put Lewis on at least an equal footing with his two sons.

With colliery royalties accounting for one third of his income and dividends and interest another, the final third derived from his land-holdings in Glamorgan and Somerset. On the Luxborough estate, the iron ore workings yielded £635 while rents and the Withiel Florey tithe made over £5,000. Nevertheless the costs of the estate were considerable and his outgoings, mostly paid through his land agent, Arthur Savill, reduced his income by well over a half. His rental income in Glamorgan was far less encumbered. His properties included land and buildings in Butetown

---

[1] PRO, BT 31/3820/23980.

and Crockherbtown, industrial land, cottages and houses in Ely, Llandaff and Canton, land and farms at Llantrisant, cottages at the collieries and property held on reversion at Gelligaer.

His country properties at Pendoylan were Ty Fry, which was run mainly as a home farm for Ely Court and as a shooting-box, rather than as a commercial enterprise and the neighbouring Warren Farm, leased from the Aubrey Estate, mainly for its shooting. Ty Fry was a mixed farm with woodland, producing both cordwood and pitwood in modest quantities; the pitwood was sold to Cymmer colliery. Pencisely Farm in Llandaff provided a home for Walter Insole and his wife and in 1880 was mostly meadow, producing hay and then pasture for cattle and sheep in a conventional rotation. There is some evidence in the accounts of sheep being brought from Ty Fry to graze Pencisely after the cows had been on the land. The hay was sold to Cymmer Colliery for the pit ponies and to Walter and Fred Insole for their horses. The remaining items of expenditure, apart from the costs of Ely Court, were his lawyer's fees and costs, about 9 per cent of his net income, and payments of £250 to each of his sons. this pattern of income and expenditure continued through the years covered by his private journal (1880–92).

James Insole had moved from the life of an industrialist to that of a rentier, his income was large and he had the time to enjoy it. He also had the pleasure of a growing family. His elder son Walter had no children but his daughter had two boys and at least one daughter. On 14 August 1878 his younger son, Fred was married to Jessy Ann David in Llandaff Cathedral. The ceremony was conducted by the Bishop of Llandaff, assisted by the Dean and the bride's uncle, Revd W. David of St Fagans. Jessy was the only daughter of Evan Williams David, who had died some years before. The Davids were a leading local family and were well represented in the public life of Cardiff and east Glamorgan. Jessy had been born at Radyr Court and was at this time living with her mother at Fairwater House. The wedding was reported at some length in the local press, including a list of presents and their donors. There were flags across the street in Llandaff and decorations in Fairwater. Over Fairwater Road, the bride's route to the cathedral and the couple's return, there were large evergreen and floral arches carrying greetings and the couple's initials and there were more arches and bunting at Fairwater House. Jessy had sixteen bridesmaids and the altar steps were strewn with flowers. A magnificent wedding breakfast followed, with a bridecake from London and afterwards the couple left for a honeymoon on the continent, throwing money to the crowd. On their return, Fred and Jessie set up home at Fairwater House. With both his sons living within walking distance of Ely Court, James Insole was near his family with whom he seems, from the apparent liberality of his financial arrangements, to have been on close and friendly terms.

In the spring of 1880 James and Mary Ann Insole went on a two-month holiday to Italy, returning through Paris. They spent nearly £400 on antiques and works of art as against £135 on travelling and hotels. Most of their heavy luggage seems to have been shipped through Livorno as Insole's account book has an item for wooden cases 'for Leghorn'. The journey would have been a lot less arduous than George Insole's early business trips since, by this time, Europe had an established and comprehensive rail network which, with the growth of what today would be called financial services and standard postage rates, made international travel easier and more reliable.

James Insole continued to play a small part in the public life of Cardiff; in 1880 he donated £1,000 to the Glamorgan & Monmouth Infirmary to name a ward 'Insole' and he became a Poor Law Guardian. He was also added to the University College Committee by Cardiff Borough Council. He subscribed to colliery management and farming periodicals and to the *Gardeners' Chronicle*. He also made donations to horticultural societies and shows, including the annual rose show.[1]

In 1881 James Insole was one of the vice-presidents of the Cardiff Fine Art and Industrial Exhibition. There were many presidents and vice-presidents, presumably asked for their patronage rather than for a commitment of time or work, which was provided by the organising committee of which Henry Lewis was a member. Insole did, however, lend a variety of objects including porcelain, ivories, bronzes, silver, jewellery and a number of paintings, some of which he may have acquired on his Italian holiday. Among his exhibits was a Turner oil painting, described as 'A Shipwreck', painted, according to the catalogue, in about 1817. The exhibition was held in the Drill Hall, Dumfries Place and the photographs in the catalogue make it look, to modern eyes, more like a house clearance sale than an exhibition. Pictures and exhibits cover the walls, display cabinets and benches clutter the floor and various objects are piled on the stage at one end of the hall; some visitors have been posed on benches or in the narrow aisles. Although the organisers had identified a number of themes and class of exhibit, it seems that they showed whatever the exhibitors chose to lend in a rather haphazard arrangement that took little account of the comfort of the

[1] CCL, Insole MSS, 4.734.

visiting public.[1]

James and Mary Ann Insole did not, however, enjoy their comfortable way of life together for long for, on 4 May 1882 Mary Ann died. She was buried in the graveyard on the north side of Llandaff Cathedral, in an area now almost exclusively reserved for bishops and eminent clerics. James erected a tall marble cross over her grave and donated a stained glass window in the north aisle of the Cathedral in her memory. He donated other stained glass windows to the parish churches at Pendoylan and Withiel Florey. At Luxborough the chancel of St Mary's church was restored in 1895 and Insole gave new altar choir stalls and the lectern in his wife's memory.

On 8 November 1883 James Insole acquired more land in Llandaff from the Ecclesiastical Commissioners for £10,750, comprising a number of fields surrounding Ely Court then used for mixed farming.[2] He removed most of the fences and hedges and converted the fields into open parkland, providing a spacious setting for his recently refurbished house.

While the coal shippers traded at the docks and James Insole lived a more leisured life, the collieries upon which they all depended continued to be worked more productively than ever. After reaching the steam coal measures at Cymmer in 1877, the Cymmer Colliery Co. was able to increase output to new and higher levels. By the year ending 30 June 1881 their annual production, on which royalties were paid, had risen to 186,000 tons of which 149,000 tons was steam coal, the remainder being No 2 Rhondda. The No 3 Rhondda seam, which James Insole had worked so furiously in the 1850s, was exhausted at Cymmer Old and New, although from 1883 it was mined with success from the Glynfach pit. Their steam coal would have been screened as part of the conditions of sale in order to remove small coal, which was not wanted by the customers, particularly the shipping lines. Cymmer steam coal was around 80 per cent large, which could be sold directly to clients. The remaining small coal presented a problem, in spite of the company's claim in their promotional book that even the dust would burn. The answer was found in the manufacture of patent fuel, an industry which grew up in Cardiff, probably as a direct result of attempts to find a profitable use for small coal. Patent fuel was produced by combining pulverised coal with a binding agent and forming bricks, which burnt with the same effect as large coal. These bricks had the further advan-

---

[1] Exhibition catalogue in CCL.

[2] Cardiff County Council, Records of the Court Estate, Llandaff, Box 21.

tage of being economical to transport and store. It was through his association with the Heath family of Northlands, Cardiff, who were pioneers in the patent fuel market, as well as his continuing interest in the coal trade, that James Insole became connected with the Star Patent Fuel Company. House coal from the bituminous seams was also screened but its small coal could be used for coke making.

Output in 1881–2 was lower than the previous year at 164,000 tons but recovered in 1882–3 to 187,000 tons. Prices, however, had fallen since 1873 when large steam coal achieved an average f.o.b. price of 23s 3d per ton. By the end of 1875 it had fallen to 10s 10d, the average for the year being 14s 3d per ton. By 1876 the average annual f.o.b. price of steam coal (large and small) at Cardiff was under 10s per ton and remained between 8s and 9s 10d until 1889.[1] In a period of rising output throughout the coalfield, these steady prices brought no additional reward to the miners who produced the coal, as their pay was governed by the sliding scale. This had been introduced after the 1875 strike and increased or reduced the miners' standard wage by 7½ per cent for every change of 1s per ton in the f.o.b. price of colliery-screened large coal at the ports. Furthermore living conditions were often poor and over-crowded and the Rhondda mining villages offered few public amenities beyond the chapel and the public house. The only consolation for the miners was that the collieries at this time did offer regular work and the wages were higher than in many other manual occupations.

The increase in output in the South Wales coalfield, when the deeper steam coal seams were being brought into production, was assisted by the widespread adoption of longwall working at the coal-face. The traditional method of working a pit or level in South Wales was known as pillar and stall. A main roadway was driven into the seam and, every 60 or 70 yards, cross-headings were driven at an angle from it. From the cross-headings, at intervals of five to six yards, a similar width of coal was cut from the seam, creating the stall in which the collier worked. The stalls could be worked for their full length of 60–70 yards leaving a wall of coal between them. It was more common for the wall to be breached every five or six yards leaving pillars to support the roof. Once the stalls had been worked to the end of the royalty, the area where they were allowed to mine, the pillars could be removed and the roof allowed to collapse on to the stone and rubbish, known as gob, which was left behind. This method was relatively slow and sometimes the pillars were abandoned in order to work the rest of the seam directly. It was therefore

---

[1] Williams, *Welsh Historical Statistics*, I, p. 337.

inefficient both in its method and in the amount of coal produced. Longwall working was a simpler procedure where two parallel cross-headings were driven off the main roadway and the coal was worked in a continuous line between them. It is still the method used with modern coal cutting machinery. It was less slow and more productive than pillar and stall, although it was not suitable for thin and heavily faulted seams. Nevertheless, in spite of initial opposition from the colliers, it was used wherever possible in the South Wales coalfield.

In 1877 the Cymmer colliery had a new manager, who satisfied the spirit and the letter of the Mines Regulation Act 1872 by having secured a manager's certificate by examination. Thomas Griffiths was a professional mining engineer, who succeeded Jabez Thomas when he retired. Jabez Thomas had served the Insoles for nearly fifty years from George Insole's first ventures on the canal wharf at Cardiff. It was probably his knowledge of coal mining, albeit without any formal qualifications, which made him useful to his employers; he seems, however, to have been both insensitive in his handling of subordinate managers and workers and slipshod in his supervision and administration. On two of the rare occasions when he emerges from the shadows of unrecorded events, he bears responsibility for a serious industrial dispute and a mining disaster. He was a founder and leading member of Bethlehem, the Calvinistic Methodist chapel in Cymmer, whose first congregation came with him from Maesmawr to Cymmer in 1844. After his retirement he continued to live next to the colliery office in a house in Three-quarters Row, with his wife Ann, who was some nine years his junior and, like him, came from the Vale of Glamorgan. He died in 1885 at the age of 87.

Thomas Griffiths was a different type of man; he was born in 1849 at Bettws near Bridgend but, by the time he left school in 1860, his family had moved to Hafod. He started work at Cymmer as a door-boy and worked for ten years at the coal-face. He became a fireman in 1869 and so started a professional career, which saw him rise to the positions of overman and agent and to the acquisition of a manager's certificate, through part-time education and private study. He had left Cymmer in the course of his progress but in 1872 he married the daughter of John Williams of Pen Rhos and he returned to work at Cymmer in 1875, possibly as engineer for the sinking of Cymmer Old to the steam coals. He was a member of the South Wales Institute of Engineers and of the Cardiff Naturalists' Society, whom he entertained at Cymmer in 1885. By that time he had been elected to the Ystradyfodwg Urban Sanitary Authority, so starting a long career of public service in local government. He was to be involved not only in colliery management but also in the direction of the Insole mining businesses over the next forty years. The Insoles' management of their collieries was always more distant than the control of their sales office and both Jabez Thomas and Thomas Griffiths enjoyed a considerable measure of freedom and delegated authority in running them. Griffiths was an early beneficiary of improvements in the professional education of engineers in South Wales, which had been fostered by the South Wales Institute of Engineers.[1]

By the early 1880s the new regime in the Insole businesses was well established, combining a still dominant family interest with professional management. Although retired, James Insole still had a direct interest in the success of the collieries and of the firm, which carried his name. He advanced loans to both firms, possibly to finance investment in a period of rapid expansion, and continued to prospect for coal and take on new leases. It was this team which would lead the enterprise through the next twenty years, the period in which both Cardiff and the Rhondda, the two areas of the Insoles' operations, would outstrip other towns and mining districts in the South Wales coalfield in their rate of growth and the value of their trade.

[1] Walters, *South Wales Steam Coal Industry*, pp. 181–4.

Chapter 7

New Ventures

1883–1901

In the last twenty years of the nineteenth century the rate of growth in the output of the South Wales coalfield accelerated and at the same time there was a disproportionately large increase in the volume of coal shipped through the port of Cardiff.[1] The market for steam coal was well established and growing, particularly for shipping, as steam replaced sail, and the demand for house coal and anthracite continued to rise as the population, business enterprise and government activities expanded. At the same time the supply of coal had been increased by new entrants to the business, including both iron companies and entrepreneurs who were anxious to join a speculative but rewarding market. Table 7.1 illustrates the expansion both of output in the coalfield and in Glamorgan and of Cardiff's export trade. Over twenty years, the growth of trade through Cardiff exceeded the growth in output in Glamorgan, showing that it had captured some of the market for Monmouthshire coal.

Table 7.1: *Growth of Coal Output in South Wales, 1881–1901*

	1881 *000 tons*	*1891* *000 tons*	*1901* *000 tons*	*Increase* *1881–1901* *000 tons*	*%*
South Wales	22,234	29,993	39,209	16,975	76
Glamorgan	15,988	21,762	27,709	11,721	73
Port of Cardiff	6,390	10,978	18,472	12,082	189

Source: John Williams, *Digest of Welsh Historical Statistics* (Welsh Office, 1985), I, pp. 300, 303, 318.

Increased demand and production in these twenty years called for expansion of the railway network and the provision of additional dock

---

[1] The customs port of Cardiff comprised Cardiff, the river Ely, Penarth and Barry.

100

capacity at the ports. Furthermore, by 1880 most of the companies which would dominate the coalfield in the years to the First World War had secured their mineral leases, so that there was little spare land available for new entrants. New winnings would therefore come from deeper mines and new sinkings in marginal areas. New sources of finance and larger businesses were needed to exploit the deeper seams. It was also necessary to attract and train a workforce and to provide their growing communities with housing, shops, transport, places of worship and social facilities.

The Insoles were at the centre of these challenges. They were mining the steam coal seams rapidly and would eventually need new sources, either by deepening and extending Cymmer or by taking new leases. Furthermore their colliery was in the lower Rhondda Valley, where the Taff Vale Railway had a monopoly and charged coal owners higher rates than in those other valleys where they faced competition. The Insoles were also, both by cost and convenience, largely confined to shipping Cymmer coal through Cardiff and Penarth.

The most urgent problem facing the coal owners of the Rhondda Valley in the early 1880s was the question of transport and dock capacity. They were in dispute with the Taff Vale Railway over freight rates and with both the Bute Trustees and the Taff Vale over congestion at the docks and on the railway. This led to delays in taking coal to the port, in loading cargoes, in getting ships in and out of the docks in the shortest possible time and in returning the collieries' trucks quickly. These problems increased the coal owners' costs, jeopardised the renewal of contracts and did not encourage the growth of new business. The Taff Vale Railway, which operated the docks at Cardiff and Penarth, extended the Penarth Dock by 6½ acres in 1880 but there was little scope for further development. The railway blamed the Bute Trustees whose only response to increased traffic had been the opening of the Roath basin in 1874 for which, with a low water pier, they had had parliamentary approval in 1866. The project had originally been a far more ambitious scheme for three new docks, with one reserved for imports, which would have proved sufficient for many years to come and might even have helped to diversify Cardiff's trade. The parliamentary committee, however, was not prepared to authorise expenditure of an estimated £2,000,000 from the trust funds of a minor, the third Marquess of Bute being 18 at the time, and the project was rejected.[1] The Roath Basin was a modest development which was achieved by enclosing the Bute Tidal

---

[1] Chappell, *Port of Cardiff*, p. 105.

Harbour, which had been in operation since the 1850s. The low-water
pier, originally intended for ocean-going passenger traffic, had been
completed in 1868. The Bute Trustees had become more circumspect in
the 1870s and, although they obtained parliamentary approval for a new
dock in 1874, they did not proceed with the scheme and the bill's
powers were allowed to lapse. The Trustees expressed concern about the
depressed trading conditions when approached by the Cardiff Chamber
of Commerce about a new dock in 1876 and their new manager, William
T. Lewis (1837–1914), was of the opinion that the coal trade was
approaching its zenith.[1] Lewis, who was appointed in 1880, was later
made a baronet and subsequently Lord Merthyr of Senghenydd. The
increase in coal exports from the port of Cardiff compared with dock
capacity provided by the Bute Trustees and the Penarth Harbour Dock
& Railway is shown in Table 7.2.

Table 7.2: *Coal exports and docks at Cardiff, 1850–90*

Year	Exports 000 tons	Dock Acreage	Coal Staithes	New Docks Opened
1850	731	19	16	Bute West Dock (1839)
1855	1,207	19	16	
1860	1,915	66	49	Bute East Dock (1856–9) Bute Tidal Harbour (1856) Ely Tidal Harbour (1859)
1865	2,354	87	61	Penarth Dock (1865)
1870	3,246	87	61	
1875	3,473	99	62	Roath Basin (1874)
1880	5,856	125	66	Penarth Dock Extension (1880)

Sources: J. Williams, *Digest of Welsh Historical Statistics*, I, p. 318; A. Bassett,
'The Port of Cardiff and the Aberdare Steam Coal Field', *Trans. S. Wales Inst.
Engineers*, IV (1864–5), p. 104.

Note: The acreage of the enclosed docks shows the area in which ships could be
accommodated and therefore gives a crude measure of dock capacity. A similar
figure for the tidal harbours would be misleading as much of the area would be
mud berths at low water. The number of coal staithes gives some indication of the
capacity of the docks for loading cargoes of coal.

---

[1] Ibid, p. 103.

The dispute came to a head in 1882 when the Bute Trustees decided to go ahead with the construction of the Roath Dock, for which they had had parliamentary approval in 1874, and at the same time, proposed an addition of 1d per ton to all Bute Dock shipments.[1] The Rhondda coal owners determined not to accept this and decided to build their own integrated dock and railway. They were led by David Davies, by now one of the dominant figures of the industrial development of Wales. Born at Llandinam in Montgomeryshire, his first ventures were the construction of railways, mainly in central Wales, before moving into coal and building up the Ocean Company. The promoters of the railway included all the leading colliery owners of the Rhondda valleys, among them the Insoles, represented by Walter. They examined both Barry and the mouth of the Ogmore River as possible choices before deciding to build their new dock at Barry. Earlier projects to develop Barry had come to nothing. A dock scheme in the 1860s was abandoned in the financial disaster of 1866, in which the confidence of industrialists throughout the United Kingdom was severely weakened by the failure of the bill discounting firm of Overend, Gurney & Co., and a plan in 1877 to turn Barry into a fashionable holiday resort met with opposition and was also abandoned, the land being sold to Lord Windsor.[2]

The Rhondda coal owners introduced their Barry Dock & Railway Bill in the 1883 parliamentary session but it was defeated, mainly by opposition from the Bute Trustees and the Taff Vale.[3] Nevertheless it was passed in the next session and received the Royal Assent on 14 August 1884. The cost to the promoters was £70,000 but they were allowed to charge both parliamentary sessions' costs to the new company. Walter Insole, who had been a member of the Parliamentary Committee,[4] was active in support of the bill in both sessions, attending every sitting through to its end.[5]

At first called the Barry Dock & Railway Company, the company's name was changed to the Barry Railway Company in 1891 in order to be listed by the Stock Exchange under railways rather than docks. The initial capital was £1,050,000 in shares with borrowing powers up to

---

[1] The Roath Dock would eventually add 33 acres to the Bute Docks and increase the number of coal staithes from 40 to 60.

[2] Chappell, *Port of Cardiff*, p. 102.

[3] D.S.M. Barrie, *The Barry Railway* (Oakwood Press, 1962), p. 158.

[4] PRO, RAIL 23/9.

[5] R.J. Rimmell, *History of the Barry Railway Company 1884–1921* (Cardiff 1922), p. 121.

£350,000. Robert George Windsor-Clive, Lord Windsor (1857–1923), who was created Earl of Plymouth in 1905 and owned much of the land at Barry, was elected chairman and remained so throughout the life of the railway. He was the son of Robert Windsor-Clive, the first chairman of the Penarth Harbour, Dock & Railway. David Davies was deputy chairman and unofficial managing director. Other directors included Crawshay Bailey, Archibald Hood and John Cory as well as Walter Insole; its secretary was Henry Lewis.[1]

The dock and railway were completed in 1889. The original main line from Trehafod to Barry was 18½ miles long with some short branches but eventually its lines spread through the steam coalfield. By 1922, when it was merged with the Great Western, which absorbed the other railways in South Wales, it had 68 route miles and comprehensive running powers over other lines.[2] As well as its coal traffic it also ran suburban passenger services, Bristol Channel steamers for a short time and holiday traffic to Barry Island, the resort which was its creation.

The dock at Barry contained 73 acres and the total cost of the original project was £2 million. The first sod was cut by Lord Windsor on 14 November 1884. Water was let into the dock on 19 June 1889 and the ceremonial opening took place on 18 July 1889 and was attended by two thousand guests. The ceremony was conducted by David Davies, since Lady Windsor, who should have opened the dock, was unable to attend.

The Barry Railway, promoted by its customers, the Rhondda coal owners, in order to provide the transport for their expanding trade, was an important element in the coal boom of 1890–1914. It was an instant success as a business venture and a second dock was opened in 1898. In the following year the dock was used by 3,000 ships and handled 7 million tons of coal and, by 1913, its traffic totalled 4,000 ships and 11 million tons of coal.[3]

This growth was achieved to a limited extent by building new lines of its own, most significantly to the Rhymney Valley and into Cardiff; also by alliance with the Vale of Glamorgan Railway, which it operated to Bridgend and Tondu; and, most importantly, by securing running powers over other companies' lines. It was also greatly assisted by the competitive prices it was able to offer, largely as a result of being an integrated dock and railway business. Its entire history from 1883 to 1922 was a story of continuous expansion and at the end of its life it had

---

[1] Barrie, *Barry Railway*, p. 159.

[2] Ibid., p. 160.

[3] Ibid., p. 153.

parliamentary approval to extend its line into Monmouthshire. Its development was not, however, easy since it was continually attacked by the Taff Vale and others, both through litigation and by competitive pricing and marketing. Its minute books record opposition to its schemes as well as its own opposition to the plans of other railways and dock undertakings.[1]

The Barry Railway lasted less than 40 years but, among companies based in South Wales, was second only to the Taff Vale, established fifty years earlier, in size and importance; it paid annual dividends of 9½ and 10 per cent and was prosperous. In 1913 the 11 million tons of coal which were shipped from Barry was nearly one-fifth of the production of the coalfield; the railway and dock thus played an essential part in achieving the record output of 57 million tons that year. The enterprise was a vindication of the resolve of the Rhondda steam coal owners and demonstrated their power and their independence from the dock and railway companies that had, until then, exerted a monopolistic influence on the coal trade in South Wales. In some ways they were following the example of the ironmasters who built the Glamorganshire Canal in the 1790s and the Taff Vale Railway in the 1830s and, unlike the builders of the Penarth Dock and Railway, were determined to be independent of other undertakings. Not only did they build a successful railway and docks but they created the new town of Barry. It was a town, however, in which the railway, the docks and the people depended almost entirely not just on a single commodity but on one product, the steam coal of Glamorgan.

Walter Insole was a director of the company from the start and appears to have been more assiduous in his attendance at both board and general meetings of the Barry Railway than his father had been with the Penarth Railway. He rarely missed a meeting although his role in the business seem to have been confined to attending Parliamentary hearings and to helping in the organisation of the sod cutting and opening ceremonies. His holding of 5,000 shares was less than other coal owners, such as Richard and John Cory and David and Edward Davies, who held 150,000 between them.

Transport was but one of the necessary conditions for the rapid growth of the South Wales coalfield at the end of the nineteenth century: capital, business organisation and labour also played their part. Earlier in the century the financial requirements of new colliery owners were small, compared for example with entrants to the iron industry in the

---

[1] PRO, RAIL 23/1–2.

same period, and could often be provided by the entrepreneur and his family, assisted by his business associates and his bank. The patches, levels and shallow pits of South Wales encouraged the growth of small scale enterprise by leaseholders, rather than the widespread development of their mineral holdings by landowners, which occurred in some English coalfields, where pits were deeper and more expensive techniques developed earlier. In the later nineteenth century the growth of the South Wales steam coal trade and the exploitation of deeper seams made greater demands on the colliery owners and increased their risks.

In the 1860s and 1870s, a number of family colliery firms took advantage of the Joint Stock Companies Act of 1856, which allowed a company with seven or more owners to be incorporated with limited liability for the shareholders. The Insoles may have been one of these family firms and the identity of their business was discussed at the start of the previous chapter. If they did set up a company, albeit unregistered, there is no record of who the original shareholders were, but the Insoles and their wives would probably have held the majority of the shares, with one or two trusted employees or business associates having taken small shareholdings.

The move to limited liability reduced the risks run by the entrepreneur and, by allowing a group of owners to be a corporate body without the obligations of a partnership, facilitated the raising of new capital in a wider market. The financial crisis of 1866 had an impact on the growth of limited liability companies in the coalfield and coal output in South Wales, which had been 13.8 million tons in 1866, remained at the same level for five years, not advancing to 14 million tons until 1871.[1] During the early 1870s there was a recovery in the formation of joint stock companies, largely as a result of the spectacular rise in steam coal prices from 8s 6d per ton for large steam coal f.o.b. at Cardiff to 23s 3d in 1873. Although prices fell back to under 10s per ton by 1876 and did not start rising for another dozen years, the creation of new larger joint stock companies in the coalfield continued. The available reserves of coal and the ever-increasing demand overcame any fears over the strength and resilience of the financial system. Indeed the next financial crisis, in 1878, in which two important regional banks failed, helped rather than hindered the development of publicly owned companies with large registers of shareholders.

In the closing months of 1878 the City of Glasgow Bank and the

---

[1] Williams, *Welsh Historical Statistics*, I, p. 300.

West of England & South Wales District Bank failed.[1] They had both been heavily involved with industry in their respective regions and their collapse had a profound effect on the behaviour of British banks, which even today are unwilling to establish the kind of close partnership with their industrial and commercial customers, including taking shares in the client's company, which characterises much commercial banking on the European mainland.

The West of England & South Wales District Bank had been established in Bristol in 1834 and had opened a branch in Cardiff in 1835. The bank expanded its activities on both sides of the Severn and by January 1836 its paid-up capital was £178,610 held by 465 share-holders, of whom only eleven came from Wales. Over the years the bank established a tradition of supporting industry and was noted for supplying loans to collieries in the Rhondda and to iron and tinplate firms. The bank's customers included George Insole, Hill's Plymouth Ironworks and the Booker partnership at Pentyrch and Melingriffith. The 1860s saw a rise in the strength of the bank which in 1864 reported to its shareholders that its confidence in the future was so great that it was extending its operations and increasing the number of branches, although this would lead to lower dividends in the short term. In the late 1870s, before its demise, the West of England & South Wales District Bank's paid-up capital was £562,500, divided between more than 2,000 shareholders, compared with the National Provincial Bank's paid-up capital of £1,080,000. The shareholders represented a broad social spectrum but included 750 widows and spinsters; the bank was thus obviously regarded as a safe place for the savings of people living on modest fixed incomes.

Nevertheless, the bank's position was vulnerable. By December 1878 the book value of the bank's investments was £777,000, but they were only expected to realise £160,000. Of the total £747,000 was lent to or invested in South Wales firms, in particular two companies, Thomas W. Booker & Co. Ltd of Pentyrch and Melingriffith and the Aberdare & Plymouth Co. Ltd, with ironworks at Aberdare and Merthyr Tydfil. Of the two commitments Booker's was the bigger and consisted of debentures, preference shares, ordinary shares, insurances and life policies, an involvement which had grown from a small account held by T.W. Booker-Blakemore, when principal partner in the Melingriffith

---

[1] The following account is mainly based on R.O. Roberts, 'Banking and Financial Organisation, 1770–1914', *Glamorgan County History. V. Industrial Glamorgan* (1980), pp. 394–9.

works, at Towgood & Co.'s Bank in Cardiff, which was taken over by the West of England & South Wales District Bank in 1855. The debts grew and in 1858 Booker-Blakemore, the managing partner, died of apoplexy and was succeeded by his two inexperienced sons, Thomas William and John Partridge Booker. By 1861 the bank was so concerned about the size of the firm's loans and overdraft and the performance of the partners that it took a hand in the management of the business. In 1868 J.P. Booker died leaving his elder brother in sole ownership of the business which was still heavily in debt to the bank. It was decided that further outside assistance was needed and in 1872 the heavily indebted partnership was converted into the limited liability company of Thomas W. Booker & Co. Ltd and the company was floated with a nominal share capital of £400,000 and £150,000 in debentures.[1]

The Aberdare & Plymouth Co. owed about £170,000 but its property was mortgaged to other creditors including a Mr Morton from Glasgow for £320,000 and its arrears of rent and royalties were approaching £40,000. The bank's crisis started with the failure of the Aberdare & Plymouth works and the difficulties of the mortgagees, including Morton, who had failed in the wake of the collapse of the City of Glasgow Bank in November 1878. In December the West of England & South Wales District Bank, like its Scottish counterpart, having received no effective help from the Bank of England, suspended payments. Many depositors had been making discreet withdrawals for some weeks and both the National Provincial Bank and the London & Provincial Bank offered to make advances and other arrangements with commercial customers of the failed bank. This was probably when the Insoles moved to the National Provincial, who remained their private and business bankers for many years. There was great distress among the poorer shareholders, who had to meet demands to repay the bank's creditors, and committees were set up for their relief in a number of towns.[2]

Nevertheless, the prudence of wary depositors and the keenness of other banks to take over the customers mitigated the effect of the crisis on the business life of South Wales. Colliery output continued to increase and doubled in the twenty years following the bank's crash. In the longer term the effects were, however, more profound. Lending to industry had always been regarded by the banks as highly risky and the acquisition of shares in customers' companies was, at the very least, frowned upon by most bankers as it further exposed a bank's position.

[1] E.L. Chappell, *Historic Melingriffith* (Cardiff, 1940), pp. 64–7.

[2] Roberts, *Glamorgan County History*, p. 399.

These opinions were reinforced by the crisis and lending against the security of fixed assets was regarded as the only safe way for a bank to provide financial support for industry, a view that is still evident today. The 1878 banking crisis thus had a profound effect on British banks. In the aftermath of the crisis, they became even more cautious in providing investment funds for industry, especially one as risky as the coal trade. The sinking or deepening of a shaft could be expensive with no guarantee of reward at the end, while even when a seam was won there remained the unknown but likely problems of faulting, drainage and ventilation and even the disappearance of seams, which could hinder the progress of the enterprise and make the prospect of profit an illusion or only a distant possibility.

For the Insoles the crisis was significant, not so much because they had to change their bank but because their approach to financing their business had to be reviewed. Although the colliery side of the business was a company and employees had been promoted to both the company's board and to membership of the trading partnership, it was still in all important respects a family business that was dependent upon its own financial resources. The West of England & South Wales District Bank, which was willing to invest in the enterprise, had been useful to them, as a provider both of short-term support and longer-term loans. During the 1880s they would have had to raise money privately, whether for investment or working capital. In particular, both businesses borrowed from James Insole, who himself had loans, of over £50,000 in the early 1880s, from Elder & Maitland and the National Bank of Wales and arrangements for an overdraft with the National Provincial Bank. He paid no more than 4 per cent on his loans and charged his creditors 5 per cent. The Cymmer Colliery Co. further increased its available funds by taking out mortgages on its wagons, a common practice among coal owners, and there is also some evidence of its delaying the payment of rent and royalties to James Insole. It is unlikely that the Insole businesses would have survived for long in this way as an independent concern, in an industry where the issue of shares was becoming the favoured way of financing new investment and where the size of companies was growing, with the emerging combines benefiting from economies of scale. The Insoles needed to increase their production to survive and were being driven inexorably towards offering shares to the public.

In 1896 Walter Insole, his brother Fred and Henry Lewis registered Insoles Ltd, with the view to its taking over the Cymmer Collieries. In March the following year they issued their prospectus and invited the public to subscribe. The nominal capital was £240,000, of which £120,000 was in ordinary shares of £10 each, £60,000 in 6 per cent £10

cumulative preference shares and £60,000 in 5 per cent debenture bonds
of £100. The preference shares and debentures were redeemable by the
company after 1 January 1907, the debentures at £105. The ordinary
shares, which carried voting rights, were taken by the owners, who were
described as the partners or shareholders of Insole & Co. They were
Walter and Fred Insole and their wives, Maria Georgina and Jessy,
Henry Lewis and his wife, Martha, and Thomas Griffiths, the colliery
manager. Of these 12,000 shares retained by the owners, the Lewises had
1,318, Tom Griffiths 51 and the remaining 10,631 were held by the
Insoles. The directors of the new company were Walter and Fred Insole,
Henry Lewis and Tom Griffiths, whose holding of 51 was just over the
minimum of £500 which was specified as a director's qualification in the
articles of association. The board's remuneration was £200 per annum,
which was to be divided by the directors.

By this time the collieries consisted of two pits, the well established
Cymmer Old and New, sunk to the steam coal measures, as well as a
drift to the No 2 Rhondda and two shafts at Upper Cymmer to the No
3 Rhondda and Hafod seams. The collieries had two ventilating fans, one
Waddle and one Schiele, winding engines and newly installed air
compression equipment which was expected to achieve savings of the
order of £3,000 per annum in underground haulage costs. The Upper
Cymmer pits also had coke-making plant, including ovens and coal
crushers. In addition to the pits and their equipment the prospectus listed
a full range of surface buildings, including a gas works and 139
leasehold cottages. The transport facilities included sidings, trams, two
locomotives and horses, as well as 700 railway wagons, of which 600
were mortgaged and partly redeemed. Of these 500 were to be redeemed
in 1899 and 100 in 1900.

The surface area of the collieries was 1,100 acres and six steam coal
seams were reported to have been won; in addition to the four seams
opened in 1877, the company had won the upper and lower Five Feet
seams. The Hafod bituminous seam, which was good for coke, and No
2 Rhondda were also available. George Insole & Son were to be retained
as selling agents for a term of 15 years 'on terms advantageous to the
Company' and it was emphasised that coal could be shipped at Barry,
Cardiff, Penarth or Newport at the same rate.

The average annual profits for the previous eight years were certified
by David Roberts & Sons of Cardiff, the company's auditors, to have
been £18,589. After deducting £3,000 for the 5 per cent preference
shares and £3,600 for the 6 per cent debentures a margin of £11,989 was
left, out of which the dividend on ordinary shares was not to exceed 5
per cent or £6,000. In addition the average annual net revenue from the

cottages had been £1,150.

The company put its annual output at 400,000 tons, which was four to five times more than the amount on which they paid royalties in the years leading up to 1891. Although some of a colliery's output was used by the colliery itself or sold at reduced rates to the workforce and was thus exempt from royalties, this total represents a considerable expansion of output and may indicate that the two Five Feet seams had been recently won. The promoters expected this level of output to be sustainable for a further 37 years and Thomas Forster Brown, the Cardiff consulting mining engineer, certified that the undertaking was ample security for the preference shares and for the debentures.[1]

The flotation was announced at the beginning of March 1897 and the shares and debentures were to be paid for in four instalments by the end of June. The issue was a success and all the shares were taken up in the first year. Initially there were 197 preference shareholders; 64 had no occupation, of whom nearly a half were women, and 34 were in the professions, 29 were merchants and 28 industrialists, 15 were in finance and 14 in the retail trade. There were also seven clerical workers, two overmen and five colliers. It was not uncommon to find working class shareholders at this time, although even a single £10 share represented nearly seven weeks wages or more than a year's rent of an Insole cottage, for one of the Cymmer colliers.[2] Some initial trading in the shares must have taken place as, by 19 October 1897, there were 210 preference shareholders. As well as the preference shares the debentures were fully subscribed and on 26 February 1898 a mortgage was raised, creating a charge on the property to secure the debentures.

The flotation of Insoles Ltd brought the business new capital of £120,000. The boom in South Wales steam coal was still growing and the company was able to prospect and win four more steam coal seams over the following fifteen years and extend its royalty of bituminous coal by taking new leases. The reorganisation of the business enriched the company but did not dilute the Insoles' control, as they held nearly all the ordinary voting shares. As the proceeds of the sale came to the Insole brothers and their immediate associates, it would have helped them not only with the expansion of the Cymmer Colliery but also with their other venture, the Windsor Colliery in the Aber Valley.

[1] GRO, D/D Xcv, Insole Records, Prospectus for the flotation of Insoles Ltd (1897); PRO, BT 31/31496/51497.

[2] Insole MSS, Cymmer Colliery Pay Sheets, cited by Lewis, *Rhondda Valleys*, p. 237n.

Whereas the flotation of Insoles Ltd was a reorganisation of an existing colliery business, the launch of the Windsor Steam Coal Co. Ltd on 6 August 1896 was a new venture to take leases and sink mines in virgin areas, particularly at Abertridwr, north of Caerphilly. The list of the new company's subscribers was headed by the Insole brothers and Henry Lewis; they were joined by Robert Forrest of St Fagans, who was Lord Windsor's land agent, Forster Brown, the civil and mining engineer of Guildhall Chambers, Cardiff, who had advised on the launch of Insoles Ltd, and his partner, Ithel Treharne Rees, as well as G.C. Downing, a partner in the firm of Downing & Handcock, the Insoles' business solicitors in Cardiff. The Insole brothers, Lewis, Forrest and Forster Brown were the first directors and two of Lewis's sons, William North Lewis and Arthur North Lewis, were respectively manager and company secretary.

Of the authorised capital of 10,000 shares (nominally £10 each), 7,500 had been taken up by the end of August. The share register on 29 August 1896 shows the following distribution:

James Walter Insole	1,700
George Frederick Insole	1,700
William Henry Lewis	1,700
Robert Forrest, St Fagans, land agent	500
George Cottrell Downing, Cardiff, solicitor,	250
John Just Handcock, Cardiff, solicitor,	250
Thomas Forster Brown, Guildhall Chambers, Cardiff, mining engineer	500
Charles Smith Morris, Guildhall Chambers, mining engineer	50
Westgarth Forster Brown, Guildhall Chambers, mining engineer	50
Ithel Treharne Rees, Guildhall Chambers, mining engineer	150
Joseph Shaw, 36 Bryanston Square, London, barrister	100
John Bell Simpson, Bradley Hall, Wylam-on-Tyne, gentleman	100
Thomas Griffiths, Porth, colliery manager	300
William North Lewis, 3 Bute Crescent, manager to private company	100
Alfred North Lewis, 3 Bute Terrace, secretary to public company	50

By 12 July 1899 the call on the shares was raised to £3 10s each and the paid-up capital increased to £30,322 10s, with £12 10s outstanding in unpaid calls. Furthermore more investors had been persuaded to take shares in the venture, including three shipowners, Burnhall Bros of Bute Docks, Cardiff, James Hall Rea of 16 James St, Liverpool, with 200 each and Henry Radcliffe of Dock Chambers, Cardiff, who had 100. The shares had also been spread by transfers: in June 1898 William North Lewis had transferred 50 to his wife and Alfred North Lewis had disposed of his 50, while Fred Insole and Henry Lewis had transferred 450 each in December 1898. Of these 950 shares, 300 were taken by Dr

Ivor Lewis and 500 by William Mathias, a contractor from Porth and a substantial figure in the district; the promoters probably saw his agreement to take shares as a significant statement of confidence in the company. Mathias later lived at Tyn-y-cymmer Hall and may well have been the lessor of the mineral rights of Insoles Ltd. One hundred of the remaining transferred shares were taken by David Jenkins, a timber merchant of Porth, and 50 by William Radcliffe Saunders, an electrical engineer from London.

A year later the directors appear to have been feeling confident about the eventual success of the Windsor Colliery and at extraordinary general meetings held on 4 and 22 August 1900 a resolution was passed and confirmed to increase the company's capital by £150,000 through the issue of 5,000 £10 preference shares. In the following year the steam coal seams were proved. The directors now had more to offer the public and needed both more money and a redirection of the company towards colliery operation. They decided on a reorganisation rather than a new issue of shares and, by resolution of extraordinary meetings in June, July and August 1901, the company was wound up and its assets sold to a re-formed company, the Windsor Steam Coal Co. (1901) Ltd, with the primary objective of mining and selling coal rather than prospecting and winning seams.

In area the Windsor Colliery's mineral resources exceeded those of George Insole's original undertaking at Cymmer. The intention was to work the steam coal seams and achieve advantages over other collieries by concentrating on a single product, by using modern technology and by being close to the ports: by the end of the century Abertridwr had a connection to Barry through the Walnut Tree Gap as well as the Rhymney Railway's line to Cardiff. The sinking of the pits, which began in 1897, leads directly into the period of the colliery's development in the early years of this century and is dealt with in the next chapter.

The two limited liability companies set up by the Insoles and Henry Lewis had different objectives and served different purposes for their founders. Insoles Ltd was formed to run an existing business, to increase its capital and to spread its risks; it would provide a regular income, with some variety in its products. The Windsor Steam Coal Co. Ltd, on the other hand, was a speculative venture with a high level of risk and no prospect of immediate returns; it would specialise in the production of steam coal and provide new resources to meet the continually rising demand, which seemed at the time to have no limit. The pattern of shareholding in the two companies was also different. The preference shares and debentures of Insoles Ltd were sold to the public and their full value was raised within five months, while all the voting shares were kept by the promoters. The 8,170 Windsor ordinary shares constituted its entire capital at first and were all voting shares, of which the George Insole & Son partnership held or controlled 5,600 or 69 per cent. The Windsor shareholders, essentially a syndicate of speculators, were mostly associates of the Insoles and the five who seem to have no link to the family business were probably friends or clients of the promoters. The Windsor flotation was far more risky and less popular than that of Insoles Ltd; at first none of the wives was involved, payment for shares was spread over a longer period and the take-up of shares was less than the authorised capital.

These two flotations allowed the Insoles to raise further capital and to win more reserves; they put them in a position where they were able to compete with the larger companies that were emerging in the South Wales coalfield at that time and in the years leading up to the First World War. They also demonstrated that, even if the second generation of Cardiff Insoles had joined the rentier class, the third generation was prepared to do its own pioneering. The Insole brothers further followed family tradition in supporting a railway and dock enterprise and were involved with the Barry Railway throughout its life.

Of the factors contributing to the accelerated expansion of the South Wales coalfield after 1880, the Insoles were involved in improving transport, increasing investment and in extending the coalfield. They appear to have little to do with attracting or providing for labour at Cymmer or Abertridwr. Their 139 cottages advertised in the prospectus for Insoles Ltd, which had been built in the middle of the century, seem to be their only venture into workers' housing in the Rhondda. Nevertheless, the demand for housing was great and the number of houses in the Rhondda Valleys increased from 9,193 in 1881 to 26,250 in 1911,[1] while in the village of Abertridwr, still a hamlet in 1896, some 700 houses had been built by 1911. These houses were small, often overcrowded and lacking bathrooms, built by contractors out of local stone, albeit by this time with slate rather than tile-stone roofs.

While these changes were taking place in the businesses, the Insole family was growing. Fred and Jessy Insole continued to live in Fairwater House and had six children, two daughters, Jessie and Violet, born in 1881 and 1884, and four boys. The children were all baptised at St Fagans by their great uncle. Their first boy, Frederick Harvey, was born in 1885 but died the same year and was buried at Llandaff. Claud, the eldest son to reach manhood, was born in 1887 and his brothers, Eric

---

[1] Lewis, *Rhondda Valleys*. pp. 202–3.

and Alan, in 1889 and 1895, by which time Fred was 48 and Jessy 42. Walter and Maria Georgina Insole, who had no children, lived at Pencisely House, with her mother, Marian Eagle and her sister, a young widow called Marian Carey; they also stayed at Luxborough and at Parich's Hotel, George Street, Hanover Square, which the Insoles described as their London residence. The farm at Pencisely appears to have been run by James Insole's farm manager, William Evans, who lived at Ty Fry with his wife Eliza; they came from Llantrisant and were Welsh-speaking.[1]

In 1890 James Insole married again after eight years of widowhood. His bride was Marian Carey, his son Walter's sister-in-law, who was some forty years his junior. The wedding took place in the summer at St George's, Hanover Square and James Insole provided a jointure of £25,000 for his new wife in the marriage settlement. He was in his seventieth year and did not have any more children. He continued to follow an active life and the couple were not at any of their homes at the 1891 census. He also made further alterations to Ely Court. In 1895 he had new entrance gates erected at a cost of £289 and in 1898 he had two towers built on the end of the north wing for £775.[2] These alterations were carried out by W. Clarke of Llandaff and to judge from the two prices the gates must have been very imposing.

He was also involved with the Fine Art, Industrial and Maritime Exhibition of 1896, an event which caused some excitement in Cardiff and drew attention to the town's growth and prosperity. This was a far more ambitious and better conceived project than its predecessor in 1881. The organisation had a single president, Lord Windsor, albeit with the usual retinue of vice-presidents, headed by the Marquess of Bute and including James Insole. It took place in Cathays Park in a specially constructed site with an exhibition building, concert hall, shops, restaurants and a bar, as well as a bicycle track, switchback, lake, canal, gardens and a branch line laid by the Taff Vale Railway. Ithel Rees, Forster Brown and Tom Griffiths were all members of the mining committee and James Insole again lent his Turner for the painting section. The architect was Edwin Seward, who had been an honorary secretary of the 1881 exhibition.[3]

The turn of the century was, however, a time of sorrow for the family.

[1] William was the son of the Revd William Evans of Tonyrefail, and grandfather of Madam Clara Novello Davies (inf. from Brian Ll. James).

[2] W.C. Clarke, Bill Book 4 (1895–7), Bill Book 5 (1898).

[3] See catalogue in CCL.

On 23 April 1898, while staying in London, Walter underwent an operation for cancer of the mouth and jaw, from which he had been suffering for some months. At first he made a good recovery but after a week he contracted an infection from which he died on 3 May. His obituary noted his enjoyment of the life of a country gentleman, as well as his 'geniality and general bonhomie' and wide circle of friends.[1] He left his entire estate, including his partnership and his shares in the Cymmer and Abertridwr collieries, to his widow; his place on the boards of the Barry Railway and the Insoles and Windsor colliery businesses was taken by his brother Fred. Walter was buried in the municipal cemetery at Llandaff. The funeral was organised by W. Clarke of Llandaff, including the return of Walter's body to Cardiff, a hearse and carriages to meet it at the station, the construction of a brick vault with a strong cover and the arrangements on the day of the funeral.

James Insole survived his son by less than three years and he died at Ely Court on the evening of Sunday 20 January 1901. On 22 January Queen Victoria died and the passing of one of Cardiff's oldest surviving coal shippers was overshadowed by national mourning. Nevertheless his funeral was well attended and many of his friends and associates who were unable to attend sent their carriages. It was also arranged by W. Clarke whose bill came to £59. His widow donated a stained glass window to the cathedral in his memory, it is a crucifixion but without inscription, in the south aisle, immediately opposite James's memorial to his first wife. His will was long and complex, entailing most of his estate in trust, possibly in order to limit Fred's freedom of action. The Somerset estate was entailed to his grandson, Claud Insole, and his widow was to have the use of Ely Court until her death or re-marriage. She was also left a further £25,000 in addition to her jointure. At the time of James Insole's death, Marian's sister Maria Georgina Insole was also very ill at Ely Court and she died on 28 February. Her will contained a long list of bequests to relations, godchildren, friends and servants but the main part of her estate, Walter Insole's share of the businesses, she left to Marian, her sister and executrix. Marian Insole thus became not only a rich widow, comfortably provided for by her late husband, but also a major shareholder in Insoles Ltd and the Windsor Steam Coal Co. Ltd, and a partner in the firm of George Insole & Son.

[1] *Western Mail*, 5 May 1898.

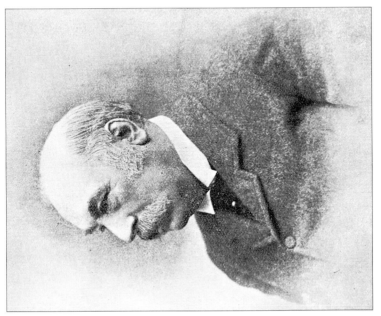

11. *Left*: James Harvey Insole; *Right*: William Henry Lewis (both from *Contemporary Portraits*, 1896).

In the High Court of Justice.
(CHANCERY DIVISION).   SECOND EDITION.
VICE-CHANCELLOR MALINS.

RE THE LUXBOROUGH ESTATE, DEVISED BY THE WILL OF SIR THOMAS BUCKLER LETHBRIDGE, BART., DECEASED.

SOMERSETSHIRE.

Particulars and Conditions of Sale

OF AN

EXTENSIVE FREEHOLD DOMAIN,

KNOWN AS THE

LUXBOROUGH ESTATE,

Situate in the Parishes of Luxborough, Kings Brompton, Treborough, Withiel Florey, Cutcombe, Exton, and Old Cleeve ;

Five miles from Washford Station on the West Somerset Railway, in direct communication with the Great Western Main Line ; Four miles from Dunster ; Six from Wiveliscombe ; Eight from the seaports of Watchet and Minehead and the town of Williton ; Ten from Dulverton ; and Eighteen from Taunton.

IT COMPRISES A

PICTURESQUE AND COMMODIOUS SHOOTING BOX,

KNOWN AS

"CHARGOT HOUSE,"

DELIGHTFULLY PLACED ON RISING GROUND, WITH

GOOD STABLING AND OUTBUILDINGS,

NUMEROUS FARMS, WITH DWELLING HOUSES AND HOMESTEADS,

SMALL OCCUPATIONS, COTTAGES,

EXTENSIVE WOODS & PLANTATIONS,

AND

VALUABLE BEDS OF IRON-STONE;

EMBRACING ALTOGETHER AN AREA OF

7217 A.   3 R.   27 P.

ALSO

The Advowson or Perpetual Right of Presentation to the Vicarage of Withiel Florey, and the great Tithes of that Parish, commuted at £155 per annum.

The whole of which will be offered for Sale by Auction by

MESSRS. BEADEL,

The Persons appointed by Vice-Chancellor Sir R. Malins, to whose Court this matter is attached,

AT THE MART, TOKENHOUSE YARD, LONDON, E.C.,

On THURSDAY, 25th NOVEMBER, 1875, at ONE O'CLOCK PRECISELY, IN THREE LOTS.

Particulars, with Plans, may be obtained of Messrs. J. and C. LONGBOURNE, Solicitors, 7, Lincoln's Inn Fields, W.C.; Messrs. BEADON & SWEET, Solicitors, Taunton ; at the Mart ; and of Messrs. BEADEL, 25, Gresham Street, London, E.C., who will issue Orders to View on application.

12. Luxborough Estate sale catalogue, 1875. *(Courtesy Somerset Record Office, Luxborough Estate Collection)*

13. Entrance front of Ely Court, Llandaff, after the additions of the 1870s *(Stephen Rowson Collection)*

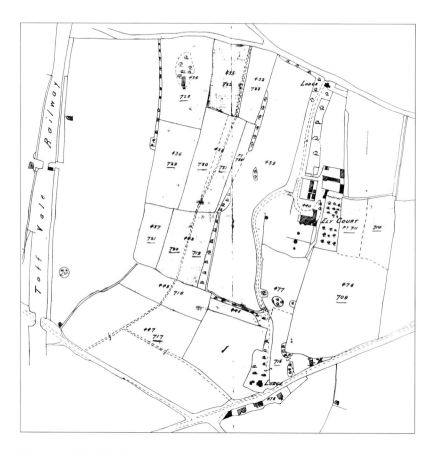

14. Plan of the Ely Court estate. J.H. Insole acquired the house, garden and lodge in 1856–79; the numbered parcels on this plan show the additional land bought in 1883. *(Courtesy Cardiff County Council)*

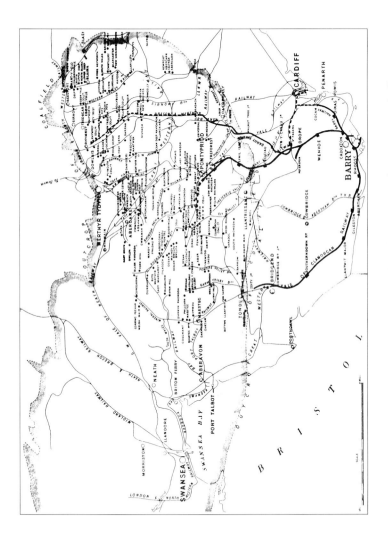

15. The Barry Railway. The solid bold lines show the company's own network; lines over which it had running powers are dotted. *(From Rimmell*, Barry Railway Company)

16. The entrance to Barry Docks. *(From Rimmell,* Barry Railway Company)

17. A group of members of the Cardiff & County Club, including Ithel Treharne Rees (top left), Walter Insole in front of him, Fred Insole in the centre, and Robert Forrest (second from front on right), who were all directors of the Windsor Steam Coal Co. Ltd. *(Courtesy Cardiff & County Club, per Arthur Weston Evans)*

18. *Above left:* Herbert Homfray; *right:* Robert George Windsor-Clive, Lord Windsor, Earl of Plymouth; *below left:* Robert Forrest; *right:* James Walter Insole.

19. Private owner wagons, including Insoles', at Barry Docks (*Courtesy Living Archive Centre, Barry*)

20. Windsor Colliery, Abertridwr *(Bill Styles Collection).*

21. *Above left:* Tom Griffiths; *right:* William North Lewis; *below left:* George Frederick Insole; *right:* Eric Raymond Insole.

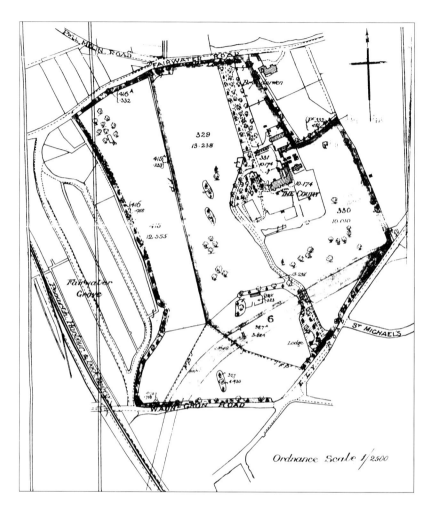

22. Plan of The Court Estate, Llandaff, *c.* 1930, showing a section of Western Avenue (numbered 6 on the plan). *(Courtesy Cardiff County Council)*

Chapter 8

Edwardian Prosperity

1901–13

The early years of the twentieth century were a period of prosperity and contrast. The lavish living of the well-to-do, the increasing comfort and security in the lives of salary and wage earners and the confidence and optimism of an unashamedly imperial nation contrasted with the penury of the poorest and least fortunate, the growth of fresh political and industrial conflicts, the increasingly belligerent tone of foreign affairs and the eventual descent into war in Europe. The coal industry in general and the Insoles' businesses in particular were typical of the age. The prosperity and importance of the South Wales coal trade reached its climax in 1913.

As in the last years of the previous century the growth of coal output was largely achieved through the deeper and more extensive mining of existing collieries by established companies. Nevertheless some new pits were sunk and the South Wales coalfield experienced record growth in both coal production and exports (Table 8.1). To achieve this expansion the numbers employed in the industry grew from 73,328 in 1874 to 233,134 in 1913,[1] a massive increase for areas that had been, in many cases, sparsely populated rural backwaters in the memory of their indigenous inhabitants.

In order to cope with the increase in coal shipped through Cardiff the Bute Docks Company, which had been formed by the Bute Trustees in 1887,[2] decided to build a new dock. Their early ideas were ambitious and included a plan to form a trust to manage all the docks on the Taff and Ely, build an import dock and enclose the estuaries. Caution, however, prevailed and their parliamentary bill, which was successful in 1895, was for a simpler scheme, for a new dock to be constructed on reclaimed ground to the south of the Roath Basin, with a channel to the Roath Dock. Work began in 1898, coinciding with the opening at Barry of the No 2 Dock of 34 acres and a deep water lock.[3] The new Queen

---

[1] Williams, *Welsh Historical Statistics*, I, p. 300.

[2] Chappell, *Port of Cardiff*, p. 111.

[3] Ibid., p. 113.

Alexandra Dock was opened on 13 July 1907 by King Edward VII, on a visit to Cardiff which the leading citizens and the newspapers treated as a festival. The dock was of 52 acres and, in addition to coal staithes, included import berths along its north side, all the wharves being furnished with the most modern equipment. Its construction had required the enclosure and reclamation of 320 acres of the foreshore and the whole enterprise cost some £2,000,000. A number of social events took place in connection with the opening, including a luncheon given by the fourth Marquess of Bute (1881–1947) and a garden party in Sophia Gardens, organised by the Chamber of Commerce. Fred Insole and William North Lewis, with their wives and daughters, were present at these events as well as at the opening ceremony itself.[1]

Table 8.1:
Coal Output and Shipments from the South Wales Coalfield,
for the peak year in each decade, 1874–1913

	1883 000 tons	1892 000 tons	1903 000 tons	1913 000 tons
Coal output in South Wales	24,975	31,207	42,154	56,830
Shipments from South Wales ports	12,332	16,575	29,170	33,196
Shipments from the port of Cardiff	7,759	11,741	19,721	25,400

Source: John Williams, *Digest of Welsh Historical Statistics* (Welsh Office, 1985), I, pp. 301, 315, 318. The port of Cardiff included the Bute Docks, Ely Harbour, Penarth and Barry.

Coal output and shipments increased throughout the Edwardian period, reaching a peak in 1913, when the total trade of the customs port of Cardiff was 30,074,000 tons, of which 13,677,000 tons passed through the Bute Docks, 4,661,000 tons through Penarth Dock and Ely Harbour, and 11,736,000 tons through Barry Docks.

This success, however, hid two weaknesses which did not bode well for the future. In the first place nearly 85 per cent of Cardiff's trade was in the export of coal. Of this the majority was steam coal, making the

[1] *Western Mail,* souvenir edition 15 July 1907; *Cardiff Tide Tables,* 1907.

base of the local economy of Cardiff and, to a greater extent, Barry very narrow and their prosperity vulnerable both to changes in fuels and technology and to events overseas which the Cardiff shippers were powerless to control. In addition Cardiff's share of the sea-borne coal trade from South Wales, as a proportion both of coal output and of total shipments, was shrinking.[1] Furthermore, the rate of increase in output was slower than in earlier years: in the 1860s increases of over 5 per cent on a moving five year average were not uncommon, whereas in the ten years leading up to 1913 a figure of 4 per cent was not reached.[2] Since there was as yet no shortage of resources, it is probable that the coal market was becoming mature and therefore in the future its prices would become even less elastic and its competitiveness more dependent than ever on lowering costs.

The South Wales coalfield was becoming increasingly dominated by large companies and combines. Of these Powell Duffryn was the oldest, having been established in 1864, after the death of Thomas Powell, by his sons and business associates. The company grew to dominate the coalfield between the two world wars and owned most of the collieries of South Wales on 1 January 1947, when the coal industry was nationalised. The Ocean Company, the first of the combines to sell shares, had been formed by David Davies in 1889 by bringing together six collieries in the Rhondda valleys. It also survived through the inter-war period and was still in business at nationalisation. In the years before the First World War the largest of the combines was the Cambrian, which was formed by an aggressive policy of acquisition between 1906 and 1916 by David Alfred Thomas, later Lord Rhondda (1856–1918). Thomas was the son of a colliery proprietor from Clydach Vale; after taking the mathematical tripos at Cambridge he studied his father's trade and was convinced that, with co-operation, the owners could control the market. At first he approached the Monmouthshire & South Wales Coal Owners' Association but found little support. The members came together to co-ordinate their actions in labour disputes and the sliding scale negotiations but they were not all willing to act together in trying to control the market. Thomas was also pursuing a political career: he was Liberal MP for Merthyr Tydfil from 1888 to 1910, but he was disappointed by not getting office in the Campbell-Bannerman government of 1905. He then concentrated his energies on building up the Cambrian Combine, which by 1913 had an authorised capital of

[1] See Appendix E.
[2] See Appendix A.

£2,000,000. By 1916 the output of his collieries had reached 7,355,000 tons per annum, one fifth of the coalfield's production.

In the early years of the century the coal owners were faced by their increasingly belligerent workers in a more united front, the newly formed South Wales Miners' Federation. The miners were as suspicious of surrendering their freedom of action to a central organisation as the owners and the union was still based upon local districts, which cherished their independence and restricted the size of its central funds. Nevertheless it provided a common forum for the workers in the coalfield and was affiliated to the national union, the Miners' Federation of Great Britain.

In the early 1890s the miners were still organised in district unions, such as the Cambrian Miners' Association in the Rhondda and were divided, particularly over the issue of the sliding scale. This method of assessing wage rates was opposed by the Miners' Federation of Great Britain, which set up a branch in South Wales under the leadership of William Brace of Monmouthshire. Brace and the Federation favoured a minimum wage, while Mabon and the older leaders remained committed to the scale and wanted a strong Welsh union. Among the members, however, there was widespread indifference to the issue, which was aggravated by the divisions in the leadership. In 1893 Brace and his allies failed to convince the members to abandon the scale in a ballot and they began a campaign of persuasion throughout the coalfield. This was successful and in September 1896 the South Wales miners voted to terminate the sliding scale on condition that the new agreement had a minimum wage. In 1898 there was a general strike by the employees of members of the owners' association for a minimum wage. In the settlement of the strike it was agreed that the sliding scale would end on 1 July 1902 and a conciliation board take its place. The employers' commitment to a minimum wage, however, was equivocal and the uncertainties of this vague agreement brought the workers together and led to the formation of the South Wales Miners' Federation on 11 October 1898.

The Conciliation Board was set up in 1902 and at first appeared to function well, possibly because wages continued to rise. The South Wales Miners' Federation concentrated its attacks on the employment of non-union labour in the early 1900s and grew from 60,000 members in 1898 to a pre-war peak of 144,579 in 1908. This was also the year when the Eight Hours Act became law, causing some turmoil in labour relations; the employers claimed that costs would rise but the miners disputed this on the ground that productivity would increase. The miners were concerned that there was no agreement about work in 'abnormal places', those difficult to mine. In the event both sides were proved right. These differences added to the growing division between employer and employee and the deteriorating labour relations in the coalfield. In August 1909 Insoles Ltd entered the conflict when the company prosecuted an employee for breach of contract over work in abnormal places.

As well as the arguments over the working day there was also growing discontent among the miners both with the workings of the Conciliation Board and with the union itself; membership fell to 114,207 in 1912. Discontent finally came to a head in the Cambrian Combine strike of 1910–11. It started with a dispute about the rate for a seam with abnormal areas which the Conciliation Board failed to resolve. The strikers held out for ten months, eventually returning to work in September 1911; they received strike pay from the union but little other support either locally or nationally. The ineffectiveness of the Conciliation Board, which was often unable to reach a decision, gave substance to the stand of the union's more belligerent wing and the 1912 annual conference of the Federation elected new leaders, imbued with the ideas of class struggle rather than conciliation. Mabon resigned but other moderate leaders came to terms with the new leadership. On 1 March 1912 the Miners' Federation of Great Britain began a national strike for a minimum wage. The government's response was immediate and conciliatory: on 19 March they introduced the Minimum Wage Bill, which was quickly enacted and one of the main aims of the miners' unions had been achieved.[1]

From its flotation Insoles Ltd, the operator of the Cymmer colliery, continued to invest and to increase its output and workforce. It was one of the larger collieries in the coalfield employing over 2,500 men by 1912. There were also changes in the company's board, which further reduced the family's control of the company's policy and operations. Walter Insole, on his death in 1898, was succeeded as chairman by his brother Fred and, in the same year, Herbert Homfray became a director. Homfray was agent for the estate of his elder brother, John, and he was then living at Bonvilston House in the Vale of Glamorgan. In 1904 he was elected to the board of the Taff Vale Railway. By 1906 his brother was living in Brighton and Herbert was living at the family seat, Penllyn Castle, near Cowbridge.

Insoles Ltd was a profitable company, providing regular returns to its

---

[1] E.W. Evans, *The Miners of South Wales* (Cardiff, 1961), pp. 150–208; Lewis, *Rhondda Valleys*, p. 178.

200 preference shareholders, who had a reputation for loyalty; in 1908 E.T. Lyddon & Sons, the Cardiff stockbrokers, reported that Insoles' preference shares and debentures 'are well held and it is seldom either come to the market'.[1] Between 1899 and 1906 the company's ordinary shares gave an annual return of 5 per cent, except in 1899 and 1905, when the dividend was 2½ per cent, and in 1903 when it was 15 per cent. In 1907–13, however the ordinary shares were more profitable, only dropping below 10 per cent in 1910 (2½ per cent), while reaching 20 per cent in 1908 and 1913. The earlier 2½ per cent dividends were paid in the years of lower output in the coalfield; 1910 was the year of the Cambrian Combine strike; and the 20 per cent dividends reflect the years of high output in 1908, the last year before the upheavals of the Eight Hour Act, and 1913, the coalfield's peak year. Throughout the period the company paid its 6 per cent dividend to preference shareholders and 5 per cent interest on its debentures. The dividends on ordinary shares went overwhelmingly to the Insoles and the Lewises. Of the 12,000 ordinary shares only 51 shares held by Tom Griffiths and 36 by Herbert Homfray and George Bevan were not owned by members of the Insole and Lewis families. During the period leading up to the First World War, the company continued to invest in Cymmer colliery and to increase its output. In contrast to James Insole's retreat from industry to land, members of the new generation on the board were proving themselves to be enthusiastic investors in the colliery businesses.[2]

They were not all, however, long livers. Walter Insole had died in his fifties and, in the early hours of Tuesday 24 October 1905, Henry Lewis died at the age of 65 at his home, Bryn Rhos, Llanishen. He had a successful career, first as a trusted employee, then as manager of the business. In 1872 he became a member of the chamber of commerce, of which he was vice-president in 1900 and president in 1901. He amassed considerable wealth which he devoted to his garden at Bryn Rhos which, with playing the harp, seems to have been his principal recreation. He was also a benefactor of a number of charities and educational bodies; for example, he gave £200 to University College, Cardiff. He attended St Margaret's Church, Roath, since 1872 a stronghold of the High Church Oxford Movement, although he came from a nonconformist background, and he was chairman of Llanishen Conservative Association. He left a widow, four daughters and four sons. Of these, at the time of their father's death, Henry North Lewis was a partner with the solicitors,

[1] E.T. Lyddon & Sons, *The South Wales Investment Circular*, 2 Nov. 1908.
[2] PRO, BT 31/31496/51497.

Downing & Handcock, running their London offices, and William North Lewis was commercial manager of the Cymmer and Windsor collieries; he was soon to succeed his father on the boards of both companies and as a partner in George Insole & Son.[1] The Cardiff docksmen included a number of closely knit groups and one of Lewis's daughters married into the Ferrier family, of whom J.B. Ferrier was the manager of the Cardiff office of Burnyeat, Brown & Co., who were the Insole's tenants in Bute Crescent. Henry Lewis's funeral took place at Llanishen on the Friday following his death and a special train was laid on from Cardiff for the 'great gathering of commercial men' reported in the *Western Mail.*[2]

In 1909 Cardiff became the target for the backers of the British Antarctic Expedition, which was to be led by Capt. Robert F. Scott RN (1868–1912).[3] Lieut. E.R.G.R. Evans R.N., the expedition's second in command, had connections with Cardiff and in the autumn of 1909 he came to the city to seek support. He met a number of docksmen and civic leaders, as well as W.E. Davies, the editor of the *Western Mail.* Davies was impressed by Evans and became an enthusiastic supporter; on 1 November 1909 he wrote a leading article, entitled 'Our Pole' (in contrast to the Americans' North Pole), lavishing fulsome praise on the expedition, while that afternoon Evans gave a public lecture at City Hall. Their efforts were successful and a number of docksmen agreed to give support, including gifts of 300 tons of patent fuel from the Crown Preserved Coal Co. Ltd, 50 tons of steam coal from the Ynyshir Steam Coal Co. Ltd and 50 tons from Insoles Ltd. Other donations included money and supplies, giving Cardiff and its merchant elite a key role in the expedition, while, in the hopes of Davies and his associates, spreading the fame of the city's progress and wealth. Overall, however, the expedition was not well financed and Cardiff's support was particularly welcome as other towns and cities were not as responsive.[4] On 10 June 1910 Scott's ship *Terra Nova, RYS,*[5] arrived in Cardiff Roads and was met by a welcoming party, led by the Lord Mayor, on board the tug

[1] *Western Mail*, 25 Oct. 1905.

[2] Ibid., 28 Oct. 1905.

[3] The Insoles' connection with Scott's Antarctic expedition is part of local oral tradition in Cardiff.

[4] A.M. Johnson, *Scott of the Antarctic and Cardiff* (Cardiff, 1984), p. 12.

[5] The *Terra Nova* was a secondhand Antarctic whaler but she was registered and sailed as a yacht in order to avoid merchant shipping regulations; she was also allowed by the Admiralty to fly the white ensign. Scott had been elected, temporarily, to the Royal Yacht Squadron.

Falcon. The party included William North Lewis among the representatives of the Cardiff Chamber of Commerce but their excitement was
muted by heavy rain and overcrowding on the tug's decks, where they
all had to travel.

Once in port the *Terra Nova* tied up at the Crown Company's berth
in Roath Dock to take on their 300 tons of patent fuel; by way of
greeting, the company's offices were bedecked with bunting.[1] The next
day she was towed to the Bute East Dock to take on steam coal, while
the expedition's members and crew enjoyed the city's hospitality. On
Monday 13 June a dinner was held for members of the expedition and
their Cardiff supporters at the Alexandra Room (now the Scott Room) at
the Royal Hotel. They still needed money and a collection was taken up
after the dinner, raising £1,000, of which North Lewis contributed five
guineas. The dinner was followed by a smoker where they were joined
by the crew of the *Terra Nova,* who had been entertained to dinner at
Barry's restaurant. Two days later the *Terra Nova* left Cardiff for the
Antarctic amid a rousing farewell.[2]

In the years leading up to the First World War Insoles Ltd profits
varied from under 7 per cent to 28½ per cent. Between 1908 and 1913
the annual balances on the profit and loss account, at 30 June, were:

1908	£73,786	1911	£42,342
1909	£58,231	1912	£54,890
1910	£51,652	1913	£81,598

The company deployed its profits in different ways. In 1909 the value
of the colliery increased while cash and stocks were run down, indicating
a period of relatively heavy investment; the profit for the year was
£12,045. 1910 was similar although stocks were rebuilt, while in 1911
stocks were run down and cash balances grew. 1912, on the other hand,
appears to have been a quiet year, leading into 1913, a very profitable
year. In fact 1913 was to prove the *annus mirabilis* of the South Wales
coal trade; in 1910 the Coal and Shipping Exchange had been founded
to bring the management of the Coal Exchange under the control of its
members and, in the following two years, the interior of the building was
transformed by its original architect, Edwin Seward; the prospects for the
coal trade seemed limitless.

At the ordinary general meeting of Insoles Ltd, held on 7 August

---

[1] *Western Mail*, 11 June 1910.

[2] Ibid., 14 and 16 June 1910.

1913, the directors reported a profit of £51,307 17s 1d, the second highest since the company had been formed sixteen years before. As a result, while the 6 per cent dividend was paid to the company's preference shareholders, the final dividend on the ordinary shares was 15 per cent, making 20 per cent for the year, with a bonus dividend of 50 per cent per ordinary share. In addition the company's debenture debt was reduced to £22,500. The chairman referred, in his report, to a proposed increase in capital. He pointed out that large sums had been spent on the colliery, which had increased its capacity from 400,000 tons a year when the company was floated to 880,000 tons. The meeting was followed by an extraordinary general meeting to deal with capital restructuring. It was agreed to divide each £10 share into ten £1 shares and to issue a further 60,000 ordinary shares, which would be offered to the public. It was also agreed to make a new issue of 500 debentures of £100 each. The chairman claimed that even with a 50 per cent increase, the company's capital would be less than many other colliery companies with similar output. Fred Insole was unable to chair these meetings on account of his health. His place was taken by William North Lewis and, by the end of the year, Herbert Homfray had been elected chairman.[1] The 60,000 new ordinary shares were issued and were fully subscribed in small amounts but the new debentures were less successful: of 500 £100 debentures only 375 were taken up. Earlier in 1913 Eric Insole had been made a director and his election was confirmed at the meeting. He joined the chamber of commerce at the same time and was the only one of Fred's sons to show any interest in the business.[2]

Where Cymmer provided income and an opportunity for profitable investment for the Insoles and the Lewises, the Windsor colliery required a great deal of money for sinking and development before it made any return. The sinking of two pits, the north (upcast) and south (downcast) began in the summer of 1897 and the reports to T. Forster Brown & Rees's office in Cardiff, presumably from their site engineer at the colliery, for eighteen months from September 1897,[3] have survived together with an engineer's (possibly Forster Brown's own) notebook of the same period.[4]

Two contractors were employed: the first, J. Jenkins, using steam cranes hired for the purpose, opened the shafts to a depth of about 100

---

[1] *Western Mail*, 8 Aug. 1913.

[2] PRO, BT 31/31496/51497.

[3] GRO, D/D DJ 91/1.

[4] GRO, D/D DJ 91/2.

feet, where a solid rock base was found, and erected the sinking headgear. During the summer of 1897 the company tried to complete the heavy work of excavating the mountainside and preparing the site before the summer was over. By September the north pit was sufficiently deep for the sinking engine's headgear to be erected. This was done between the end of September and the middle of December and was followed by three weeks spent in clearing water from the pit. On 3 January 1898 the main contractor, Thomas Rees & Sons of Llantrisant, began sinking the north shaft. The south pit took longer to get ready and, although work on the headgear started in the third week of October, sinking did not start until the end of July 1898. Rees & Sons were paid £19 per yard for sinking and £1 per yard for 18in. thick walling; the company retained 10 per cent of the payment but also made advances to the contractor in each monthly bill.

The sinking of the north pit continued for twenty weeks at a rate of five to ten yards per week with curbs placed every 25–30 yards. The intervening space between the curbs was walled with either 9 in., 18 in. or 27 in. brickwork. When walling the sinkers worked on cradles, suspended from the winding gear, close to the face of the shaft. At first all went well and the reports show that there was steady progress, but at 6 a.m. on 27 May 1898 they struck water at a depth of 142 yards. During sinking the normal flow of water was up to 1,000 gallons per hour and could be pumped clear but the flow now increased to 4,500 gallons per hour and after twelve hours ineffective baling the water was allowed to accumulate until Tuesday 31 May. It was Whit week and both the Monday and Tuesday were holidays. By the time they returned to work the water was nearly 140 ft deep, filling one third of the shaft, and took 52 hours to empty with a 290 gallon barrel. The following week was spent in keeping water down but after some shot firing the flow of water increased to 6,000 gallons per hour and sinking was stopped to clear it. Work was further interrupted twice in the following week, when the hourly flow reached 5,000 gallons. These events led to disagreements with the contractor, mainly over the power of the winding engine and its ability to move the quantity of water, and there was an angry exchange of letters between Tom Griffiths, the colliery manager, and Thomas Rees & Son, the contractor. The argument continued until the end of July when Forster Brown, acting as arbitrator, secured an agreement and Rees & Son resumed sinking on 4 August, but with only six to eight men to a shift. Further problems with water led to the work being abandoned and water winding continued until 2 September, when sinking was resumed, but by company's own men. Rees & Son started sinking the south pit at 2 p.m. on Monday 25 July, although they had had instructions from Griffiths to begin on 7 July. They stopped work at a depth of 62 yards on Saturday 20 August and the work was taken over by the company's men the following Wednesday.

Once the company had taken over in both pits steady progress was maintained through the autumn and winter. Sinking in the north pit was between three and four yards per week, with walling curbs at intervals of between 25 and 33 yards, and had reached 190 yards by Christmas, when water stopped work again and it was decided to up-grade the winding engine. There were delays in getting a part but sinking resumed in early February 1899 and had passed a depth of 207 yards by the middle of March. Progress in the south pit was faster, between five and six yards per week, with walling curbs at 20 to 32 yards. A depth of 172 yards had been achieved by the middle of March. Apart from the problems of water, in both pits, the air was reported to be becoming thick at about 80 yards depth and wooden ducts were laid from the ventilating engine to the shafts.

As the colliery was on a virgin site, everything had to be built from new. The company had to construct surface buildings and earthworks, including a reservoir for the boilers, ventilation ducts and railway sidings. They also had to install services for the pits themselves, including pumps, engines, fans and electric light. The work also included stone quarrying, and between September 1897 and September 1898 3,362 trams of stone, of about 50 cwt each, were brought down from the Garth quarry, on the top of the mountain to the west of the colliery, on a reopened tramway.

The reports only started to record wages and payments to contractors from 1 January 1898. At this time the contractors received monthly payments varying from £351 to £455 and the company's fortnightly wage bill varied from £95 to £150. Soon after the company took responsibility for sinking, it changed to weekly payments, which were in the range £150–£314, although Christmas week was lower at £120. There was, however, less variation than the figure implies, as half were between £220 and £250. The average wage bill increased gradually as the pits deepened. The cost of sinking was calculated weekly and ranged from £19 to £33 per yard, with two exceptional weeks at £38, when a new feeder was found, increasing the hourly flow of water to 6,800 gallons, and £47 when two accidents to the machinery caused delays.

The wage rates illustrate a wide variety of working patterns, which were further complicated when, after 27 October, the sinkers were paid on the basis of the sliding scale, at their own request. The underground workers were led by the foreman sinker who earned £2 per week. The sinkers were paid by the eight-hour shift: 6s 6d for a leader sinker, 6s for a second leader sinker and 5s for a sinker. When the sliding scale was adopted these rates became 5s 9d plus 17½ per cent, 5s 3d plus 17½ per cent and 4s 9d plus 17½ per cent. Two adjustments were made in the sliding scale in the following four months: on 8 December there was a 2½ per cent advance and on 9 February a 1½ per cent reduction. Day workers were paid by the twelve hour day, except for the smith and his men who worked nine and a half hours. Daily rates varied from 5s for the banksman and engine driver to 2s 8d for the smith's striker.

The stores held were mostly building and digging tools, grease, oils and candles but also included gelignite at £75 per ton which was used at the rate of about £6 worth or 1½ cwt per week. Some protective clothing was kept and either issued or sold to the men. Oilskin suits, at 10s each, were essential for the work and cost just under a quarter of a sinker's weekly wage. Walling gloves, at 1s 2d per pair, were also kept. Bricks were used in quantities of 100,000 to 300,000 at a time for walling and were stacked on site; on one occasion they were stacked in between the shafts, preventing work on vent ducts.

By May 1902 Forster Brown was able to note that sinking was nearing completion and that in a year's time coal working would begin. The sinking of the north pit was still in progress but the south pit was now 673 yards deep and the installation of its winding engine, from Markham & Co. of Chesterfield, was expected to be completed in six weeks. The carpenters' and smiths' shops were complete and the building of the offices in progress. The pits had been connected at 325 yards with a lodge house and pump. A further connection at 608 yards in the 4 ft seam was not complete and the ventilation was poor. A twelve foot down-throw had been found 125 yards west of the pit bottom in the 4 ft seam and it had been decided to drift up to the 2 ft 9 in.

The problems of the Windsor were not yet over. On 3 June 1902 there was a fatal accident in the north pit, when the staging on which a shift of nine sinkers was working collapsed into twenty-four feet of water and six of the men were drowned. There had been a 'huge fall of rubbish' inside the shaft on the Sunday before and the men had spent the previous day clearing it away. It was when they had almost completed the job on the Tuesday afternoon that the accident occurred. Sinking had reached a depth of about 630 yards and the staging had been erected, supported on a curb, possibly at 608 yards, where the shift was engaged in turning a heading off the shaft. No reason for the failure of the staging was immediately apparent but the accident was sudden and only one of the men was able to save himself from falling into the water at the bottom of the shaft and climb into the headings. Of the eight who fell six were either too seriously injured to reach the surface or were trapped under the water by the debris. Two men did escape, one having helped the other extricate himself from the floating timbers.[1]

The previous year had seen the launch of Windsor Steam Coal Co. (1901) Ltd on 2 July. The company's directors were the directors of the predecessor company but with the addition of W.H. Mathias from Porth, originally a successful railway contractor but now also concerned with collieries as a director of the Albion Steam Coal Co. Ltd. The chairman was Fred Insole and Henry Lewis was the managing director. Tom Griffiths was not a director of either Windsor company but he had a ten-year contract as colliery manager with the new firm. The company's bankers were the London & Provincial Bank, whereas Insoles Ltd banked with the National Provincial.

The company's principal assets at the time were its partly completed colliery, its mineral leases and the coal seams won. The mineral leases had been taken out for periods of 99 years from 1 January 1896 for royalties of 8d for large and 4d for small coal with certain rents as listed in Table 8.2. Most of the coal measures were under Lord Windsor's land and could be worked free of wayleave, while the others were expected to be won with a single wayleave.

Table 8.2:
Leases taken out by the Windsor Steam Coal Co. Ltd

Landowner	Acres	Rent 1898/9	Rent 1900/1	Rent 1902/3	Rent there-after	Paid to 30.6.01
		£	£	£	£	£
Col. Lewis Sheddon	272	400	400	400	400	2,200
Lord Windsor	1,425	0	700	1,500	3,000	3,350
Margaret Thomas	28	14	28	42	70	112
Eleanor Powell and others	213	107	213	319	532	848
John Rowlands and the Trustees of Richard Thomas	36	18	36	54	90	144
Total	1,974	539	1,377	2,315	4,092	6,654

Source: PRO, BT 31/6969/49072, Sale agreement between Windsor Steam Coal Co. Ltd. and Windsor Steam Coal Co. (1901) Ltd.

[1] *Western Mail*, 1 June 1902.

The seams won at the time of flotation were:

Name of seam	Proven thickness
2 ft 9 in	3 ft 5 in
4 ft	6 ft 9 in
6 ft	3 ft 6 in
Red Coal	4 ft 7 in
9 ft	5 ft 7 in

The claims in the company's prospectus were alluring. The mineral area was large and virgin, railway rates were low (6.652d to Cardiff) and they would soon have connections to Penarth and Barry. The services of Tom Griffiths as manager for ten years, the appointment of George Insole & Son as sales agents and of Forster Brown & Rees as consulting engineers, each for 21 years, would bring benefits and the money being raised was considered sufficient to provide working capital, pay interest on debentures during development and bring output to 600,000 tons per annum. Eventually one million tons per annum for fifty years were expected from the colliery and predictions were made of profits, on half that quantity, of over £31,000, leaving a net surplus of nearly £14,000 after meeting the company's obligations to the preference shareholders and debenture holders.

The new company's authorised capital was £275,000. There were 15,000 ordinary shares of £10 each, of which only 10,000 were issued as fully paid up shares, providing £100,000 to purchase the assets of the Windsor Steam Coal Co. Ltd; in effect this amounted to an exchange of shares, from one company to the other, by the original promoters and their friends. There were also 12,500 6 per cent cumulative preference shares of £10 each, which were being offered to the public, in this issue, for an initial call of £6 per share. In addition the company issued 12,500 5 per cent debenture bonds of £100 for an initial call of £60 each.

At the statutory meeting of the company on 12 October 1901 the directors reported that 9,516 preference shares had been allotted realising £52,027. This was about £5,000 short of the call money and the issue was undersubscribed by nearly 2,984 shares. The debentures were slightly more successful, realising £61,890 by the date of the directors' report (2 October 1901). The issue should have realised £75,000 and the difference could have been caused by either late payments or insufficient subscribers. The sale price from the previous company was £250,000 to be paid with £100,000 in ordinary shares and £150,000 in cash and it was agreed to accept 2,984 preference shares for £29,840 of the cash. In this way the Insole and Lewis families, unusually for original proprietors, became holders of preference shares as well as ordinaries. By 6 August of the following year when the debenture trust deed was executed the debentures had been fully subscribed and the deed was for the full amount of £125,000. The debentures were important to the directors as the proceeds were to be used to help fund the sinking and opening out of the pits. This was unusual as debentures were normally used to provide additional working capital.[1]

By 1904 the company needed more money, turned to the London & Provincial Bank and, on 22 October 1904, issued another two hundred 5 per cent debentures of £100. They were not offered to the public but were assigned to the bank as security for loans with a second charge on the property. On 27 December 1906 a further seven hundred 5 per cent debentures of £100 were issued and were also assigned to the company's bank. By this stage all calls had been made on the preference shares, which were fully paid up at £10.

By the end of December 1905 more changes had occurred on the board. Henry Lewis had died in the October and T. Forster Brown had been succeeded as a director by his partner, Ithel Treharne Rees. Foster Brown lived in Somerset and may have found the travelling irksome, he was by now an old man and he died two years later on 23 October 1907. Rees lived at Blaenypant, Malpas (Mon.), which was thus closer to the colliery. William North Lewis was company secretary in succession to his brother Alfred, who was by now living in South Africa.[2] On 10 August of the following year William North Lewis was elected to the board and his place as secretary was taken by F. Athol Barrass.

As Forster Brown had predicted, the colliery was not operational until 1903 and was slow to produce the promised levels of output at reasonable cost. The pit was deeper than Cymmer: seams which had been won at around 300 yards in the lower Rhondda were 600 yards deep in the Aber valley. The pit was in an area which had been completely rural in the 1880s and was not close to other mining communities, apart from the Universal Colliery at Senghenydd, which was almost contemporary; this created problems both in manning the pit and in building the new village community at Abertridwr. The work-force, which had been less than 100 during sinking, had reached 250 by April 1903, when the miners formed their own lodge in the East Glamorgan District of the South Wales Miners' Federation[3] and by 1905 the Windsor colliery employed 850

[1] Walters, *South Wales Steam Coal Industry*, p. 129.

[2] *Western Mail*, 25 Oct. 1905.

[3] J.B. Phillips, *Abertridwr through the ages* (Newport, 1991), p. 115.

men. The Insoles had not built a miner's cottage since George Insole's early days at Cymmer, but it was now found expedient to build houses at Abertridwr, as well as encouraging speculative builders and building clubs. By 1906 over five hundred houses had been built and, in the following four years, a further two hundred were built by clubs and private contractors. Nevertheless the population continued to grow and reached 4,500 in 1910, with overcrowding still a problem.[1]

The first years of operation were not profitable, as the costs of sinking and opening out were not recovered in high output and sales. The company was having difficulty with the geological conditions at the coal-face, including faults and roof falls, and had problems with underground haulage. The company's cumulative loss on 30 June 1908 was £30,888 18s, which included that half-year's profits of £11,498 13s 5d. Output reached 368,000 tons in the same year, still well short of the promised 600,000 tons per annum. The interest on the preference shares had been guaranteed for the first two years but had not been paid since 1903, with the result that £37,500 was outstanding by June 1908. As the company owed £135,000 to sundry creditors, had an overdraft in excess of £50,000 and debentures of £125,000, the directors had accumulated debts of over £347,000 for a company with share capital of £225,000, a debt-to-equity ratio approaching 5:3. The company was in need of either a rapid improvement in output and profit or of capital restructuring.

The directors' hopes of an immediately prosperous future received a further setback, when an accident in the north pit shaft later in 1908 stopped winding and disrupted work for a number of months. By 30 June 1909 they had spent £381,657 on acquiring, sinking and developing the colliery, which was over £70,000 more than had been raised by shares and debentures. The company had also increased its cumulative loss to £56,917, including £26,028 in the previous twelve months. In order to remedy their difficult situation the directors decided to go to the market for more funds. They called extraordinary general meetings, on 30 September and 19 October 1909, at which they sought approval to increase the company's share capital. It was agreed to increase the authorised capital to £375,000, by the issue of 10,000 first preference shares. These were to have the first call on the company's assets in the event of liquidation and were to be paid a fixed dividend of 10 per cent per annum, having priority over all other dividends. The 'directors and their friends' subscribed for £30,000 and the remainder were offered first to existing shareholders and debenture holders, who took £25,000, and

[1] Ibid., pp. 121–2.

then to the general public, from whom it was hoped to raise the balance of £40,000. The directors published their prospectus in December 1909, saying that they needed further capital to complete the equipment and development of the collieries and to provide working capital, explaining that the accident in the previous year had drained the company's resources. The prospectus was supported by a letter from T. Forster Brown & Rees and Tom Griffiths explaining how flooding, a major fault and remedial work following the accident in the north pit, had required a heavy outlay, but reassuring prospective shareholders that these 'exceptional mining difficulties' had been surmounted. They also restated their belief that an annual output of 600,000 tons could be achieved. Tom Griffiths had been elected to the board in April that year and his successor as manager was Walter B. Jones. A new agent, Edmund Creed, was appointed at the same time and he wrote a second supporting letter, which was included in the prospectus, assuring potential investors that with less 'slack' working by the men and more capital investment, particularly for compressed air secondary haulage and increased winding capacity, a profitable future was in prospect. The expected investors, however, resisted the generous terms of the offer and the professional blandishments of the mining engineers, who were either directors or employees of the company, and the offer was under-subscribed. Only 1,387 of the new shares were taken, leaving the company £26,130 short of its target. The director's troubles were not eased by the death of Robert Forrest on 5 February 1910. He was not only a director of the company but also the agent for Earl of Plymouth's estate; he had been agent for the earl's St Fagans lands since 1874 but in later years was responsible for the entire estate of some 40,000 acres in England and Wales. He was an influential figure in South Wales, being Deputy Lieutenant of Glamorgan, a J.P. for Cardiff and the county and a Conservative county councillor.[1]

The village continued to grow and in 1911 the Workmen's Hall and Institute was opened. Mabon was invited to perform the ceremony on 9 August and Lord Roberts to open the miniature rifle range. As neither was able to attend the institute was opened by Walter Jones, the general manager, who was a local district councillor and president of the management committee, while Lord Windsor fired the first shot on the range.[2] As well as providing official support for the miners' welfare, the company was also involved in national, coalfield and local labour

---

[1] W. Linnard, "'Lord' Forrest of St Fagans', *Morgannwg*, 33 (1989), 55–68.

[2] Phillips, *Abertridwr*, pp. 142–3.

disputes. At first the chief cause of antagonism was the use of non-union labour but a number of other issues arose, including demarcation disputes and the high rents and poor maintenance in company houses, which came to a head over the company's offer to collect the building clubs' payments from the men at the colliery offices. By this time labour relations in the valley had been further soured by the parsimonious terms of compensation for the bereaved following the huge explosion at the Universal Colliery at Senghenydd on 13 October 1913 which claimed 436 lives.[1]

The company continued to build up liabilities for the future by deferring dividends on preference shares and by the summer of 1912 were eight years in arrears, a contingent liability of £60,000. Creditors were owed £93,000 and £50,900 was owed to the bank. The company's debt was now nearly £330,000 but the paid up share capital was £300,000, producing a small improvement in their debt-to-equity ratio. By now the company's cumulative loss was £95,211, having increased by £14,400 over the previous year. By June 1913 capital investment had reached £405,849, making Windsor an expensive pit. Cymmer, by contrast, was a more extensive colliery, had nearly twice the output but was valued at £263,000 in the balance sheet.

The twelve months ending on 30 June 1913, however, was the year the directors had been waiting for. At the annual general meeting, held in the Park Hotel in August 1913 (Insoles' ordinary general meetings were usually held at the company's offices), they announced a profit of £30,000, the payment of the preference shareholders' dividends and the reduction of sundry creditors to £6,000; they also declared a dividend of 15 per cent on the ordinary capital. The cumulative loss was reduced to £51,000 and the company's debt to some £130,000. It must have seemed, as the chairman congratulated the shareholders on their company's performance, that success had finally been achieved.[2] The meeting took place soon after the annual meeting of Insoles Ltd and Fred Insole was still ill. Once again his place was taken by William North Lewis, who was by now the managing director, and was becoming the pre-eminent figure in the business. Eric Insole had been appointed to the board in May and his election was confirmed at the meeting.

It is probable that Fred Insole was starting to reduce his involvement in the business, possibly because of ill-health but also, more probably, on account of his age; he was 65 in 1912. Although Fred had been

[1] Ibid., pp. 149–57.
[2] PRO, BT 31/6969/49062.

chairman of Insoles Ltd and a director of the Barry Railway he seems to have sought to make his mark as a founder and later the chairman of the Windsor company. He appears to have been more vigorous in business than his brother, Walter, and more adventurous than Henry Lewis. His father, on the other hand, may have considered him to have profligate tendencies, as his will entailed his estate to the next generation and, after Walter's death, he removed Fred as his executor. Nevertheless in 1903 Fred marked his father's memory by the donation of a teak case for the new organ at Llandaff Cathedral; it was decorated with carvings and was made by W. Clarke at a cost of £582 10s. It was later destroyed by enemy action in 1941, although some of the carved angels survived and were used to decorate the cathedral's concrete pulpitum.[1]

Fred was involved in the wider business life of the docks and the social circles of the Cardiff docksmen. He was a member of the chamber of commerce although, unlike his father and brother and the Lewises, did not hold office. He joined the Cardiff coal owners' pitwood cartel in the early 1900s, through which the owners sought to control the price of this important commodity. From 1908 until 1917 he was president of the Cardiff & County Club, where he was a popular member. His father had joined the club when it was founded in 1868 and his brother Walter and two of his sons, Claud and Eric, were members He was also a county magistrate but did not seek political office, although he was probably helpful to the Conservative cause: there is a picture of a Primrose League garden party on the lawns of the Court, as he renamed his father's house.

The refurbishment and extension of the Court was his other main occupation in these years. He was not able to occupy the house until 1905, following the marriage of his stepmother, Marian Insole, to Lieut.-Col. William Aitchison, which was celebrated, like her marriage to James Insole, at St George's, Hanover Square. Fred Insole thereupon took over Ely Court and, between 1906 and 1909, carried out a massive reconstruction costing £16,433. He remodelled a number of the rooms in the fashionable English Renaissance Revival style, took the roof off the tower and made it a castellated turret, and added a large service wing to the east of the house. He was appointed a trustee of his father's estate in 1903, on the death of Arthur Savill, and with the other trustees started to develop the lands of Pencisely Farm for housing. Some houses at the northern end of the west side of Palace Road were built in the early years of the century but the rest of the Palace Road development took place between 1910 and the outbreak of war. Building on the north side

---

[1] Llandaff Society, *Llandaff* (Chalford Press, 1996), pp. 83–6.

of Pencisely Road began in 1913. Pencisely House itself was let from 1905 to P.A. Vyvyan Robinson, who had been succeeded before 1913 by William Jones.[1]

On 13 September 1906 Fred's elder daughter, Jessie, married Richard O'Callaghan from Swords in Co. Dublin, an artillery captain, who later transferred to the Irish Guards. The wedding was a magnificent occasion, with bunting and mottoes decorating the bride's road to the cathedral, which was full to capacity long before the ceremony began at 2.30. The event, reminiscent of her parents' wedding, was extensively reported in the *Western Mail*, which included a long list of presents. Among the bridesmaids was Jessie's younger sister, Violet; she did not marry but became a well known horticulturist and a leading member of the British Iris Society. Fred's sons were at school and university for most of the period. Claud went to Harrow in January 1902 and to Trinity College, Cambridge, in 1907, where he was a member of the university polo team, in 1910, the year he graduated BA (Ordinary), having also passed the Law Special Examination; Eric joined him at Harrow in 1903 and followed him to Trinity in 1908, where he took the Law Special Examination but did not graduate. Like most of Fred's family he was a motoring enthusiast and at the start of the Michaelmas term in 1910 he had his motor car sent by rail to Cambridge. Alan went to Harrow from 1908 to 1913 and then to Trinity but, on the outbreak of war, he joined the army. Claud, to whom the Luxborough estate was entailed, does not seem to have played much part in Cardiff life but Eric joined the business and was 24 in 1913 when he was elected to the boards of Insoles and the Windsor company. Alan is reputed to have become an artist and, after the First World War, he lived in London. By 1914, therefore, it was clear that the Insole family was not going to have a fourth generation of enterprising coal owners. Although they were still the largest shareholders, they were ceding the leading position in the business to others, in particular William North Lewis. The next four years would, of course, bring more profound changes to the family.

[1] *Western Mail Cardiff Directory* (1905 and 1913 eds.).

Chapter 9

Polite Decline

1913–40

The coal owners and miners of South Wales were soon to find that 1913 had been the peak of prosperity for the coalfield and for the port of Cardiff. Along with many others, the Insole businesses never again attained that year's performance. The years that followed were a period of disruption and decline through which, nevertheless, an almost blind optimism about the future prosperity of the coal industry still prevailed. For example, Prof. H.S. Jevons, writing in 1915, made forecasts of coal demand and production for well over 100 years. He did not see any diminution of Britain's annual coal output occurring until the twenty-second century, although he warned that in future 'Englishmen (*sic*) must ... rely less upon exploiting our vast store of natural wealth, and more upon the resources which scientific skill and practical education can place at our disposal'.[1] Similarly, for a number of years from 1926, the *South Wales Coal Annual* included an article previewing the coming year, which usually forecast an early return to prosperous trading.[2] The industry's leaders and workers do not seem to have realised the likelihood or the consequences of coal being no longer the only bulk source of energy.

The coal industry's history between 1914 and 1940 can be divided into four periods. In the First World War, with the emphasis on maximum production, the industry was taken by stages under government control. In the years from 1919 to 1921 the war-time controls remained and the industry enjoyed a brief boom, while its future was the subject of wide debate. In 1921 the industry returned to private hands and a policy of uncontrolled *laissez-faire* largely prevailed until 1929. From 1930 the government gradually re-imposed controls on the industry, which became total in the Second World War and were eventually superseded by nationalisation in 1947.

For much of the First World War the production of some of the principal European coalfields, for example in Belgium, Northern France,

---

[1] H.S. Jevons, *The British Coal Trade* (1915), pp. 10, 752.
[2] *South Wales Coal Annual* (1926–33).

Polish Silesia and Galicia, was lost to the international market.[1] The coal shippers of Cardiff and other ports were hit by the closing of markets and the loss of trade, while the output of the coalfield was affected by reductions in the workforce caused by the number of miners enlisting.[2] Furthermore, the war brought rising prices, food prices having increased by 24 per cent by March 1915 and working class living costs by 20 per cent. The price of coal also increased, raising the suspicion among the miners of profiteering by owners but leading in 1915 to government control of the export trade and of the domestic market. A claim for an increase in pay by the South Wales Miners' Federation in February 1915, to meet the rising cost of living, was ignored by the owners but, when a strike was called in July, the owners appealed to the government, who settled within a week on the men's terms. By 1916 coal distribution was under government control but in South Wales a further dispute threatened to lead to another strike and on 29 November 1916 the government issued the necessary orders, under the Defence of the Realm Act 1914, to take the South Wales coalfield under public control. In early 1917 the government extended the orders to the rest of the industry and for the remainder of the war the government controlled output, distribution, sales policy, recruitment, wages and prices but not profits. Operations and the deployment of men were left in the hands of the owners and the miners' unions.[3]

Table 9.1:
Insoles Ltd: Annual Profits, Ordinary Share Dividends and Profit and Loss Account Balances, 1914–19

Year	Annual Profit £	Dividend %	P. & L. Balance £
1914	23,745	6	16,843
1915	30,692	10	35,535
1916	42,682	20	36,882
1917	54,616	20	51,599
1918	34,344	20	46,343
1919	64,208	20	57,464

Source: PRO, BT 31/31496/51497.

[1] B. Supple, *The History of the British Coal Industry*, IV (Oxford, 1987), p. 45.
[2] Ibid., p. 48.
[3] Ibid., pp. 62–76.

Insoles Ltd remained profitable throughout the war, with bonus dividends on ordinary shares in 1916–19: Table 9.1 shows the annual profits, dividends on ordinary shares and the balance on the company's profit and loss account in the war years.

The company's return to shareholders was thus maintained, in most years the annual profit exceeding the balance carried forward on the profit and loss account. The directors, moreover, had increased their pay to £750 in 1914. The company invested little money in Cymmer during the war, as development work was discouraged by the emphasis on production for the war effort and the company had to manage with a smaller workforce with fewer skilled men. The colliery's value depreciated in the balance sheet, partly as a result of lack of investment and partly through the closure of Upper Cymmer in 1915, leaving Cymmer Old and New and the No 2 Level as the operational mines.[1] Stocks fluctuated between £9,000 and £15,000 in the early years of the war as they had done in the years before but were higher at £19,000 and £18,400 in 1918 and 1919. Cash balances were higher: the figure of £59,981 in 1916 was more than 50 per cent higher than the pre-war maximum and, by 1919, the cash balance was £153,000. Investment in securities also increased, more than doubling from £41,500 in 1914 to £99,000 in 1916 and to £158,000 in 1919.[2]

Table 9.2:
Windsor Steam Coal Co. (1901) Ltd
Annual Profits and Profit and Loss Account Balances, 1914–19

Year	Annual Profit	P. & L. Balance
	£	£
1914	14,243	(37,018)
1915	42,790	3,893
1916	30,000	3,473
1917	26,502	16,482
1918	26,065	35,055
1919	51,438	42,120

Source: *Colliery Guardian*. The profit for 1916 is an estimate, as it was not reported in the *Colliery Guardian*.

The performance of the Windsor colliery continued to improve during the war but the percentage profit was lower than Cymmer's and was probably less than the owners had hoped and expected. The annual

[1] *South Wales Coal Annual* (1916).
[2] PRO, BT 31/31496/51497.

profits and the balance on the company's profit and loss account are
shown in Table 9.2. Of these figures the annual profit for 1915 was the
best that the company had achieved and represented a 10 per cent return
on the capital employed in sinking and equipping the colliery. The profit
in 1919, including the last four and a half months of the war, was the
company's highest ever.

During the war labour relations at Cymmer and Abertridwr seem to
have improved as, apart from national or district confrontations, there
were only two local disputes, one at each pit, which were referred to the
Conciliation Board; both concerned pay rates for working particular
underground districts. In both pits the size of the workforce declined, at
Cymmer from a pre-war peak of 3,115 to 2,123 in 1916 and at the
Windsor from 2,246 to 1,664. (After 1916 the reported numbers were not
changed for a number of years, casting doubt on their reliability for
longer than that year.)[1]

Both Insoles and the Windsor Steam Coal Company did well in the
war, particularly Insoles, which supplied the Royal Navy. Cymmer
colliery was on the Admiralty list of suppliers and, as a listing was only
given to collieries which met the Admiralty's high standards for the
performance of their fuels, it was eagerly sought by every owner in the
steam coal districts. The companies advertised regularly in the *South
Wales Coal Annual* and other publications and from 1915 Insoles added
'on Admiralty List' to their standard advertisement.

At the outbreak of war the young men of the family all volunteered.
Claud Insole joined the Red Cross and served with the British Expedi-
tionary Force, driving his own car.[2] He served at Mons and was
awarded the Mons Star with ribbon. He joined the Welsh Guards on the
formation of the regiment on St David's Day 1915 and was commissioned on 8 April. He was promoted to lieutenant on 16 June 1915 and
was posted to France. He survived the first battle of Loos and a cold
winter in the trenches and was promoted to captain on 2 February 1916.
On 1 July that year he led his company in an assault at Mortaldje in the
Ypres salient and, although wounded, continued to direct his men until
relieved, an action for which he was awarded the Military Cross. He was
evacuated to hospital in England and spent nearly two years recovering
and attending weapons courses before returning to France in 1918. His

---

[1] *South Wales Coal Annual* (1913–16).

[2] A number of motor car owners, generally at this time well-to-do, joined the Red
Cross with their vehicles. The Red Cross Museum at Wonersh near Guildford has the
records of their activities.

brother-in-law, Richard O'Callaghan, served in the Irish Guards. Eric
Insole stayed at home in the Territorial Army, serving as the garrison
intelligence officer at Cardiff and Barry, for which he received a royal
commendation at end of the war. Alan Insole enlisted in the Royal
Artillery in 1914 after one year at Trinity College Cambridge.

On 11 February 1917, after a long illness, Fred Insole died. His
obituary recalls not only his business career but also his pastimes and
interests. In his youth he had held a commission in the Third Artillery
Volunteer Company of the Glamorganshire Volunteers and he was an
excellent shot. He was regarded as an all-round sportsman; he enjoyed
shooting at Ty Fry and Warren Farm (Luxborough was entailed to his
eldest son) and was a member of the Taff & Ely Fishing Association, of
which his father had been a founder. He was a good cricketer and rackets
player, playing for the Cardiff Cricket Club in its early days. He was a
member of the Royal Porthcawl and Southerndown Golf Clubs and was
a supporter of the Cardiff Horse Show. He had also taken an early
interest in the motor car and employed a chauffeur rather than a
coachman; when petrol was in short supply in the war he had to go to
some trouble to engage a new chauffeur who could drive a carriage. His
obituarist also noted that he was a kindly and generous but retiring man.
His funeral at Llandaff Cathedral was arranged by W. Clarke and cost
£76 17s 6d, it was the last funeral that they organised for the family
which used a horse-drawn hearse. The service and interment were
conducted by the Dean and the Archdeacon of Llandaff and, as well as
the family, there was 'a large gathering of county business gentlemen'.[1]

The war brought further sorrow to the family. After his return to
France, Claud was soon back at the front and, during an attack near
Arras on 12 April 1918, he was killed by shellfire while leading a patrol
to capture a prisoner from the German lines. He seems from the records
of the Welsh Guards to have been a well regarded officer with a
reputation for quiet determination. He was tall, slightly stooped, with
sandy hair and a moustache. He was also quietly spoken, with a slight
lisp, apparently unable to shout or say his 'r's'. He left a number of
personal bequests, including his baby Peugeot motor car to his sister
Violet, £25 to Guardsman Jones, who had been his soldier servant since
he was commissioned,[2] and £50 to his commanding officer to distribute
among the men 'in his discretion'. His family erected a memorial in the

---

[1] *Cardiff Daily News*, 12 Feb. 1917.

[2] Soldier servant is the term used in the Household Brigade to describe an officer's
batman.

Cathedral, a figure of an angel holding Claud's sword; the figure and the
sword are lost, as is the nearby stained glass window in the Jasper
Tower, which was Jessy Insole's memorial to her husband. Both
memorials were the work of Felix Joubert. Alan was wounded in the last
year of the war and was invalided out. Eric Insole and Richard O'Callaghan both survived the war and the latter was to play an important part
as a trustee of the Insole Estate.

The immediate aftermath of the war until 1921 was a period of
changing fortunes for the owners and the miners. At first coal was scarce
and at the end of 1918 100,000 miners were quickly demobilised, while
the government used its wartime control of the mines and railways to
improve distribution. The war had also seen a considerable rise in the
cost of living and, as a result, domestic coal prices were subsidised.
There was debate about the future structure of the industry but the
government had no plans. The owners, represented nationally by the
Mining Association of Great Britain (MAGB) were thinking in terms of
a return to pre-war conditions with the continuation or even extension of
the consultative machinery. The Miners' Federation of Great Britain
(MFGB), representing the workers, wanted nationalisation, although there
were those who advocated the syndicalist approach of workers' control.
Both approaches were comprehended by the recently written constitution
of the Labour Party.[1]

In 1919 the MFGB submitted a claim for a 30 per cent increase in
wages. In order to avoid the problems of handling the claim in isolation
from the wider issues, the government set up a commission to deal with
the pay claim urgently and to investigate and make proposals on the
future of the coal industry. It was led by Sir John Sankey,[2] and had
equal representation from the MAGB and MFGB, together with four
independent businessmen. It became a trial of strength, played out in
public and fully reported in the press, which the miners effectively won.
The Commission reported quickly on the pay claim and recommended
a wage settlement, broadly on the miners' terms.

The Commission produced four final reports: the MFGB members
recommended nationalisation of the mines, the MAGB members and
three of the independent businessmen rejected nationalisation but
supported consultation and profit-sharing. The fourth independent

---

[1] Supple, *British Coal Industry*, IV, pp. 117-20.

[2] Sir John, later Viscount Sankey (1866–1948), was called to the bar by the Middle
Temple in 1892 and gained his early experience in South Wales, particularly on workmen's
compensation cases. He took silk in 1909 and became a judge in 1914. He was later to
serve as Lord Chancellor under Ramsey MacDonald, 1929–35 *(DNB)*.

member, Sir Arthur Duckham, proposed regional amalgamations of colliery companies with workers on their boards, profit limitation and government oversight of the industry. Sir John Sankey recommended nationalisation to end 'the present atmosphere of distrust and recrimination'. All four reports recommended nationalisation of the mineral royalties, on the ground that 'the fragmentation of private ownership and decision making led to inefficiency in the use of a natural resource'. The government, however, dithered and the owners improved their presentation, under the leadership of Evan Williams of the Monmouthshire & South Wales Coal Owners' Association, while, throughout the summer of 1919, there was less public support for nationalisation, particularly among the miners' allies, the railway and transport workers.

On 18 August Lloyd George gave the government's response to the Sankey Commission. There was to be nationalisation of royalties but no nationalisation of the collieries; the government also proposed regional amalgamations along Duckham's lines, with workers on higher level boards but with government sponsorship, not oversight, and without profit limitation. The miners rejected these proposals and demanded nationalisation, although they did not support their demand by calling strikes.[1] The Mining Industry Act of 1920, which was Parliament's formal response to the Sankey Commission, set up the Mines Department in the Board of Trade and extended control until 31 August 1921. The Act established the Miners' Welfare Fund financed by a levy of 1d per ton of output and set up consultative committees which, however, never met as both sides refused to co-operate.[2]

Since the war the coal trade had been recovering and prices had risen even faster than in the war; average annual prices per ton of large steam coal f.o.b. at Cardiff increased from 16s 5d in 1913, to 30s 9d in 1918, 41s 1d in 1919 and to 61s 5d in 1920.[3] The miners demanded reductions in the prices of domestic coal and increases in wages to compensate for their increased cost of living. Output, however, was falling and the government made any offer contingent upon the achievement of a given level of output, 'the datum line'. The miners refused to accept this condition and called a strike which was quickly resolved. The miners were awarded an increase tied to output and the export price of coal. In 1921 this fell from over £3 to 39s 5d per ton at Cardiff and to 26s 2d in the following year. The miners had won a battle but the owners had won

---

[1] Supple, *British Coal Industry*, IV, pp. 123–35.

[2] Ibid., p. 145.

[3] See Appendix B.

the war.[1]

On 28 January 1921 the government announced that it would end its control of the coal industry and return the collieries to the coal owners on 31 March of that year. The coal owners set out their terms, which include a longer working day, lower pay and the termination of all district contracts. The miners called a strike which lasted until the end of June but failed to achieve any change; they returned to work on the owners' terms.

The return of *laissez-faire* coincided with a period of recession in the coal industry, only slightly relieved by a brief recovery, following the French occupation of the Ruhr in January 1923 and an American pit strike.[2] The recession was caused by the replacement of coal by oil in world shipping; greater efficiencies in fuel technology among the major coal users (iron and steel, railways, gas, electricity); the decline of world trade, formerly carried in British ships; German war reparations providing substitutes in British markets; the growth of rivals, such as Poland, Germany and the US; declining relative productivity (particularly in South Wales which had low levels of mechanisation); the resumption of production in the war-affected areas and excess colliery capacity. The difficulties, in the export trade in particular, were aggravated by the pound sterling's return to the gold standard in 1924.

The attitudes of owners and miners remained firmly entrenched in hostile confrontation, culminating in the General Strike and the lock-out of 1926. This long dispute led to the loss of markets, many of which were never recovered and a new threat to the hegemony of the MFGB in the creation, with the owners' backing, of new 'non-political' unions, formed by those miners who had returned to work during the lock-out.

The industry's decline continued; in 1922 Cardiff prices per ton had fallen by a third in one year to 26s 2d per ton, they rallied to 28s in 1923, fell back to 27s 3d in 1924 and declined thereafter to 14s 8d in 1929, the year of the Wall Street crash and the onset of the depression.[3] Nevertheless the owners and their supporters remained optimistic and even cavalier about the future, as contemporary articles in the *South Wales Coal Annual* and the companies' annual reports show. By 1928, a particularly difficult year with reduced output and prices, the optimism of most of the owners was diluted, as they realised that wage cuts and longer hours had not arrested the industry's decline. The owners in the

---

[1] Supple, *British Coal Industry*, IV, p. 154.

[2] Ibid., p. 216.

[3] Williams, *Welsh Historical Statistics*, I, p. 337.

South Wales coalfield agreed to co-operate in sales and formed the South
Wales Coal Marketing Association.

As shippers of steam coal with dependence on the export trade, the
Insole businesses had to weather these storms. France and Italy, for
example, two countries receiving German coal as war reparations, were
among their principal markets. At the end of the war, Fred Insole having
died in 1917, the partnership of George Insole & Son was reconstituted
and a new deed was drawn up in 1919, with Eric Insole, William North
Lewis and Marian Aitchison as the partners.

The directors of Insoles Ltd were Eric Insole, William North Lewis,
who was chairman and managing director, Tom Griffiths and Herbert
Homfray. The Insole and Lewis family holdings in the company
amounted to £107,950 out of a total of £180,000. Tom Griffiths held 510
£1 shares and Herbert Homfray 360; the remaining £71,180 were held
by about 300 preference and some 660 ordinary shareholders. In 1920
they capitalised a large part of their £153,000 cash balance and rewarded
themselves and their ordinary shareholders with a 2 for 3 scrip issue.
This increased the company's nominal capital by £120,000 to £300,000
and brought the value of company's equity closer to that of its assets.[1]

In 1921 Insoles Ltd dropped the list of customers which had been a
feature of their advertisements, a possible portent of the loss of business
which lay ahead. Nevertheless, profits and the dividend on ordinary
shares were maintained until 1924, although losses were recorded for the
remaining years to 1929, when the cumulative loss was £106,000 (Table
9.3). The company did not, however, default on the payment of the
annual dividend on its 6 per cent preference shares in these years.

Table 9.3:
*Insoles Ltd: Annual Profits and Losses
and Ordinary Dividends, 1920–9*

Year	Profit (Loss)	Dividend	Year	Profit (Loss)
1920	£57,418	20%	1925	(£37,346)
1921	£43,124	10%	1926	(£3,303)
1922	£78,594	20%	1927	(£39,295)
1923	£66,818	20%	1928	(£16,600)
1924	£33,953	10%	1929	(£31,781)

Source: Colliery Guardian

[1] *Colliery Guardian*, 4 June 1920.

At the end of the war the Windsor directors were Eric Insole, William North Lewis, Tom Griffiths and William Mathias, with North Lewis as chairman and managing director. Mathias died on 8 May 1922 and his place was taken by George Walter Insole Burness, the son of James Insole's daughter, who was a coal merchant, living at Farnham in Surrey. The company had made investments in the Treforest Electrical Consumers Co. Ltd and the South Wales Electrical Power Distribution Co. Ltd, as well as £20,000 in 5 per cent War Loan. These were to provide funds to redeem the company's debentures, although at that time electricity companies might have been considered rather speculative for such security. In 1918 they had raised a mortgage of £15,000 on 150 of the company's twelve-ton railway wagons, from the London Provincial & South Western Bank Ltd. Of these wagons, 100 had been built by the Gloucester Railway Carriage & Wagon Co. Ltd in 1908 and 50 by the Cambrian Wagon Co. Ltd of Cardiff. At an extraordinary general meeting on 3 May 1920 the shareholders agreed to divide the company's £10 shares into 10 of £1 each, following a similar move by Insoles Ltd, to promote the easier purchase of their shares.

In the year ending 30 June 1920 the company made a profit of £50,767, only £671 short of the previous year's record, but in 1921 the profit fell to £35,724 and in the following year the company made a loss of £24,059, its cumulative balance on the profit and loss account being a loss of £17,484. In spite of a profit in 1923 of £11,985 the loss in 1924 of £33,617 pushed the cumulative loss to £39,116. At the same time the company took out a further mortgage to supplement the security for the company's original debentures. Two years of arrears on the 10 per cent first preference shares and four years on the 6 per cent preference shares added £59,991 to the company's liabilities. Its entire capital of nearly £300,000 and its debentures of £120,000 had been spent on sinking and developing the colliery, although development had probably been curtailed in the war. The colliery now needed more investment, which would have required further borrowing or a new share issue, neither of which was likely to have been successful. The directors, therefore, recommended that the company seek voluntary liquidation. Accordingly, at an extraordinary general meeting on 5 June 1925 it was agreed that the colliery be sold to Powell Duffryn for £250,000 and the company wound up. The directors announced that they hoped that the sale proceeds would be sufficient to repay the debentures of £125,000 and other debts and creditors and leave some money for the holders of the 10 per cent first preference shares, whose nominal value was £74,950. The holders of the 120,000 6 per cent preference shares and the 100,000 ordinary shares, mostly the Insoles, Lewises and their associates, would receive nothing.[1] The sale represented a revaluation of the colliery from over £400,000 in the company's books. It had been an expensive venture for the Insoles and Lewises, they not only lost nearly all their capital invested in the project but the company had never paid a dividend on its ordinary shares, the bulk of which they held. Powell Duffryn, however, was able to revive the colliery's fortunes and by 1932 it was showing an operating profit.[2] The Windsor colliery was in Powell Duffryn's hands at nationalisation and it remained in production for a further thirty years; from 1976 its seams were worked from the Nantgarw Colliery in the Taff Valley and it finally closed in 1987. In 1997 the site was being reclaimed for industrial development by the Welsh Development Agency.

The recession in the coal industry affected the Insoles' other activities. The Luxborough Estate had been entailed by James Insole in his will to Claud and thence in tail male. In 1922 the Insole trustees decided to sell the estate, probably to find a more profitable, secure and less burdensome investment. The sale was effected that year and, by Christmas, the estate was in the hands of Lt-Col. Sir Charles Henry Malet Bt DSO OBE JP. The estate has been considerably reduced but it is still owned by the Malet family and is highly regarded as a sporting estate.

Although the Insole family's fortunes were somewhat in decline, William North Lewis continued to prosper, in spite of his losses in the Windsor colliery. His standing in the coal industry, based on nearly forty years experience, made him one of its leading authorities, his views carrying exceptional weight for the head of what was, by that time, one of the smaller firms in the coal trade. He was also a director of the Treforest Electrical Consumers' Co. Ltd, the Monmouthshire and South Wales Employers' Mutual Indemnity Society and of the Taff Vale Railway until it was absorbed by the Great Western in 1923. He had been president of the Cardiff Chamber of Commerce in 1912, of which he had been a member since 1893 and was also a member of the executive council of the Association of British Chambers of Commerce and of the International Chamber of Commerce, whose inaugural meeting he attended in Paris in 1920, as one of the representatives of the Mining Association of Great Britain. He was a member of the South Wales and Monmouthshire Coal Freighters' Association and had been chairman in 1911. He had also been one of the promoters of the South Wales and Monmouthshire School of Mines and was a member of the board of

---

[1] PRO, BT 31/6969/49062; *Western Mail*, 12 June and 18 Dec. 1925.

[2] Powell Duffryn Ltd, *A Short Survey of the Organisation, Growth and Development of Powell Duffryn Ltd* (Cardiff, 1946), pp. 2–5.

management. Outside the coal trade, he was a governor of the King
Edward VII Hospital, now the Cardiff Royal Infirmary, a founder of the
Welsh Hospital at Netley and, during the war, had been a member of
many committees. It may be indicative of North Lewis's standing in the
coal industry that in 1919, when the Prince of Wales visited South
Wales, he came to Cymmer colliery where he was welcomed by North
Lewis and, having been taken underground, allowed a newly worked
district to be named after him.

Tom Griffiths was also present for the royal visit but he was by this
time one of the veterans of the company and on 24 January 1924 he
retired at the age of 74. As one who had started work as a door boy, he
had come a long way. By the time of his retirement he was a director of
Insoles Ltd and the Windsor Steam Coal Co. Ltd, a member of the
Conciliation Board, a past president of the South Wales Coal Owners'
Association and a life member of the South Wales Institute of Engineers.
He was particularly well known, trusted and admired for his work in
colliery rescues and disaster explorations; he was at the Pentre disaster
in 1871 and, after becoming manager at Cymmer, led the following
rescues (the number of men who had been killed is shown in brackets):

1879	Dinas	(3)	1892	Great Western	(58)
1880	Naval, Penygraig	(96)	1894	Albion, Cilfynydd	(276)
1883	Gelli	(4)	1896	Tylorstown	(57)
1885	Naval	(14)	1899	Llest, Garw	(19)
1885	Mardy	(81)	1901	Senghenydd	(82)
1887	Wattstown/Ynyshir	(37)	1905	Clydach Vale	(31)
1892	Park Slip	(110)	1905	Wattstown	(0)

In 1906 he retired from rescue work and was presented with a full-
length portrait and a silver plate for his role in rescues and his public
service by 'all classes' in the Rhondda Valleys. He was a Liberal
member of the Rhondda Local Board and its successor, the urban district
council, of which he was the second chairman in 1891–2. He was also
a JP, known for his 'kindness on the bench', and a governor of the
University of Wales.

Griffiths was Welsh speaking and his early experience underground
had helped him to gain the confidence of the men, being known for his
fairness, understanding and sound judgement. According to Col. Watts
Morgan MP DSO he was once asked to become the miners' agent. He
retired to West Cross on the Gower where he died three years later on
11 February 1927. His funeral, conducted by the Congregational minister

at the cemetery, was attended by Eric Insole and Arthur North Lewis.[1] He was succeeded by William B. Davies, the son of a county alderman from Pentre, who had been his deputy. Before coming to Cymmer Davies had a varied industrial career and had qualified as a civil, electrical and mining engineer. Davies's three brothers were a Cardiff doctor, a Harley Street specialist and a major in the Territorial Army, a very different background from both of his predecessors, Jabez Thomas and Tom Griffiths.

By 1930 it was clear, even to many of the coal owners themselves, that unregulated competition in a free market was enfeebling if not destroying the industry, particularly as other countries and their coal industries were not so encumbered. The results for the owners were the loss of markets, declining sales, lower or non-existent profits and no dividends for ordinary shareholders: Cambrian Collieries paid none from 1921 until taken over in 1928, Ebbw Vale Steel, Iron & Coal Co. none from 1921 and Powell Duffryn none between 1927 and 1932. Of the large South Wales companies only the Ocean Coal & Wilsons Co. Ltd managed to maintain a dividend in most years (it paid no dividend in 1928, 1932 and 1935). In South Wales there was widespread restructuring in the 1920s, as small businesses were taken over by combines, leaving only Powell Duffryn and the smaller Ocean Coal & Wilsons Co. Ltd as the two dominant coal owners in the eastern areas of the coalfield. If matters were bad for the owners, they were far worse for the industry's workers, who suffered low pay, short-time working, unemployment and poverty. Conditions were particularly bad in the South Wales coalfield, which was so dependent on the export trade and had few alternative industries.

In 1930 the Labour government introduced a new bill to regulate the coal market. Part I of the Coal Mines Act 1930 compelled the industry to set up schemes, of which membership was compulsory, run by central and district committees, to regulate output and to set minimum prices in the districts. As these schemes required 85 per cent support from the owners for their implementation, Part I was not at first a success but in 1934 the administration was tightened and more compulsion was introduced. The scheme mainly affected collieries serving the home market but was welcomed by some South Wales owners including William North Lewis. Part II of the Act sought to establish a Coal Mines Commission, to promote district amalgamations, but this proved

---

[1] *South Wales Daily News,* 25 Jan. 1924, 13 Feb. 1927; *Colliery Guardian,* 18 Feb. 1927.

powerless in the face of opposition from the owners. In 1938 it was renamed the Coal Commission with powers to nationalize royalties and compel firms to amalgamate. Its implementation was delayed until 1940 and royalties were eventually taken into public ownership in 1942.[1]

In the early thirties, following the crash of 1929, the depression deepened, unemployment increased and the spread of poverty in the South Wales Valleys went from bad to worse. For those in work wages were low and, although prices were also falling, were both insufficient to maintain the miners' former standard of living and were often reduced by short-time working. In the collieries the South Wales Miners' Federation was faced not only by the owners, who continued to seek cost reductions, while waiting for something to turn up in the coal trade, but also by the 'non-political' South Wales Miners' Industrial Union which had been formed, with the owners support and assistance, by miners who returned to work in the 1926 lock-out. Even the departure from the gold standard in 1931 did not achieve any improvement in the export trade, as it coincided with a further depression in Europe. With unemployment endemic in the Valleys, the miners and their families faced further privations, poverty, hunger, disease and the realisation that little was being done to improve their situation. Even when, in the mid-1930s, a recovery had begun in the more prosperous parts of Britain it had little effect in the Rhondda.

Cymmer was by now an old pit and Insoles, one of the last firms in the Rhondda to be independent of the combines, lacked the resources or the impetus to modernise it. By 30 June 1931 its cumulative losses were £153,251 and, although it made modest profits in 1932 and 1933, in 1934 it returned to losses, as Table 9.4 shows.

From 1933 to 1938 the company's ordinary general meetings were fully reported in the *Western Mail*, usually with a picture of William North Lewis, the chairman and managing director. On 9 September 1933 North Lewis was moderately optimistic. The company had achieved its best results since 1924 in spite of the depressed state of coalfield and the fact that there had been many days when the colliery was not worked on account of the want of trade. North Lewis even announced investment in a new boiler and a plant to dry clean small coal, the first of its kind in the coalfield. He also gave notice of the directors' plans for capital reconstruction: they proposed to reduce the value of ordinary shares and to liquidate the outstanding debt of £32,400 on the preference shares with cash and a partial issue of ordinary shares.

---

[1] Supple, *British Coal Industry*, pp. 296–7.

Table 9.4
*Insoles Ltd: Annual Profits and Losses
and Profit & Loss Account Balances, 1930–8*

Year	Profit (Loss)	Balance
1930	(£42,045)	(£148,306)
1931	(£4,944)	(£153,251)
1932	£7,097	(£140,918)
1933	£21,435	(£119,483)
1934	£7,466	(£112,017)
1935	(£14,735)	(£126,752)
1936	(£25,122)	(£62,988)
1937	(£17,638)	(£80,626)
1938	£2,643	(£77,982)

Sources: 1930–6, *Colliery Guardian*; 1937–8, CCL, Periodicals, Insoles,
Directors' Reports and Accounts.

North Lewis also supported Part 1 of the Mines Act 1930, saying that Insoles had 'had bitter experience of unregulated competition under conditions of declining demand'. He believed that the industry would need regulation until trade returned and wondered if bankers would support an industry 'frittering away its resources in cut-throat competition'. He said that Great Britain as a whole and South Wales in particular had held their share of world trade, although 2,000,000 tons of merchant shipping was laid up and the coaling depot trade had slumped. Railways in Argentina and others were less busy, access to the main markets of France, Germany, Belgium and Spain was rationed but the Italian trade was holding up.[1]

By early 1934 North Lewis saw some hopeful signs. At a dinner on 20 January 1934, when he and his wife were entertained by the colliery officials and a number of the workforce to mark his fifty years with the business, he pointed out that they had been bunkering steamers which had been laid up for a long time; he had expectations from government-led bilateral trade agreements, e.g. with Argentina; and he once again defended the operation of Part 1 of the 1930 Mines Act and the imposed quotas. William Davies, the colliery manager, who was by now a JP, presided at the dinner and he also was optimistic about the Rhondda's future, citing its extensive steam coal reserves. North Lewis was presented with a pair of George III salt cellars, a pair of silver entrée

---

[1] *Western Mail*, 8 Sept. 1933.

dishes and an electric hotplate, while his wife received a jewel case. None of the Insole family nor his other fellow directors were present at the dinner.

A few months later his statement at the 1934 ordinary general meeting was less positive. He attacked James Griffiths, the leader of the South Wales Miners' Federation (and later a Cabinet minister and first Secretary of State for Wales), for making threats of strike action in support of a wage claim, on the grounds that 'the men always lose'. He also censured the Coal Mines Industrial Board (set up by Coal Mines Act 1930) because it was unrepresentative of the industry, since both the MAGB and the MFGB had decided not to recognise it. He referred disparagingly to the experience of national agreements in 1921–6. The capital restructuring, proposed at the previous year's general meeting, had been deferred for two years.[1]

In 1935 North Lewis once again reported a loss, for which he blamed underground conditions and a pay increase, which added £4,200 to the wages bill. The capital restructuring would now have to wait for better trading results and the outlook was further clouded by the loss of much Italian trade through difficulties in getting payment. Nevertheless the company was still exploring new seams and had hopes for the future.[2]

In 1936, facing a cumulative trading loss of £151,873, the directors decided to deduct from the figure the general reserve of £71,827 and a sum of £17,058, the profit from the sale of investments. At the general meeting North Lewis reported the death of George Walter Burness, at his home near King's Lynn, in December 1935 and the death of Athol Barrass, the company secretary, a faithful servant of the company for over forty years.[3]

In 1937 North Lewis reported increased demand and a smaller loss aggravated by an explosion in early June. He regretted the loss of lives but prompt rescue efforts had fortunately saved many more. Profit in South Wales generally had reduced from 3½d per ton to 2d, partly from a wage increase granted in advance of any improvement in trade. He thought that the District Control Board should prevent sudden drops in prices.[4]

Earlier in the year on 15 January 1937 Marian Aitchison, James Insole's widow, died at her home in Paddington. She was a partner in

[1] *Western Mail*, 8 Sept. 1934.

[2] Ibid., 7 Sept. 1935.

[3] Ibid., 26 Aug. 1936.

[4] Ibid., 4 Sept. 1937.

George Insole & Son and a major shareholder in Insoles Ltd. She had made her will as a widow in 1931 when she was living in Mayfair. Her daughter, Lylie Evelyn, son-in-law, John Walter Beresford Merewether,[1] and her solicitor, Lawrence Gardner Williams, who was also a director of Insoles Ltd, were her executors and her daughter and granddaughter, Dorothy Lylie Corbyn, were the main beneficiaries. Under the terms of the deed of partnership dated 14 August 1919 between herself, Eric Insole and William North Lewis, she appointed Herbert Homfray to succeed her. His name, however, does not appear on some surviving stationery on which hers has been crossed out.

At what was to be the company's last ordinary general meeting, on 3 September 1938, North Lewis reported an improvement in the accounts of £20,000, leaving a small profit of £2,643 but the position was far from satisfactory. The colliery had had more underground trouble, including a fault in a previously good seam, and efforts to increase production in other areas had been slow to bring results. Recovery, he believed, depended on the settlement of troubles in Europe and the Far East but the system of control would prevent 'unnecessary' price falls. The directors were not happy with the introduction of paid holidays, since in their experience the men had taken extra days unpaid leave.[2]

The company, however, did not survive for long. Early in 1939 the decision was taken to close the colliery and the last tram was raised in March. On 30 March 1939 a letter was sent from the secretary of Insoles Ltd resigning from the South Wales Coal Owners' Association with effect from 30 June 1939 as a result of closing of the colliery.[3] Cymmer colliery had been operational for over a hundred years and its usefulness was not at an end; it was sold to Powell Duffryn, who partially sealed the shafts to the depth of the Rhondda No 3 seam and used the pit to minimise the water flows and thus assist in draining the Lewis Merthyr colliery at Trehafod. Cymmer thus stayed open until Lewis Merthyr was itself closed in 1983, to be transformed into the Rhondda Heritage Park. The Cymmer site was eventually released by British Coal for industrial development and now contains a Co-op supermarket. The Abergorci colliery, which the Insoles sold in 1873, in order to concentrate on finding the steam coal at Cymmer, finally closed in 1967 and is now

---

[1] Lylie had previously been married to a Mr Corbyn and they had had a daughter. They were beneficiaries of her marriage settlement which had been made while her mother was married to James Insole.

[2] *Western Mail*, 3 Sept. 1938.

[3] NLW, Coal Owners D/179, Insoles Ltd.

open grass and scrubland.

The family as well as the business experienced changes of fortune in the 1930s. In the summer of 1932 Fred's younger daughter Violet, a well known horticulturist, contracted peritonitis for which she underwent an operation for the removal of her appendix. Unfortunately complications followed and she died on 1 July. She was a member of the British Iris Society and was a breeder as well as a successful exhibitor. She presented a trophy which is still awarded at the society's annual show. She was president of the South Wales Spring Flower and Daffodil Society at which she won prizes for her rock plants. She maintained a rock garden and iris garden at the Court, which was well-known among gardeners, who often came to visit. She also suffered from heart problems, which may have caused concern earlier in the year, as on 28 January she made what appears to have been a hurried hand-written will on a standard stationer's form. She left the bulk of her property to her sister's children, Bryan, who had followed his father into the Irish Guards and Maureen O'Callaghan. She ended her will, 'No one to wear mourning or go to the funeral'. Her wishes were not carried out, although her funeral was less elaborate than her father's and W. Clarke supplied a motor hearse and one car.

The family, however, was moving away. Alan Insole had lived in London since the war and the Burness and O'Callaghan cousins were living in East Anglia and the Home Counties. Lena Insole, Julia's daughter, had died in 1928, leaving bequests to a far-flung number of relations and friends. So, after Violet's death, only Fred Insole's widow, Jessy, and her son, Eric, were still living in Cardiff; they occupied the Court, while the farm at Ty Fry was run by a manager, as in James Insole's day. They had made an agreement in 1924 with the trustees of James Insole's estate and the other members of the family to transfer the Court from James Insole's trustees to those of Fred Insole, i.e. themselves, and, after the passing of the Settled Land Act 1925, they obtained possession of the Court.

In 1931 Cardiff Corporation served a compulsory purchase order on them to acquire some of the Court's land for the construction of Western Avenue. The Insoles thereupon, as the law allowed, required the council to purchase the entire property. After protracted and not altogether good tempered negotiation,[1] it was agreed that Jessy and Eric would sell the

---

[1] The Insoles' solicitors wrote to the Corporation in Nov. 1931, asking that Violet Insole be allowed to remove her rock plant and iris collection, saying that they required her personal and specialist attention and suggesting that it was most unlikely that 'in the present circumstances your council could indulge in such an expensive hobby'.

Court for £26,250 and would be allowed to remain in occupation for two years from completion as tenants of the corporation for a peppercorn rent. The agreement was signed on 23 December 1931 with completion set for 11 January 1932, although the conveyance was not signed until 13 February. The corporation retained the house and gardens but released the parkland for low-density development with typical 1930s detached and semi-detached suburban houses; the development was completed by the outbreak of war.

The trustees of James Insole's estate, meanwhile, had been developing the Pencisely House land for housing. Building on the north side of Pencisely Road continued throughout the first World War and by 1920 they had leased fifteen building plots. St Michael's Road, Caewal Road and Chargot Road were developed during the 1920s and by 1934, in addition to the houses in Palace Road, the estate consisted of 141 houses, producing total annual ground rents of £1,180 3s. In the same year the last crop of hay was mown on the land to the south of Pencisely Road and the area was developed, between then and the outbreak of war, by the trustees of James Insole's estate, similarly to the area surrounding the Court. On a couple of occasions Alan Insole and the trustees borrowed money on the security of the estate.

Jessy Insole moved to London, where she died at her home, 2 Mansfield Street, Marylebone, on 9 September 1938, at the age of 85. She was buried at Llandaff on 13 September and her funeral was well attended, although more modest than Violet's, costing under £25. The mourners were led by her son Alan, as his elder brother Eric was unable to come because of illness. Eric, however, was the sole beneficiary of her will, both by bequest and appointment, and Alan was not mentioned.

Eric Insole moved to the Manor House, Stoke Charity (Hants.), where he lived the life of a country gentleman. He was a keen fisherman and, like his father, a member of the Cardiff & County Club. He also owned Porthkemys Farm in the parish of Llanfair Discoed and the Bridge Inn with nine acres of land at Kemys Commander, both in Monmouthshire. These properties included a riverside cottage, known as Chain Bridge, which he kept for fishing trips. In the early 1920s he had had extensive works carried out on the cottage and the river bank, costing some £800. Eric never married and does not seem to have played a very active part in the business, although he kept his directorships. He died on 20 January 1946 at the Manor House at the age of 57. He seems to have had minor health problems throughout his life. He did not take his degree at Cambridge and served on garrison duties throughout the First World War. His obituary states that he was an extensive traveller and records that he accompanied Lord Baden Powell, as a secretary, on a trip round the world.[1] He was buried at St Michael's parish church in Stoke Charity. In his will, having made a number of personal bequests, he required his properties to be sold and the proceeds held in trust for the Gentlefolks Help Friends of the Poor, the Guild of Aid for Gentlepeople and the Distressed Gentlefolks' Aid Association.

After Eric's death the trustees sold the various Insole properties. Of those devised or entailed in the wills of James and Fred Insole, the Luxborough Estate had been sold in 1922, Windsor colliery in 1925, The Court in 1932, Cymmer colliery in 1940 and the Bute Docks property soon after. They now sold the Pencisely property to the General Life Insurance Society for £59,311 17s and also disposed of 82 terraced houses in Grangetown and 78 in Canton.

Eric's brother, Alan, was not present at the funeral, nor was he mentioned in his brother's will. He had lived at various addresses in London and was, for eleven years from 1922, a Fellow of the Zoological Society of London. In the late 1950s went to live in South Africa where he died, at Durban on 2 August 1964, leaving a widow but no children. Under his power of appointment he left his widow an annuity to be paid from the investments representing the sale of the Luxborough Estate and left all his property in England to his niece, Maureen Priest, the daughter of Richard and Jessie O'Callaghan, on trust to be divided between her two sons.

After Eric's death the sole survivor of the leading members of the Insole businesses was William North Lewis, who, when the company went into liquidation, had been chairman and managing director for over twenty years. He was over 70 years old when Insoles was wound up and the partnership of George Insole & Son dissolved and he seems to have taken the opportunity to retire, as he had resigned from the Chamber of Commerce and from his associated national and international commitments in 1939.[2] He had, over the years since the First World War, extended his holdings at The Orchard in Lisvane, by further acquisitions of neighbouring land and a farm, to make a small country estate. Here he lived in as much style as the war allowed until his death on 6 May 1947 after which his Lisvane properties were sold.[3] He was buried at Llanishen parish church, as was his widow, Rosa, who died aged 91 on 20 September 1963.

[1] *Western Mail*, 22 Jan. 1946.

[2] GRO, D/D COM/C 1–7.

[3] P. Riden and K. Edwards, *Families and Farms in Lisvane, 1850–1950* (Cardiff, 1993), p. 137.

By the time North Lewis died, the coal industry had been nationalised and was to begin, in spite of pit closures and the reduction in the size of the workforce, a 40-year renaissance as a supplier of industrial and domestic fuel and, above all, as the basis of a national electricity service, which would probably have given the coal owners of the inter-war years some food for thought.

Little trace now remains of the Insoles. Their pits have all closed and their offices in the docks have been demolished. Apart from headstones and title deeds their name survives in a Cardiff public house, some streets in Llandaff and in their old house now named Insole Court. Some descendants survive, including a branch of the family in South Africa.

Chapter 10

Conclusions and Assessments

Although in later years, the Insoles' income was derived from a variety of investments, including land, railways, docks and other industries, the foundation of their fortune was the expanding South Wales coal trade. At the beginning of the nineteenth century most coal mined in South Wales was used by the metal industries and the sale coal trade was modest by comparison; coal was sold in much the same way as agricultural products, taken to local markets or to merchants at the ports. During the century, however, coal quickly overtook wood and charcoal, as well as water, wind and animal power, to become the dominant source of energy and a major industry in its own right and, by 1914, South Wales had become the most productive coalfield in the United Kingdom achieving and benefiting from success in all markets, particularly the steam coal trade. After the First World War the region's dependence on a single product made it vulnerable to the vicissitudes of a volatile market and aggravated the effects of falling demand and economic depression.

The spectacular success of the South Wales coal trade was caused by both the expansion of existing markets and the establishment of new market sectors during the nineteenth century. Demand was increased by the growth of the principal industries of the Industrial Revolution, metals, textiles and engineering, and by the increased population, which led to the growth of towns and the expansion of housing. New markets and products added further opportunities. When George Insole came to Cardiff the use of steam ships was confined to estuaries and coastal waters but by the outbreak of the First World War steam had superseded sail in almost all classes of shipping. The steam coals of South Wales found a ready market in the shipping lines and navies of the world. The railways also brought a number of new opportunities for the use of coal, including fuel for the locomotives, power for the factories and workshops of the railway companies and energy for the manufacture of the iron, and later steel, rails of the permanent way. Rails in particular not only proved a boon to the ironmasters of South Wales but also helped to keep them out of the sale coal trade. Thus the market was more open to the smaller sale coal businesses and to new entrants to both colliery ownership and the coal trade like the Insoles. Coal also found new markets in gas production and, by the end of the century, electricity generation. The

170

demand for coal, however, was so great that the coal owners invested neither time nor money, to any great extent, in either new products or diversification. The new products which they did develop were, in the main, only modest diversifications, such as the manufacture of patent fuel and the production of coke. Some companies, including Powell Duffryn, later moved into electricity generation but the industry did not develop an associated chemical industry, as the oil industry was to do in the twentieth century. The coal owners concentrated on their raw but lucrative product, without seeming to give much thought to the possibility of detrimental change occurring and, when it did, they waited for something to turn up.

The Insoles were active participants in the development of the coal trade. No sooner had George Insole set up his yard alongside the canal basin in Cardiff than he was looking for ways of selling directly to customers in large orders rather than to ships' masters in smaller cargoes. He travelled to the ports of south west England and visited Irish coastal towns from Limerick to Belfast. He engaged in regular correspondence with his customers, both to retain their loyalty and to look for new uses and markets for coal. When he started to develop sales of steam coal from the Cynon Valley, he prepared promotional letters in order to advertise the product to potential customers at home and abroad. His successors in the 1880s compiled a book giving a history of the company, pictures of the colliery and lists of customers and agents, as well as detailed analysis of Cymmer steam coal, in order to advertise its qualities and promote its sale. The Insoles also sold through overseas agents and established depots around the world. They did not have as many depots as those coal traders who had their own shipping lines but they remained at the centre of the Cardiff coal trade until the end. Even as late as the 1930s, William North Lewis was a major figure in the industry and was using the company's annual meeting to support the government's efforts to improve the marketing and to control the production of coal.

As colliery proprietors, the Insoles seem to have been careful in choosing their pits and levels and, until the sinking of the Windsor Colliery, circumspect about committing their resources to more than one site. George Insole's first colliery lease at Maesmawr was a safe choice. Its coal had a good reputation, it had been one of the leading sale coal collieries using the Glamorganshire Canal, and it had ceased production because of the financial difficulties of the proprietor rather than the exhaustion of its coal seams. His bid for Maesbach, however, was probably a more opportunist venture. The Insoles' move to Cymmer, in the sparsely populated and largely unspoilt Rhondda Valley, owed much to the success of Walter Coffin and the No 3 Rhondda seam which he had won at Dinas. It was, nevertheless, a speculative venture as the No 3 seam had not been proved at Cymmer, where only the No 2 Rhondda had been won. Although George Insole & Son had been shipping steam coal for 30 years, the Abergorci colliery, acquired in 1862, was the firm's first steam coal colliery, apart from James Insole's briefly held share in Deep Duffryn and offered the chance of winning the steam coal seams at shallower depths than at Cymmer. The family's final venture, then in alliance with the Lewises, the Windsor colliery at Abertridwr, was a more risky enterprise, since the site was between the great anticline and the southern outcrop of the coalfield, which was not the most promising area for profitable colliery development. They did, however, enjoy good relations with Lord Windsor, the principal landowner and, although they sunk a lot of money in the venture and eventually lost it, the colliery itself did became profitable in the early 1930s and was worked successfully for a further 50 years. Colliery ownership secured regular supplies for the coal shipper but also brought with it entry into a very competitive business. Owners of collieries exploited the coal seams rapidly, endeavoured to differentiate and promote their products and engaged in aggressive marketing. There was very little co-operation among them and the Insoles in particular seem to have stayed out of any of the owners' associations until the twentieth century, when the day-to-day operations of the businesses were no longer exclusively in the family's hands.

The Insoles managed their collieries at arm's length. For the first fifty years, their manager and agent, Jabez Thomas, appears to have had full control at Maesmawr and Cymmer. There is only one recorded incident when James Insole appointed a senior member of the colliery staff and two where he came into direct conflict with his men. Thomas's management was probably very effective at achieving and maintaining a high level of production; it was not, however, conducive to good labour relations. He seems to have had both an autocratic style and a devious manner, although it must be said that when he moved from Maesmawr to Cymmer he persuaded a number of the workforce to move with him. During their weekly visits to their collieries, when Thomas was manager, George and James Insole probably only looked at output, new investment and any problems which Jabez could not handle or where he needed the owners' support. His successor, Tom Griffiths, was a different sort of manager; he had worked his way up from the coal-face and enjoyed the confidence of his own workers and, it seems, of the South Wales Miners' Federation as a whole. He was also a leader in rescue operations after mining disasters. He was not only an active colliery manager but also took part in local politics and in the activities of the South Wales Institute of Engineers, the South Wales Coal Owners' Association and the Conciliation Board. In later years, no doubt under his influence, the managers of the Insoles' collieries, in spite of a number of industrial disputes, did take an active part in the development of the miners' institutes and in welfare activities. The Insoles sank new shafts at all their collieries but they do not appear to have been great innovators in colliery methods and technology; like many other owners they continued with pillar and stall until the 1870s, changing to longwall for the steam coal seams. It also took them a long time to abandon furnaces and adopt fans for ventilation, possibly as a result of the influence of Jabez Thomas, who seems to have been inherently conservative. Eventually, after the First World War, Cymmer was an old pit and lacked modern equipment, which the owners could not or would not provide.

Safety was always a key issue at the collieries, particularly at Cymmer after the 1856 disaster, especially when the deeper seams had been won. The second half of the nineteenth century saw a gradual strengthening of the powers of HM Inspectors of Mines and of the laws and regulations governing colliery operations. The years before 1856 showed James Insole's relations with Herbert Mackworth, the inspector, to have been very poor and it seems that his commitment and that of his manager to safety and indeed to the welfare of the workers was weak. In addition, some of the attitudes and practices of the colliers themselves did not help to promote their own safety. Eventually, however, safety procedures improved at Cymmer and the commitment of the management and of the workers to safe practices increased. From tentative beginnings in the 1840s, the government increasingly regulated the operation of the coal industry, until, during the First World War, it took powers for the overall direction of the industry and the comprehensive regulation of the management of collieries, in order to ensure adequate production for the war effort. Government action after the war aimed to combat the effects of volatile demand and, in the 1930s to redress the effects of *laissez-faire* economics and the subsequent depression. In these years the response of William North Lewis, the chairman of Insoles Ltd, to government controls was one of support, albeit as a temporary expedient and as the lesser of two evils.

Although the Insoles eventually became very rich people, in the early years they needed capital, both for their work in the coal trade and in particular for their colliery operations. George Insole, like other entrepreneurs, provided capital from his own resources but he also had support from his bank, which allowed him to borrow and to run an overdraft. James Insole also used his own money and in later years, when he became to all intents and purposes a landowner, he acted both as landlord and banker to the Insole businesses. Coal owners, however, needed other sources of capital beyond their own resources. In the early days they were able to make use of bills of exchange in order to improve their cash flow and working capital and they relied on their banks for overdrafts, loans and, sometimes, investment. Later these became inadequate or put the family fortunes totally at risk and many coal owners, possibly including the Insoles, sought the security provided by limited liability. By the end of the century the quantity of capital needed to sink and expand collieries and to develop the infrastructure of the coalfield were so great that they could not be provided even by a rich family like the Insoles. The spread of risk and the increase in capital resources provided by a joint stock company increased the attractiveness of flotations. The sale of shares in Insoles Limited, the operator of the Cymmer Colliery, in 1896 raised money for the family and for the Lewises, part of which they were then able to invest in the Windsor venture, which had been launched the previous year. Although Insoles Ltd was able to pay regular dividends, the Windsor colliery required injections of capital and loans at later dates both for sinking and for development, which would have strained the resources of a family business and could only be met through a stock market flotation.

The new coal owners of South Wales, in the early nineteenth century, came to a sparsely populated territory and they had to attract labour for their operations. The colliers, who often came from established areas of the coalfield, had a tradition of independence, in particular they expected to be consulted by their employers in matters where their own safety was concerned. The dialogue with their workmen was an important element in the Insoles' history. At first it does not appear to have been very satisfactory and even in later years the workers were often in dispute with either the owners as a group or with the Insoles themselves. In 1842, George Insole employed some 150 men and boys, a workforce which grew until, by 1914, it exceeded 5,000 men at the two collieries. The education and skills of both management and men improved over the century, particularly after the appointment of Tom Griffiths at Cymmer. Improved training and better qualifications both for managers and senior staff and for those colliers who were ambitious to succeed, either through promotion or in the union, was a feature of the coalfield during the latter years of the nineteenth century. The Insoles seem to have been, on the whole, a typical coal owning family, leaving the operation of their collieries to managers and were probably no more or less liberal or dictatorial in their approach to their employees than other owners. The blatant autocracy of the 1840s and 1850s became, towards the end of the colliery's life, a benevolent despotism, which was exercised by North Lewis and was tempered by regulation from the authorities and consultation with the workers and their unions. In response to the coal owners, the workers improved the organisation of their associations and trade unions until, by the end of the First World War, they were able to sit as equal partners with the owners at the sessions of the Sankey Commission. A number of colliers from the Insoles' pits became prominent in the work of the South Wales Miners' Federation.

George Insole had no land when he came to Cardiff but he soon acquired it. He built up his holding in Crockherbtown, which provided a comfortable home for his family, and acquired fields nearby but his major acquisitions, both by purchase and lease, were in the coalfield. The landowners from whom he leased minerals included local freeholders like Evan Morgan of Tyn-y-cymmer Farm, Glamorgan gentry such as Dr Casberd and the Phillips estate, absentees like the Aubreys and the local magnate, the Marquess of Bute. Nearly all his leases, except an early Aubrey lease, were on the standard terms with a dead rent, a royalty, which usually varied depending on the size of coal mined and a wayleave. The Insoles also sub-leased, from time to time, the Glynfach colliery, the Upper Cymmer Colliery and the Cymmer Level, while they concentrated on the two pits of Cymmer Old and New. Sub-leasing was particularly common in the middle years of the nineteenth century. It allowed more capital to be brought into the colliery and provided the principal lessee with a regular income. When he retired from colliery ownership, James Insole effectively sub-leased the entire Cymmer holding to his sons and Henry Lewis, which provided over a third of his gross income. In addition to their collieries and mineral leases, the Insoles also acquired land, mainly in Cardiff, but also in Llantrisant, Gelligaer and the pit villages, including farms to keep their horses or to provide them with fodder. The bulk of the urban land was used for housing and for a limited amount of industry and commerce. The estate provided James Insole and his successors with a second source of income outside the coal trade. In terms of the Insoles' social ambitions, however, the more significant land acquisitions were their country estates with their houses, gardens, parkland, sporting facilities, farms and even minerals. These brought them status and a place among the county gentry and included land at Llandaff and Pendoylan in Glamorgan, Luxborough in Somerset and riverside properties in the Monmouthshire countryside. By 1914 the Insoles were not only the lessees of extensive mineral rights but also landowners themselves on a fairly large scale.

Before the Industrial Revolution the South Wales valleys were covered with woods, small, mostly freehold, farms, rivers, primitive parish roads and ancient trackways. By the time George Insole arrived in South Wales the canals and their associated tramroads were well established. Road transport, however, apart from the turnpike from Cardiff to Merthyr Tydfil, had shown little improvement. George Insole used the Glamorganshire Canal both to receive consignments from his suppliers and to ship his own Maesmawr coal to his yard near the canal sea-lock in Cardiff. It was the coming of the railways that opened up the valleys of South Wales and the building of docks at Cardiff and other ports which enabled the coalfield to compete in the world-wide coal trade. The docks and railways provided faster transport and new methods of handling and shipping coal, which encouraged the colliery proprietors and coal shippers to expand their horizons. This was not always an easy business, as the problems which George Insole had with the Taff Vale Railway illustrate.

Vested interests, competition between colliery proprietors and the problems of getting increasing traffic down what was always a narrow rail corridor aggravated the problems of the coal owners in trying to get their output to market as quickly as possible in the best possible condition. When George Insole started shipping coal, it was moved from canal boat to wharf and from wharf to ship in wheelbarrows pushed by hand. By the end of the century coal was lifted from railway wagons into ships holds or bunkers by mechanical hoists or tips and was screened at the same time. Railways and docks, however, brought new problems as so often happens with new technologies, as people learnt how to handle the facilities and learn the new techniques, such as steam traction, traffic management, marshalling and timetables as well as problems like congestion and turn-round. In addition, both the docks and the railways were monopolies and had the means and the will to maintain their control of transport in South Wales. The Insoles were involved in efforts to break these monopoly powers. George Insole had been anxious to get a railway line or siding to transport his coal from Cymmer to the docks in the face of opposition from Walter Coffin. Later his son, James, was invited to join the promoters of the Ely tidal harbour and he thus became a director of the Penarth Harbour, Dock & Railway Co. This undertaking was originally set up as a rival to the Taff Vale and the Bute Docks although, in the end, it became a virtual subsidiary of the Taff Vale and was eventually managed and operated as an integral part of Cardiff Docks. James Insole's sons, Walter and Fred, as well as Eric his grandson, were all in turn involved in the establishment and direction of the Barry Railway, the strongest competitor to the Taff Vale, which proved to be highly successful as an integrated dock and railway company. It had less track than the other large railways in the coalfield but had extensive running powers on other lines and a high volume of both passenger and goods traffic, as well as a willingness to experiment and a flair for enterprise. Together the docks and the railways gave the coalfield a comprehensive network and ample port facilities but, in the end, both suffered from the region's dependence on one product with little diversity. In particular, the port of Cardiff and its associated valleys, the scenes of the Insoles' endeavours, were particularly badly hit in the 1920s and 1930s by their dependence on the export of steam coal.

George Insole had a reputation as a pioneer of the steam coal trade, although this was challenged by others. His claim, however, is strong; he was the first to take an order from a London merchant for steam coal from the Thomas's Waun Wyllt colliery and he moved quickly into the export trade. He was also one of the first to open up, on a large scale, the coal trade of the Cynon Valley, selling its steam coal to the Royal Navy and to merchant shipping lines. He was also an innovator in his trading methods, particularly by using direct sales to customers rather than relying on ships' masters. He also brought imaginative ideas to the trade, including advertising his products with enthusiastic promotional letters, in order to find new markets. His success was all the more remarkable in a man who did not enter the trade until he was nearly 40 and who suffered from a bad heart. George Insole's pioneering tradition does not seem to have survived to the next generation. James Insole was a consolidator and was more concerned to spread his investments and to diversify his sources of income. He seems to have been a more cautious man in business and to have been happier as a rentier rather than an entrepreneur. Of his two sons, Walter appears to have followed him in preferring the life of a country gentleman; Fred, however, may have inherited some of his grandfather's pioneering spirit and the Windsor venture was a exciting enterprise, very much in George Insole's tradition. He may well have been a profligate man, at least in his father's eyes. There is no evidence of the pioneering spirit in the last generation of the family, at any rate in the male line, although Violet Insole was a leading plant breeder and introduced new varieties.

The Insoles' success and their fortunes contributed to the growth of Cardiff and of the Rhondda Valleys, although their ambitions lay more in the advancement of their family than in the development of their communities. The Insoles were early users of the Bute Dock and played a prominent part in the growth of the railways, while George Insole was elected to Cardiff Borough Council. Furthermore, James Insole was the first president of the Chamber of Commerce, the organisation which represented the docksmen, sometimes in opposition to the townsmen, who formed the Borough, and later City, Councils. His sons, one grandson and the Lewises were all members of the Chamber. These activities were, however, probably the limit of the Insoles' influence in local political or commercial affairs; after George Insole's death none of them took any part in local politics nor do they do figure to any extent in charitable or community subscription lists, apart from the Infirmary, although James was appointed to the Borough Council's university committee. They were, however, modest contributors to the growth of Cardiff: James leased land for and built some high density housing, which would have helped, albeit marginally, to alleviate the shortage of working class housing in the town and the two Llandaff estates eventually became areas of fashionable suburban housing.

The rise of the Rhondda Valleys was rapid and its increase in population spectacular. There was, therefore, a great need for housing and urban amenities but these tended not to be supplied by the leaders of local industry. It is true that George Insole built some houses at Cymmer and Porth but, apart from the establishment of Bethlehem Chapel, under the leadership of Jabez Thomas, and of the miners' institute at Cymmer, there does not seem to have been any involvement by the Insoles or their firms in the provision of public amenities in the Rhondda. At Cymmer and Porth, therefore, as in other parts of the South Wales coalfield, the supply of housing was left to the self-help of the workers themselves supported by building societies and clubs. The other major feature of valley towns was the spread of the chapels, which were not only places of worship but also centres of community activities and, in the early days, schools. The Insoles took no part in the erection of chapels or schools. In their venture at Abertridwr, which lasted some 25 years, the Insoles' involvement in the community followed a similar pattern, with some houses built for rent and the management of the colliery playing an important part in building and overseeing the running of the miners' institute.

The nineteenth century saw an enormous change in the fortunes of the Insole family and thus their social status. George Insole was an independent artisan, a member of a class which had prospered in England for many years, usually in a modest way but, following his move to Cardiff and his entry into the coal trade, he quickly became wealthy. James Insole started his working life in the coal trade under his father's tutelage but, once his father had died and he had established his control of the business, he started to diversify his interests. He acquired land for housing and for business use, which gave him an alternative source of income, and he invested in railways and companies with which he had business connections. He also bought land for enjoyment and status as well as investment, as he moved from participation in the coal trade to the life of a country gentleman. By his mid-fifties he had become a holder of stocks, shares and leases, rather than a working coal owner. His style of living was very different from that of the simple home where he had been born in High Street, Worcester. His sons went to public school and followed him as wealthy men having the interests and pursuits of the gentry; they also ceded day-to-day control of their businesses to those who had worked their way up through the firm or from the coal-face. They enjoyed their country houses, rural sports and activities, while Fred sent his sons to Harrow and Cambridge. Although they were a rich family, they never quite made the top rank of South Wales society; they were recognised as important in the coal trade and, as local gentry, they had influential friends, including the Windsors and the Homfrays, but they do not seem to have had a powerful position either in the county or in Cardifff politics.

The fourth generation of Insoles seems to have had, at the most, a semi-detached relationship with the coal trade. Claud Insole took no part in the business and from his twenty-fifth birthday in 1912, would have had the income of the Luxborough Estate to support him in leading the life of a country gentleman. Similarly the youngest brother, Alan, had no shares or other stake in the businesses and played no part in their affairs; he left Cardiff to live in London after the First World War and rarely returned. Eric Insole, although a director of both colliery companies and a partner in George Insole & Son, does not seem to have played a very prominent part in the business; he was more interested in travel, motor cars and fishing and left the leadership and management of the business to others.

From James Insole's retirement in the 1870s, the Lewises played an increasingly important part in the running of the businesses. Henry Lewis was an equal partner with Walter and Fred and probably provided a professional counterweight to Walter's amateurism and any tendency to profligacy by Fred. His son brought the same approach to his career and, by the time Fred Insole died, he was the unchallenged leader of the Insole businesses and an influential figure in the commercial life of Cardiff. At the same time the managers of the Insoles' collieries, from Tom Griffiths onwards, were independent and knowledgeable professionals who could be relied on to run the collieries with the minimum of oversight and top-level direction.

The Insoles were in many ways typical of the successful industrialists and their families in their day. They maintained their success and good fortune through four generations, their businesses lasted for over a century, they changed from artisans to industrialists and then to gentry although they never quite made the top rank either as coal owners or in county society. To their credit they provided employment for many people and so underpinned the livelihoods of the coal mining communities but they did little more to develop and enrich the towns and villages where those communities lived. They left no reminders in the Rhondda or in Abertridwr and very little of their legacy remains in Cardiff, apart from their family home, a few streets and a public house. By their activities they enriched themselves, earning the regard and respect of their peers, while their wealth continued to support many in the family long after the collieries and the coal trade fell on hard times and their businesses had disappeared. George Insole was considered individualistic, sometimes rather awkward to deal with but determined to be successful. James Insole was a wealthy man even when he succeeded his father and when he died was an important figure in Cardiff's coal society. Walter and Fred Insole were very different characters but they did maintain an involvement in the coal business, as well as enjoying the family's fortunes and status. The fourth generation lived on the fruits of their forebears' achievements and did little to add to the family's wealth, standing and influence.

Most of the ladies of the Insole family are shadowy characters owing to the lack of family records; about George Insole's wife, Mary, and James's first wife, Mary Ann, very little survives. James's second wife, however, Marian Eagle, with her three marriages and her inheritance, became an important shareholder in the collieries and a partner in the trading business, although she seems to have played no part in running them. Of the others, Julia Insole led a quiet life through a long widowhood, supporting herself on her own investments and her father's legacy. James and Fred Insole had married daughters, whose husbands were brought into the family's business and private affairs. Fred Insole's wife was a member of the David family which figured prominently in nineteenth-century Cardiff. Finally Violet Insole led an independent life and made a name for herself in the world of British horticulture.

In conclusion, the Insoles were a family who made their fortune in the risky but rewarding South Wales coal trade, became influential Cardiff docksmen and joined the local gentry. They worked for themselves and built for themselves, they put little into the community, they left few monuments and, when the main line of the family died out, they were largely forgotten.

South Wales Coalfield
Coal Output, 1831–1938

Year	Annual output '000 tons	'000 tons	Annual change % change	Five-Year moving average '000 tons	% change
1831-35				4,000	
1835-40				4,800	20.0
1841-45				5,000	4.0
1846-50				6,500	23.0
1851-55				7,670.0	18.0
1854	8,500			7,836.0	2.12
1855	8,550	50	0.59	8,012.0	2.20
1856	8,919	369	4.32	8,261.8	3.02
1857	7,132	-1,787	-20.04	8,035.8	-2.81
1858	7,495	363	5.09	8,119.2	1.03
1859	9,600	2,105	28.09	8,339.2	2.71
1860	10,256	656	6.83	8,680.4	4.09
1861	11,666	1,410	13.75	9,229.8	6.33
1862	10,449	-1,217	-10.43	9,893.2	7.19
1863	10,992	543	5.20	10,592.6	7.07
1864	10,977	-15	-0.14	10,868.0	2.60
1865	12,656	1,679	15.30	11,348.0	4.42
1866	13,821	1,165	9.21	11,779.0	3.80
1867	13,662	-159	-1.15	12,421.6	5.46
1868	13,211	-451	-3.30	12,865.4	3.57
1869	13,455	244	1.85	13,361.0	3.85

1870	13,664	209	1.55	13,562.6	1.51
1871	14,036	372	2.72	13,605.6	0.32
1872	14,882	846	6.03	13,849.6	1.79
1873	14,342	-540	-3.63	14,075.8	1.63
1874	16,491	2,149	14.98	14,683.0	4.31
1875	14,173	-2,318	-14.06	14,784.8	0.69
1876	16,972	2,799	19.75	15,372.0	3.97
1877	16,911	-61	-0.36	15,777.8	2.64
1878	17,417	506	2.99	16,392.8	3.90
1879	17,819	402	2.31	16,658.4	1.62
1880	21,116	3,297	18.50	18,047.0	8.34
1881	22,234	1,118	5.29	19,099.4	5.83
1882	22,817	583	2.62	20,280.6	6.18
1883	24,975	2,158	9.46	21,792.2	7.45
1884	25,552	577	2.31	23,338.8	7.10
1885	24,343	-1,209	-4.73	23,984.2	2.77
1886	24,204	-139	-0.57	24,378.2	1.64
1887	26,046	1,842	7.61	25,024.0	2.65
1888	27,355	1,309	5.03	25,500.0	1.90
1889	28,064	709	2.59	26,002.4	1.97
1890	29,415	1,351	4.81	27,016.8	3.90
1891	29,993	578	1.96	28,174.6	4.29
1892	31,207	1,214	4.05	29,206.8	3.66
1893	30,155	-1,052	-3.37	29,766.8	1.92
1894	33,418	3,263	10.82	30,837.6	3.60
1895	33,040	-378	-1.13	31,562.6	2.35
1896	33,868	828	2.51	32,337.6	2.46
1897	35,806	1,938	5.72	33,257.4	2.84
1898	26,724	-9,082	-25.36	32,571.2	-2.06

1899	39,870	13,146	49.19	33,861.6	3.96
1900	39,328	-542	-1.36	35,119.2	3.71
1901	39,209	-119	-0.30	36,187.4	3.04
1902	41,306	2,097	5.35	37,287.4	3.04
1903	42,154	848	2.05	40,373.4	8.28
1904	43,730	1,576	3.74	41,145.4	1.91
1905	43,203	-527	-1.21	41,920.4	1.88
1906	47,056	3,853	8.92	43,489.8	3.74
1907	49,978	2,922	6.21	45,224.2	3.99
1908	50,227	249	0.50	46,838.8	3.57
1909	50,364	137	0.27	48,165.6	2.83
1910	48,700	-1,664	-3.30	49,265.0	2.28
1911	50,201	1,501	3.08	49,894.0	1.28
1912	50,116	-85	-0.17	49,921.6	0.06
1913	56,830	6,714	13.40	51,242.2	2.65
1914	53,880	-2,950	-5.19	51,945.4	1.37
1915	50,453	-3,427	-6.36	52,296.0	0.67
1916	52,018	1,565	3.10	52,659.4	0.69
1917	48,508	-3,510	-6.75	52,337.8	-0.61
1918	46,717	-1,791	-3.69	50,315.2	-3.86
1919	47,522	805	1.72	49,043.6	-2.53
1920	46,249	-1,273	-2.68	48,202.8	-1.71
1921	30,572	-15,677	-33.90	43,913.6	-8.90
1922	50,325	19,753	64.61	44,277.0	0.83
1923	54,252	3,927	7.80	45,784.0	3.40
1924	51,085	-3,167	-5.84	46,496.6	1.56
1925	44,630	-6,455	-12.64	46,172.8	-0.70
1926	20,273	-24,357	-54.58	44,113.0	-4.46
1927	46,256	25,983	128.17	43,299.2	-1.84

1928	43,312	-2,944	-6.36	41,111.2	-5.05
1929	48,141	4,829	11.15	40,522.4	-1.43
1930	45,108	-3,033	-6.30	40,618.0	0.24
1931	37,085	-8,023	-17.79	43,980.4	8.28
1932	34,874	-2,211	-5.96	41,704.0	-5.18
1933	34,355	-519	-1.49	39,912.6	-4.30
1934	35,173	818	2.38	37,319.0	-6.50
1935	35,025	-148	-0.42	35,302.4	-5.40
1936	33,886	-1,139	-3.25	34,662.6	-1.81
1937	37,773	3,887	11.47	35,242.4	1.67
1938	38,185	412	1.09	36,008.4	2.17

Sources: 1831–55: S. Pollard, 'A New Estimate of British Coal Production, 1750-1850', *Economic History Review*, 2nd ser. 33 (1980), p. 229 (quinquennial figures). 1854–1938: J. Williams, *Digest of Welsh Historical Statistics* (Welsh Office, 1985), I, pp. 297, 300 (annual figures). *Note:* Figures for missing years (1831-55) have been estimated, using rates of increase from R. Church, *History of the British Coal Industry*, III (Oxford, 1986), p. 3. Moving averages for 1854–7 include these estimated figures.

Appendix B

Coal Prices, 1840–1938
Large Steam Coal: Price per Ton f.o.b. at Cardiff

Year	s.	d.	Year	s.	d.	Year	s.	d.
1840	10	0	1873	23	3	1906	12	4
1841	10	0	1874	16	11	1907	14	9
1842	10	0	1875	14	3	1908	15	8
1843	9	0	1876	9	10	1909	13	9
1844	9	0	1877	9	1	1910	14	10
1845	8	9	1878	9	1	1911	14	9

1846	9	6	1879	8	6	1912	15	6
1847	9	6	1880	8	6	1913	16	5
1848	9	3	1881	8	11	1914	17	6
1849	8	9	1882	9	5	1915	20	11
1850	8	6	1883	9	8	1916	24	5
1851	8	3	1884	9	10	1917	26	11
1852	8	0	1885	9	3	1918	30	9
1853	10	6	1886	8	5	1919	41	1
1854	11	0	1887	8	0	1920	61	5
1855	10	6	1888	8	4	1921	39	5
1856	9	6	1889	10	6	1922	26	2
1857	9	3	1890	13	0	1923	28	0
1858	8	9	1891	13	5	1924	27	3
1859	8	3	1892	11	7	1925	25	1
1860	8	3	1983	9	7	1926	21	11
1861	8	6	1894	10	8	1927	21	4
1862	8	7	1895	9	7	1928	18	8
1863	8	9	1896	9	2	1929	19	0
1864	8	9	1897	9	3	1930	19	7
1865	8	9	1898	10	1	1931	19	9
1866	8	6	1899	11	1	1932	19	11
1867	8	6	1900	15	2	1933	19	11
1868	8	0	1901	16	1	1934	20	0
1869	8	6	1902	13	7	1935	20	0
1870	9	3	1903	12	10	1936	20	4
1871	10	6	1904	12	9	1937	22	7
1872	19	3	1905	12	0	1938	25	6

Source: John Williams, *Digest of Welsh Historical Statistics* (Welsh Office, 1985), I, p. 337. *Note*: 1935–8 prices have been estimated from *The Colliery Year Book & Coal Trades Directory* (1943).

Appendix C

Rules and Regulations for Cymmer Colliery 1848

Rules and Regulations agreed upon the Sixteenth of February 1849: Between Messrs. George Insole and Son, the Proprietors and the undersigned Colliers and Others working at the Cymmer Colliery Levels.

1. That each collier before entering the above work, shall sign or make his mark to an agreement to work for twelve months from the date above mentioned before one of the Agents of the said colliery to abide by the Rules, Regulations and Agreement hereinafter contained; and that he is satisfied to work on the terms, prices and conditions hereinafter mentioned.

2. That each collier before entering the work shall have delivered to him a proper set of tools, which he must produce when required or pay the value for the same.

3. That each collier on entering the above work shall peaceably, quietly, and regularly, day by day, continue his work without interfering with the other colliers or workmen, and shall to the satisfaction of the Agent for the time being at Cymmer Levels, cut and fill his coal in a clean, proper and workmanlike and marketable manner, and doing the usual work of a collier for carrying on the work in a proper and safe way; but should any collier or colliers neglect or refuse to comply with these rules and regulations, terms and conditions and notice being given him or them of it three times at least, or neglect to fill the coal in a clean, proper workmanlike and marketable manner, the Agent shall be, and is hereby authorized to call in one old experienced collier to his assistance to judge and decide as to such coal, and if they adjudge and determine that the coal has not been filled in the above mentioned condition, the collier or colliers so neglecting or refusing to attend to such notice shall be discharged forthwith.

4. Any collier or colliers, not being satisfied either with his or their work, or the price paid for such, he or they shall be at liberty to leave the work on giving a fortnight's notice (provided the number giving notice at any one time from each colliery-pay shall not exceed six) and shall peaceably and quietly leave the Levels and work, on being paid his or their wages; or if Messrs. George Insole and James Harvey Insole, Proprietors of the

Cymmer Level, shall be disposed to discharge any number of colliers, they shall and hereby in like manner, authorized and empowered to discharge any number not exceeding six at one time, on giving a fortnight's notice.

5. And we, the undersigned colliers and workmen, hereby agree to cut and fill our coal in a clean, proper, workmanlike and marketable manner and to separate the same, i.e., for all large, clean, marketable coal, 2/- per ton of 2,520 lbs. weight to the ton; and all brush or tender coal of light weight, cut and filled in a clean and marketable manner 1/10 per ton; and for small coal, cut and cleaned in a like, clean, and marketable manner, of like weight 1/4 per ton.

6. And we, the undersigned colliers and workmen agree with Messrs. George Insole and James Harvey Insole to cut and work the said coal in Cymmer Levels, and doing the usual work of colliers for carrying on the works safely for the above prices, terms and conditions for ONE YEAR from the date hereof, unless there be a general alteration in prices for cutting and working the coal in the same veins in the Cwm Rhondda Valley; and we bind ourselves to abide by any advance or reduction that takes place in the same veins. The coal to the workmen to be supplied to them as heretofore.

7. For the protection of the well disposed colliers and other workmen as well as their employers at the Cymmer Levels, it is hereby further agreed that no stops nor strikes shall be made at the said work at any time, on any pretence whatever, during the term of ONE YEAR from the date hereof.

8. Any collier or colliers having any just cause of complaint and wishing for redress, any three of their number (but no more, so that the colliery and works be not retarded), shall wait on the Agents forthwith; and if possible, such cause of complaint shall be adjusted; but if the dispute cannot be settled, the same shall be referred to the employers at their next weekly visit, whose decision shall be final.

9. The said George Insole and James Harvey Insole agree that no more colliers are to be taken into the said work unless there be a call for a greater quantity of coal than the colliers then employed will supply: and if there are more colliers in the work than will get their work out fairly, some of the last colliers taken in are to be the first drafted out.

Source: National Library of Wales, E.D. Lewis Collection.

Appendix D

George Insole & Son's Promotional Letter for Aberaman Steam Coal, 1848

Geo. Insole & Son, Coal Office, Cardiff

To the Purchasers and Consumers of Steam Coal

The immense increase of Steam Power within the last few years, among Public Companies and in the Naval Department and for Stationary Engines, in Great Britain, as in nearly every Maratime Nation on the Globe, renders the subject of Steam Coal of paramount importance; all are concerned in obtaining Coal of the best description for raising Steam cheaply.

In procuring Coal best suited for Steam purposes, great care should be taken to select that which has the highest possible evaporative power, contains the least Sulphur, emits the least quantity of smoke, leaves the smallest amount of ash and residue, does not make clinkers or cinder, or burn the bars and boiler.

As the Aberaman Merthyr Steam Coal shipped at Cardiff, by Messrs Geo Insole and Son, possesses all the qualities above stated in a higher degree than any other known Coal, they have the authority of Sir Hy De La Beche, of the Museum of Practical Geology, London, in stating "that the Aberaman, Merthyr Steam Coal is not surpassed if equalled by any other in this kingdom."

As a proof of the superior quality of the Aberaman Merthyr Steam Coal, the Lords Commissioners, not only of the Admiralty, but also of the Victualling department have been pleased to direct that <u>that</u> Coal be inserted on the list of Coal suitable for those departments, being the only Coal shipped at Cardiff so placed by their Lordships.

As per the following Copies of Letters.

Admiralty, 4th March, 1848

Sir—Referring to your letter of the first instant, I acquaint you that the Lords Commissioners of the Admiralty have directed the Aberaman Merthyr Steam Coal to be added to the list of those specified in Naval Contracts.

> I am, Sir,
> Your humble Servant,
> (Signed) R. Dundas, Storekeeper General

From the Controller of Victualling of Her Majesty's Navy

Admiralty, 5th April, 1848

Sir—A report having been received of the Abcraman Merthyr Steam Coals referred to in my Letter of the 11th Ult°, and delivered by you at Deptford Victualling Yard, I have to acquaint you that their Lordships have been pleased to direct that this description of Coal be added to the list of Welsh Coals required for the service of this department in future

> I am, Sir,
> Your most obedient Servant,
> (signed) J^{as} Meek.

As a still further proof of the superiority of the Aberaman Merthyr Steam Coal:

The Lords Commissioners of the Admiralty having directed that experiments should be made upon the merits of Steam Coal worthy of notice to the Navy,—by the third and last Report by Sir H^y T. De La Beche and D^r. Lyon Playfair, presented to both Houses of Parliament, at the Command of Her Majesty, this Coal is the best ever tested, and stands highest of all. Vidê the Report or extracts of the Summary of Welsh Coal on the next page.

Welsh Steam Coal far exceeds that of the North of England in every requisite quality, and to nearly every Port, Freights are much lower from Wales, particularly for foreign.

The Aberaman Merthyr Steam Coal is in great and increasing demand especially for Consumption abroad, being more extensively shipped Foreign than any other Coal from Cardiff, and now, by erection of improved machinery; the proprietors are enabled to meet any ordinary demand in the splendid Docks at Cardiff, where Vessels of any size can be loaded afloat. In thus bringing the Aberaman Merthyr Steam Coal, and the improved mode of Shipping more prominently before the Public, they feel warranted in stating they are offering an article unequalled by any.—In addition to the foregoing references are kindly granted as to its superior quality to the first Steam Packets Companies in the world; among whom the Royal Mail Steam Packet Company, the Peninsular and Oriental Steam Packet Company, and to nearly all the Public and Private Consumers of Steam Coal in the Metropolis.

All further particulars may be had and orders executed on application to Geo. Insole & Son, Colliery Proprietors, Cardiff.

Source: National Library of Wales, E.D. Lewis Collection; Glamorgan Record Office, Insole Industrial Records.

Extract from the Third and last Report of Sir Henry T. De La Beche and Dr Lyon Playfair on Coal suited for the Steam Navy; presented to both Houses of Parliament. by Command of Her Majesty. being a Summary of Welsh Coal. tested and named in 1st, 2nd and 3rd Reports.

Name of Coal employed in the Experiments	Economic evaporating power or pounds of water evaporated from 212° by 1lb of Coal	Specific Gravity of Coals	Results of experiments on Cohesive power of Coals (per Centage of large Coal)	Carbon	Hydrogen	Sulphur	Ash	Soot in Flues	Extracts of Remarks on the Coals
Abcraman Merthyr	**10.75**	**1.305**	**74.0**	**90.94**	**4.28**	**1.18**	**1.45**	**None**	"The Specimen examined was brilliant and granular in its structure."
Ebbw Vale	10.21	1.275	45.5	89.78	5.15	1.02	1.50	7lbs	"They coke on the Bars." "They are also found to evolve a grayish black smoke in rather considerable quantities, and from their bituminous nature require frequent stoking"
Thomas's or Wood's } Merthyr	10.16	1.30	57.5	90.12	4.33	0.85	1.68	None	"This Coal was not so firm, and perhaps little less brilliant than some others"
Powell's Duffryn	10.14	1.32	56.2	88.26	4.66	1.77	3.26	"	"This is a Coal of rather soft description"
Nixon's Merthyr	9.96	1.31	64.5	90.27	4.12	1.20	1.25	"	"Under the Boiler this Coal was found to light with difficulty." It is also liable to crumble on the fire, and fall thro' the bars"
Binea	9.94	1.30	51.2	88.26	6.43	1.33	3.96	"	"It is a soft Coal"
Bedwas	9.97	1.22	54.0	80.61	6.01	3.50	6.94	"	"It contains Iron Pyrites"
Gadley's Nine Feet	9.56	1.33	"	86.18	4.31	"	5.34	"	"Left a large quantity of Ash of a very incombustible nature, which when again thrown on the grate, was found to choke the bars and interfere with the draft"

do. do. more and more inferior, vide Reports

Table. showing the average value of Coals from different localities.

Locality	Evaporating power of number of lbs of Water evaporated from 212° by 1lb of Coal	Rate of evaporation or number of lbs evaporated per hour	Weight of lbs of one cubic foot of coal	Space occupied by One Ton in Cubic Feet	Results obtained in experiments on cohesive power of Coal	Per Centage amount of Sulphur obtained in Coal
Average of 37 samples from Wales	9.05	448.2	53.1	42.71	60.9	1.42
Average of 17 " Newcastle	8.37	411.1	49.8	45.30	67.5	0.94
Average of 28 " Lancashire	7.94	447.6	49.7	45.15	73.5	1.42
Average of 8 " Scotland	7.70	431.4	50.0	49.99	73.4	1.45
Average of 8 " Derbyshire	7.58	432.7	47.2	47.45	80.9	1.01

Appendix E

The Port of Cardiff's share of coal output and shipments, 1874-1913

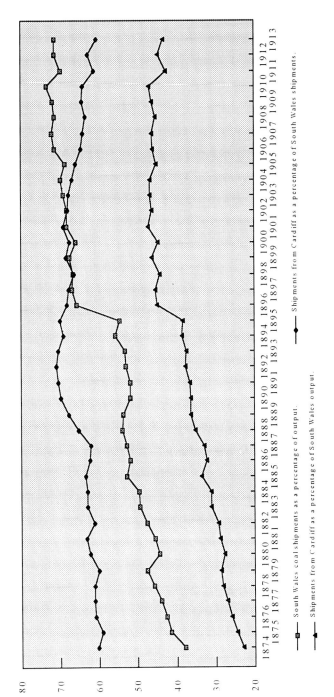

South Wales coal shipments as a percentage of output.

Shipments from Cardiff as a percentage of output.

Shipments from Cardiff as a percentage of South Wales output.

Shipments from Cardiff as a percentage of South Wales shipments.

Source: John Williams, *Digest of Welsh Historical Statistics* (Welsh Office. 1985), I, pp. 300, 315, 318.

Bibliography

Primary Sources

Public Record Office
BT 31, Board of Trade, Files of dissolved companies.
RAIL 23, Records of the Barry Railway Co.
RAIL 561, Records of the Penarth Harbour, Dock & Railway Co.
RAIL 684, Records of the Taff Vale Railway Co.

National Library of Wales
E.D. Lewis Collection.
South Wales Coal Owners Association Collection, D/179, Insoles Ltd.
NLW MS 437E, M.O. Jones ('Nil Desperandum'), 'Coal Industry in the Rhondda' (1895).

Glamorgan Record Office
D/D Xcv, Insole industrial records.
D/D Au 182, Aubrey papers.
D/D PD 7, Powell Duffryn Ltd, *A Short Survey of the Organisation, Growth and Development of Powell Duffryn Ltd* (Cardiff, 1946).
D/D COM/C Cardiff Chamber of Commerce records.
Q/DP, Deposited plans.
B/C 4, Cardiff Borough Council Minutes.

Somerset County Record Office
DD/DP 14, 15, Luxborough Estate Papers.

Cardiff County Council, Legal Department, City Hall, Cardiff
Deeds and papers relating to the Court Estate, Llandaff.

Cardiff Central Library
Insole MSS.
George Insole & Son, *Cymmer Steam Coal* (Cardiff, 1880).
Bute MSS.

Rhondda Central Library
Insole collection.

W. Clarke, Llandaff
Bill Books, day books and ledgers, 1894–1940.

Parliamentary Papers

Royal Commission on Children's Employment in Mines & Manufactories. First Report (Mines & Collieries); Appendix (1842).
Coals Suited to the Steam Navy. First Report by Sir H. De la Beche and Dr. Playfair; Appendix; Plates (1847–8).
Reports of Inspectors of Mines (1856; 1857 Session 2).

Secondary sources

Books and articles

Contemporary Portraits and Biographies (Cardiff, 1896).
Contemporary Biographies (Brighton, 1907).
'Excursion to Cymmer Colliery', *Transactions of the Cardiff Naturalists Society* 15 (1883), 40–44.
Barber, J.T., *A Tour through South Wales and Monmouthshire* (1803).
Barrie, D.S.M., *The Taff Vale Railway* (Oakwood Press, 1982).
Barrie, D.S.M., *The Barry Railway,* (Oakwood Press, 1962).
Bassett, A., 'The Port of Cardiff and the Aberdare Steam Coal Field', *Transactions of the South Wales Institute of Engineers*, 4 (1864–5), 96–110.
Chappell, E.L., *History of the Port of Cardiff* (Cardiff, 1939).
Chappell, E.L., *Historic Melingriffith* (Cardiff, 1940).
Church, R., *History of the British Coal Industry*, III (Oxford, 1986).
Cope, M., *85 Years in Newport and Cardiff* (Cardiff, 1928).
Daunton, M.J., *Coal Metropolis: Cardiff 1870–1914* (Leicester, 1977).
Evans, C., Dodsworth, S., and Barnett J., *Below the Bridge* (Cardiff, 1984).
Evans, E.W., *The Miners of South Wales* (Cardiff, 1961).
Hadfield, C., *The Canals of South Wales and the Border* (Cardiff, 1967).
Ince, L., *The Neath Abbey Company* (De Archaeologische Pers, Nederland, 1984).
James, D.C., 'The Genesis of Sanitary Reform in Cardiff, 1774–1850', *Welsh History Review*, 11 (1982–3), 50–66.
Jevons, H.S., *The British Coal Trade* (1915).
John, A.H., *The Industrial Development of South Wales 1750–1850* (Cardiff, 1950).
Johnson, A.M., *Scott of the Antarctic and Cardiff,* (Cardiff, 1984).
Jones, R., and Reeve, C.G., *A History of Gas Production in Wales* (Cardiff, 1978).
The Law Journal Reports, XXVIII (1850).
Lewis, E.D., *The Rhondda Valleys* (1959).
Lewis, E. D., 'Pioneers of the Cardiff Coal Trade', *Glamorgan Historian,* XI (1975), 22–52.
Lewis, E.D., 'The Cymer (Rhondda) Explosion 1856', *Transactions of the Honourable Society of Cymmrodorion* (1976), 119–161.
The Llandaff Society, *Archive Photograph Series: Llandaff* (Chalford Press, 1996).
Linnard, W., '"Lord" Forrest of St Fagans', *Morgannwg*, 33 (1989), 55–68.
E.T. Lyddon & Sons, *The South Wales Investment Circular* (1899–1909).
Morris, J.H., and Williams, L. J., *The South Wales Coal Industry 1844–75* (Cardiff, 1958).

Phillips, D.R., *History of the Vale of Neath* (Swansea, 1925).

Phillips, E., *A History of the Pioneers of the Welsh Coalfield* (Cardiff, 1925).

Phillips, J.B., *Abertridwr through the ages* (Newport, 1991).

Pollard, S., 'A New Estimate of British Coal Production, 1750–1850', *Economic History Review*, 2nd series, 33 (1980).

Riden, P., and Edwards, K., *Families and Farms in Lisvane, 1850–1950* (Cardiff, 1993).

Rimmell, R.J., *History of the Barry Railway Company 1884–1921* (Cardiff, 1922).

Roberts, R.O., 'Banking and Financial Organisation, 1770–1914', *Glamorgan County History. V. Industrial Glamorgan* (Cardiff, 1980), pp. 363–407.

Supple, B., *The History of the British Coal Industry*, IV (Oxford, 1987).

Vincent, J.E., *John Nixon, Pioneer of the Steam Coal Trade in South Wales* (1900).

Walters, R.H., *The Economic and Business History of the South Wales Steam Coal Industry, 1840–1914* (New York, 1977).

Wilkins, C., *The South Wales Coal Trade and its Allied Industries* (Cardiff, 1888).

Weston Evans, A., *Cardiff & County Club, 1866 to 1991* (Cardiff, 1991)

Williams, J., *Digest of Welsh Historical Statistics* (Welsh Office, 1985).

Directories

South Wales Coal Annual (1903–39).

Bird, W., *Cardiff Guide & Directory* (1829).

Ewan's Cardiff Almanack & Guide (1855).

Cardiff & County Calendar (1868).

Western Mail Cardiff Directories (1905–47).

Kelly's Somerset Directory (1875–1923).

Newspapers and periodicals

The Cambrian

Cardiff & Merthyr Guardian

Cardiff Daily News

South Wales Daily News

Western Mail

Colliery Guardian

The Builder

The Graphic

Index

All place-names are in Glamorgan, unless otherwise indicated.

195